ARTFOLDS

....

This book belongs to

....

Folded by

Classic Editions
No. 2
Snowflake

featuring

The Snow Queen and Other Tales

By Hans Christian Andersen

Studio Fun Books
White Plains, NY • Montréal, Québec • Bath, United Kingdom

ArtFolds™
Classic Editions No. 2
Snowflake
featuring
The Snow Queen and Other Tales

ArtFolds is a patent-pending process for folding pages based on a set of unique printed marks to create a sculpture out of a bound book.

This Studio Fun Edition contains the complete text of *The Snow Queen* and other tales of Hans Christian Andersen.

ISBN 978-0-7944-3224-9

To learn more about ArtFolds, visit artfolds.com.

Customized and/or prefolded ArtFolds are available. To explore options and pricing, email specialorder@artfolds.com.

To discover the wide range of products available from Studio Fun International, visit studiofun.com.

Address any comments about ArtFolds to:
Publisher
Studio Fun Books
44 South Broadway, 7th floor
White Plains, NY 10601
Or send an email to publisher@artfolds.com.

Printed in China
1 3 5 7 9 10 8 6 4 2 LPP/04/14

About ArtFolds

THE BOOK YOU HOLD in your hands is more than just a
book. It's an ArtFolds™! Inside are simple instructions that
will show you how to fold pages to transform this book into a
beautiful sculpture. No special skill is required; all you'll do is
carefully fold the corners of marked book pages, based on the
markings provided. When complete, you'll have created a
long-lasting work of art. It's fun and easy, and can be completed
in just one evening!

To add to the experience, each ArtFolds contains compelling
reading content. In this edition, you'll find *The Snow Queen* and
other fairy tales by Hans Christian Andersen, stories that have
been loved by generations of readers.

Each ArtFolds edition is designed by an established, professional
Book Sculptor whose works are displayed and sold in art
galleries, museum shops, and online crafts and art stores.
ArtFolds celebrates this community of artists, and encourages you
to support this expanding art form by seeking out their work and
sharing their unique designs and creations with others.

To learn more about ArtFolds, visit **artfolds.com**. There you'll
find details of all ArtFolds editions, instructional videos, and
much more.

The ArtFolds Portfolio

Color Editions

These smaller ArtFolds™ editions use a range of colors printed on each page to make each sculpture a multi-colored work of art. Titles now or soon available include:

Edition 1: Heart
Edition 2: Mickey Mouse
Edition 3: Christmas Tree
Edition 4: MOM
Edition 5: Flower

Classic Editions

These larger ArtFolds™ editions include the full text of a classic book; when folded, book text appears along the edges, creating a piece of art that celebrates the dignity and beauty of a printed book. Titles now or soon available include:

Edition 1: LOVE
Edition 2: Snowflake
Edition 3: JOY
Edition 4: READ
Edition 5: Sun

To see the full range of ArtFolds editions, visit **artfolds.com**.

About the Designer

The sculpture design in this edition was created
exclusively for ArtFolds by Luciana Frigerio. Based in
Vermont, Luciana has been making photographs, objects,
book sculptures, and artistic mischief for over 30 years.
Her work has been exhibited in galleries and museums
around the world. Luciana's artwork can be found at:
lucianafrigerio.com, and her unique, customized book
sculptures can be found in her shop on the online crafts
market Etsy at: etsy.com/shop/LucianaFrigerio.

Instructions

Creating your ArtFolds™ Classic Edition book sculpture is easy!
Just follow these simple instructions and guidelines:

1. Always fold right-hand pages.

2. Always fold toward you.

3. All folding pages require two folds:
   The top corner will fold down, and
   the bottom corner will fold up.

4. Grasp the top right corner of
   the page, and fold until the
   side of the page aligns exactly
   with the TOP of the gray bar.

5. Grasp the bottom right corner
   of the page, and fold upward until
   the side of the page aligns exactly
   with the BOTTOM of the gray bar.

6. Carefully, run your finger across
   the folds to make sure they are
   straight, crisp and accurate.

7. If the folded corner goes past the
   center crease of the book, simply
   fold back the paper that extends
   past the crease so the page can
   turn normally.

8. Continue on to the next page and
   repeat until your ArtFolds book
   sculpture is complete!

Extra advice

• We recommend washing and then thoroughly drying your hands prior to folding.

• Some folders prefer using a tool to help make fold lines straight and sharp. Bone folders, metal rulers, popsicle sticks, or any other firm, straight tool will work.

• Some folders prefer to rotate their book sideways to make folding easier.

• Remember: The more accurate you are with each fold, the more accurate your completed book sculpture will be!

Folding begins on page 5 and continues until page 319.

For more folding instructions and videos, visit **artfolds.com**.

The Snow Queen
and Other Tales

By Hans Christian Andersen

Table of Contents

The Snow Queen

FIRST STORY. Which Treats of a Mirror and of the Splinters

Now then, let us begin. When we are at the end of the story, we shall know more than we know now: but to begin.

Once upon a time there was a wicked sprite, indeed he was the most mischievous of all sprites. One day he was in a very good humor, for he had made a mirror with the power of causing all that was good and beautiful when it was reflected therein, to look poor and mean; but that which was good-for-nothing and looked ugly was shown magnified and increased in ugliness. In this mirror the most beautiful landscapes looked like boiled spinach, and the best persons were turned into frights, or appeared to stand on their heads; their faces were so distorted that they were not to be recognised; and if anyone had a mole, you might be sure that it would be magnified and spread over both nose and mouth.

"That's glorious fun!" said the sprite. If a good thought passed through a man's mind, then a grin was seen in the mirror, and the sprite laughed heartily at his clever discovery. All the little sprites who went to his school—for he kept a sprite school—told each other that a miracle had happened; and that now only, as they thought, it would be possible to see how the world really looked. They ran about with the mirror; and at last there was not a land or a person who was not represented distorted in the mirror. So then they thought they would fly up to the sky, and have a joke there. The higher they flew with the mirror, the more terribly it grinned: they could hardly hold it fast. Higher and higher still they flew, nearer and nearer to the stars, when suddenly the mirror shook so terribly with grinning, that it flew out of their hands and fell to the earth, where it was dashed in a hundred million and more pieces. And now it worked much more evil than before; for some of these pieces were hardly so large as a grain of sand, and they flew about in the wide world, and when they got into people's eyes, there they stayed; and then people saw everything perverted, or only had an eye for that which was evil. This happened because the very smallest bit had the same power which the whole mirror had possessed. Some persons even got a splinter in their heart, and then it made one shudder, for their heart became like a lump of ice. Some of the broken pieces were so large that they were used for windowpanes, through which one could not see one's friends. Other pieces were put in spectacles; and that was a sad affair when people put on their glasses to see well and rightly. Then the wicked sprite laughed till he almost choked, for all this tickled his fancy. The fine splinters still flew about in the air: and now we shall hear what happened next.

SECOND STORY. A Little Boy and a Little Girl

In a large town, where there are so many houses, and so many people, that there is no roof left for everybody to have a little garden; and where, on this account, most persons are obliged to content themselves with flowers in pots; there lived two little children, who had a garden somewhat larger than a flower-pot. They were not brother and sister; but they cared for each other as much as if they were. Their parents lived exactly opposite. They inhabited two garrets; and where the roof of the one house joined that of the other, and the gutter ran along the extreme end of it, there was to each house a small window: one needed only to step over the gutter to get from one window to the other.

The children's parents had large wooden boxes there, in which vegetables for the kitchen were planted, and little rosetrees besides: there was a rose in each box, and they grew splendidly. They now thought of placing the boxes across the gutter, so that they nearly reached from one window to the other, and looked just like two walls of flowers. The tendrils of the peas hung down over the boxes; and the rose-trees shot up long branches, twined round the windows, and then bent towards each other: it was almost like a triumphant arch of foliage and flowers. The boxes were very high, and the children knew that they must not creep over them; so they often obtained permission to get out of the windows to each other, and to sit on their little stools among the roses, where they could play delightfully. In winter there was an end of this pleasure. The windows were often frozen over; but then they heated copper farthings on the stove, and laid the hot farthing on the windowpane, and then they had a capital peep-hole, quite nicely rounded; and out of each peeped a gentle friendly eye—it was the little boy and the little girl who were looking out. His name was Kay, hers was Gerda. In summer, with one jump, they could get to each other; but in winter they were obliged first to go down the long stairs, and then up the long stairs again: and out-of-doors there was quite a snow-storm.

"It is the white bees that are swarming," said Kay's old grandmother.

"Do the white bees choose a queen?" asked the little boy; for he knew that the honey-bees always have one.

"Yes," said the grandmother, "she flies where the swarm hangs in the thickest clusters. She is the largest of all; and she can never remain quietly on the earth, but goes up again into the black clouds. Many a winter's night she flies through the streets of the town, and peeps in at the windows; and they then freeze in so wondrous a manner that they look like flowers."

"Yes, I have seen it," said both the children; and so they knew that it was true.

"Can the Snow Queen come in?" said the little girl.

"Only let her come in!" said the little boy. "Then I'd put her on the stove, and she'd melt."

And then his grandmother patted his head and told him other stories.

In the evening, when little Kay was at home, and half un-dressed, he climbed up on the chair by the window, and peeped out of the little hole. A few snow-flakes were falling, and one, the largest of all, remained lying on the edge of a flower-pot.

The flake of snow grew larger and larger; and at last it was like a young lady, dressed in the finest white gauze, made of a million little flakes like stars. She was so beautiful and delicate, but she was of ice, of dazzling, sparkling ice; yet she lived; her eyes gazed fixedly, like two stars; but there was neither quiet nor repose in them. She nodded towards the window, and beckoned with her hand. The little boy was frightened, and jumped down from the chair; it seemed to him as if, at the same moment, a large bird flew past the window.

The next day it was a sharp frost—and then the spring came; the sun shone, the green leaves appeared, the swallows built their nests, the windows were opened, and the little children again sat in their pretty garden, high up on the leads at the top of the house.

That summer the roses flowered in unwonted beauty. The little girl had learned a hymn, in which there was something about roses; and then she thought of her own flowers; and she sang the verse to the little boy, who then sang it with her:

"The rose in the valley is blooming so sweet,   And angels descend there the children to greet."

And the children held each other by the hand, kissed the roses, looked up at the clear sunshine, and spoke as though they really saw angels there. What lovely summer-days those were! How delightful to be out in the air, near the fresh rose-bushes, that seem as if they would never finish blossoming!

Kay and Gerda looked at the picture-book full of beasts and of birds; and it was then—the clock in the church-tower was just striking five—that Kay said, "Oh! I feel such a sharp pain in my heart; and now something has got into my eye!"

The little girl put her arms around his neck. He winked his eyes; now there was nothing to be seen.

"I think it is out now," said he; but it was not. It was just one of those pieces of glass from the magic mirror that had got into his eye; and poor Kay had got another piece right in his heart. It will soon become like ice. It did not hurt any longer, but there it was.

"What are you crying for?" asked he. "You look so ugly! There's nothing the matter with me. Ah," said he at once, "that rose is cankered! And look, this one is quite crooked! After all, these roses are very ugly! They are just like the box they are planted in!" And then he gave the box a good kick with his foot, and pulled both the roses up.

"What are you doing?" cried the little girl; and as he perceived her fright, he pulled up another rose, got in at the window, and hastened off from dear little Gerda.

Afterwards, when she brought her picture-book, he asked, "What horrid beasts have you there?" And if his grandmother told them stories, he always interrupted her; besides, if he could manage it, he would get behind her, put on her spectacles, and imitate her way of speaking; he copied all her ways, and then everybody laughed at him. He was soon able to imitate the gait and manner of everyone in the street. Everything that was peculiar and displeasing in them—that Kay knew how to imitate: and at such times all the people said, "The boy is certainly very clever!" But it was the glass he had got in his eye; the glass that was sticking in his heart, which made him tease even little Gerda, whose whole soul was devoted to him.

His games now were quite different to what they had formerly been, they were so very knowing. One winter's day, when the flakes of snow were flying about, he spread the skirts of his blue coat, and caught the snow as it fell.

"Look through this glass, Gerda," said he. And every flake seemed larger, and appeared like a magnificent flower, or beautiful star; it was splendid to look at!

"Look, how clever!" said Kay. "That's much more interesting

than real flowers! They are as exact as possible; there is not a fault in them, if they did not melt!"

It was not long after this, that Kay came one day with large gloves on, and his little sledge at his back, and bawled right into Gerda's ears, "I have permission to go out into the square where the others are playing"; and off he was in a moment.

There, in the market-place, some of the boldest of the boys used to tie their sledges to the carts as they passed by, and so they were pulled along, and got a good ride. It was so capital! Just as they were in the very height of their amusement, a large sledge passed by: it was painted quite white, and there was someone in it wrapped up in a rough white mantle of fur, with a rough white fur cap on his head. The sledge drove round the square twice, and Kay tied on his sledge as quickly as he could, and off he drove with it. On they went quicker and quicker into the next street; and the person who drove turned round to Kay, and nodded to him in a friendly manner, just as if they knew each other. Every time he was going to untie his sledge, the person nodded to him, and then Kay sat quiet; and so on they went till they came outside the gates of the town. Then the snow began to fall so thickly that the little boy could not see an arm's length before him, but still on he went: when suddenly he let go the string he held in his hand in order to get loose from the sledge, but it was of no use; still the little vehicle rushed on with the quickness of the wind. He then cried as loud as he could, but no one heard him; the snow drifted and the sledge flew on, and sometimes it gave a jerk as though they were driving over hedges and ditches. He was quite frightened, and he tried to repeat the Lord's Prayer; but all he could do, he was only able to remember the multiplication table.

The snow-flakes grew larger and larger, till at last they looked just like great white fowls. Suddenly they flew on one side; the large sledge stopped, and the person who drove rose up. It was a lady; her cloak and cap were of snow. She was tall and of slender figure, and of a dazzling whiteness. It was the Snow Queen.

"We have travelled fast," said she; "but it is freezingly cold. Come under my bearskin." And she put him in the sledge beside her, wrapped the fur round him, and he felt as though he were sinking in a snow-wreath.

"Are you still cold?" asked she; and then she kissed his forehead. Ah! it was colder than ice; it penetrated to his very heart, which was already almost a frozen lump; it seemed to him as if he were about to die—but a moment more and it was quite congenial to him, and he did not remark the cold that was around him.

"My sledge! Do not forget my sledge!" It was the first thing he thought of. It was there tied to one of the white chickens, who flew along with it on his back behind the large sledge. The Snow Queen kissed Kay once more, and then he forgot little Gerda, grandmother, and all whom he had left at his home.

"Now you will have no more kisses," said she, "or else I should kiss you to death!"

Kay looked at her. She was very beautiful; a more clever, or a more lovely countenance he could not fancy to himself; and she no longer appeared of ice as before, when she sat outside the window, and beckoned to him; in his eyes she was perfect, he did not fear her at all, and told her that he could calculate in his head and with fractions, even; that he knew the number of square miles there were in the different countries, and how many inhabitants they contained; and she smiled while he spoke. It then seemed to him as if what he knew was not enough, and he looked upwards in the large huge empty space above him, and on she flew with him; flew high over the black clouds, while the storm moaned and whistled as though it were singing some old tune. On they flew over woods and lakes, over seas, and many lands; and beneath them the chilling storm rushed fast, the wolves howled, the snow crackled; above them flew large screaming crows, but higher up appeared the moon, quite large and bright; and it was on it that Kay gazed during the long long winter's night; while by day he slept at the feet of the Snow Queen.

THIRD STORY. *Of the Flower-Garden At the Old Woman's Who Understood Witchcraft*

But what became of little Gerda when Kay did not return? Where could he be? Nobody knew; nobody could give any intelligence. All the boys knew was, that they had seen him tie his sledge to another large and splendid one, which drove down the street and out of the town. Nobody knew where he was; many sad tears were shed, and little Gerda wept long and bitterly; at last she said he must be dead; that he had been drowned in the river which flowed close to the town. Oh! those were very long and dismal winter evenings!

At last spring came, with its warm sunshine.

"Kay is dead and gone!" said little Gerda.

"That I don't believe," said the Sunshine.

"Kay is dead and gone!" said she to the Swallows.

"That I don't believe," said they: and at last little Gerda did not think so any longer either.

"I'll put on my red shoes," said she, one morning; "Kay has never seen them, and then I'll go down to the river and ask there."

It was quite early; she kissed her old grandmother, who was still asleep, put on her red shoes, and went alone to the river.

"Is it true that you have taken my little playfellow? I will make you a present of my red shoes, if you will give him back to me."

And, as it seemed to her, the blue waves nodded in a strange manner; then she took off her red shoes, the most precious things she possessed, and threw them both into the river. But they fell close to the bank, and the little waves bore them immediately to land; it was as if the stream would not take what was dearest to her; for in reality it had not got little Kay; but Gerda thought that she had not thrown the shoes out far enough, so she clambered into a boat which lay among the rushes, went to the farthest end, and threw out the shoes. But the boat was not fastened, and the motion which she occasioned, made it drift from the shore. She observed this, and hastened to get back; but before she could do so, the boat was more than a yard from the land, and was gliding quickly onward.

Little Gerda was very frightened, and began to cry; but no one heard her except the sparrows, and they could not carry her to land; but they flew along the bank, and sang as if to comfort her, "Here we are! Here we are!" The boat drifted with the stream, little Gerda sat quite still without shoes, for they were swimming behind the boat, but she could not reach them, because the boat went much faster than they did.

The banks on both sides were beautiful; lovely flowers, venerable trees, and slopes with sheep and cows, but not a human being was to be seen.

"Perhaps the river will carry me to little Kay," said she; and then she grew less sad. She rose, and looked for many hours at the beautiful green banks. Presently she sailed by a large cherry-orchard, where was a little cottage with curious red and blue windows; it was thatched, and before it two wooden soldiers stood sentry, and presented arms when anyone went past.

Gerda called to them, for she thought they were alive; but they, of course, did not answer. She came close to them, for the stream drifted the boat quite near the land.

Gerda called still louder, and an old woman then came out of the cottage, leaning upon a crooked stick. She had a large broad-brimmed hat on, painted with the most splendid flowers.

"Poor little child!" said the old woman. "How did you get upon the large rapid river, to be driven about so in the wide world!" And then the old woman went into the water, caught hold of the boat with her crooked stick, drew it to the bank, and lifted little Gerda out.

And Gerda was so glad to be on dry land again; but she was rather afraid of the strange old woman.

"But come and tell me who you are, and how you came here," said she.

And Gerda told her all; and the old woman shook her head and said, "A-hem! a-hem!" and when Gerda had told her everything, and asked her if she had not seen little Kay, the woman answered that he had not passed there, but he no doubt would come; and she told her not to be cast down, but taste her cherries, and look at her flowers, which were finer than any in a picture-book, each of which could tell a whole story. She then took Gerda by the hand, led her into the little cottage, and locked the door.

The windows were very high up; the glass was red, blue, and green, and the sunlight shone through quite wondrously in all sorts of colors. On the table stood the most exquisite cherries, and Gerda ate as many as she chose, for she had permission to do so. While she was eating, the old woman combed her hair with a golden comb, and her hair curled and shone with a lovely golden color around that sweet little face, which was so round and so like a rose.

"I have often longed for such a dear little girl," said the old woman. "Now you shall see how well we agree together"; and while she combed little Gerda's hair, the child forgot her foster-brother Kay more and more, for the old woman understood magic; but she was no evil being, she only practised witchcraft a little for her own private amusement, and now she wanted very much to keep little Gerda. She therefore went out in the garden, stretched out her crooked stick towards the rose-bushes, which, beautifully as they were blowing, all sank into the earth and no one could tell where they had stood. The old woman feared that if Gerda should see the roses, she would then think of her own, would remember little Kay, and run away from her.

She now led Gerda into the flower-garden. Oh, what odour and what loveliness was there! Every flower that one could think of, and of every season, stood there in fullest bloom; no picture-book could be gayer or more beautiful. Gerda jumped for joy, and played till the sun set behind the tall cherry-tree; she then had a pretty bed, with a red silken coverlet filled with blue violets. She fell asleep, and had as pleasant dreams as ever a queen on her wedding-day.

The next morning she went to play with the flowers in the warm sunshine, and thus passed away a day. Gerda knew every flower; and, numerous as they were, it still seemed to Gerda that one was wanting, though she did not know which. One day while she was looking at the hat of the old woman painted with flowers, the most beautiful of them all seemed to her to be a rose. The old woman had forgotten to take it from her hat when she made the others vanish in the earth. But so it is when one's thoughts are not collected. "What!" said Gerda. "Are there no roses here?" and she ran about amongst the flowerbeds, and looked, and looked, but there was not one to be found. She then sat down and wept; but her hot tears fell just where a rose-bush had sunk; and when her warm tears watered the ground, the tree shot up suddenly as fresh and blooming as when it had been swallowed up. Gerda kissed the roses, thought of her own dear roses at home, and with them of little Kay.

"Oh, how long I have stayed!" said the little girl. "I intended to look for Kay! Don't you know where he is?" she asked of the roses. "Do you think he is dead and gone?"

"Dead he certainly is not," said the Roses. "We have been in the earth where all the dead are, but Kay was not there."

"Many thanks!" said little Gerda; and she went to the other flowers, looked into their cups, and asked, "Don't you know where little Kay is?"

But every flower stood in the sunshine, and dreamed its own fairy tale or its own story: and they all told her very many things, but not one knew anything of Kay.

Well, what did the Tiger-Lily say?

"Hearest thou not the drum? Bum! Bum! Those are the only two tones. Always bum! Bum! Hark to the plaintive song of the old woman, to the call of the priests! The Hindoo woman in her long robe stands upon the funeral pile; the flames rise around her and her dead husband, but the Hindoo woman thinks on the living one in the surrounding circle; on him whose eyes burn hotter than the flames—on him, the fire of whose eyes pierces her heart more than the flames which soon will burn her body to ashes. Can the heart's flame die in the flame of the funeral pile?"

"I don't understand that at all," said little Gerda.

"That is my story," said the Lily.

What did the Convolvulus say?

"Projecting over a narrow mountain-path there hangs an old feudal castle. Thick evergreens grow on the dilapidated walls, and around the altar, where a lovely maiden is standing: she bends over the railing and looks out upon the rose. No fresher rose hangs on the branches than she; no appleblossom carried away by the wind is more buoyant! How her silken robe is rustling!

"'Is he not yet come?'"

"Is it Kay that you mean?" asked little Gerda.

"I am speaking about my story—about my dream," answered the Convolvulus.

What did the Snowdrops say?

"Between the trees a long board is hanging—it is a swing. Two little girls are sitting in it, and swing themselves backwards and forwards; their frocks are as white as snow, and long green silk ribands flutter from their bonnets. Their brother, who is older than they are, stands up in the swing; he twines his arms round the cords to hold himself fast, for in one hand he has a little cup, and in the other a clay-pipe. He is blowing soap-bubbles. The swing moves, and the bubbles float in charming changing colors: the last is still hanging to the end of the pipe, and rocks in the breeze. The swing moves. The little black dog, as light as a soap-bubble, jumps up on his hind legs to try to get into the swing. It moves, the dog falls down, barks, and is angry. They tease him; the bubble bursts! A swing, a bursting bubble—such is my song!"

"What you relate may be very pretty, but you tell it in so melancholy a manner, and do not mention Kay."

What do the Hyacinths say?

"There were once upon a time three sisters, quite transparent, and very beautiful. The robe of the one was red, that of the second blue, and that of the third white. They danced hand in hand beside the calm lake in the clear moonshine. They were not elfin maidens, but mortal children. A sweet fragrance was smelt, and the maidens vanished in the wood; the fragrance grew stronger—three coffins, and in them three lovely maidens, glided out of the forest and across the lake: the shining glow-worms flew around like little floating lights. Do the dancing maidens sleep, or are they dead? The odour of the flowers says they are corpses; the evening bell tolls for the dead!"

"You make me quite sad," said little Gerda. "I cannot help thinking of the dead maidens. Oh! is little Kay really dead? The Roses have been in the earth, and they say no."

"Ding, dong!" sounded the Hyacinth bells. "We do not toll for little Kay; we do not know him. That is our way of singing, the only one we have."

And Gerda went to the Ranunculuses, that looked forth from among the shining green leaves.

"You are a little bright sun!" said Gerda. "Tell me if you know where I can find my playfellow."

And the Ranunculus shone brightly, and looked again at Gerda. What song could the Ranunculus sing? It was one that said nothing about Kay either.

"In a small court the bright sun was shining in the first days of spring. The beams glided down the white walls of a neighbor's house, and close by the fresh yellow flowers were growing, shining like gold in the warm sun-rays. An old grandmother was sitting in the air; her grand-daughter, the poor and lovely servant just come for a short visit. She knows her grandmother. There was gold, pure virgin gold in that blessed kiss. There, that is my little story," said the Ranunculus.

"My poor old grandmother!" sighed Gerda. "Yes, she is longing for me, no doubt: she is sorrowing for me, as she did for little Kay. But I will soon come home, and then I will bring Kay with me. It is of no use asking the flowers; they only know their own old rhymes, and can tell me nothing." And she tucked up her frock, to enable her to run quicker; but the Narcissus gave her a knock on the leg, just as she was going to jump over it. So she stood still, looked at the long yellow flower, and asked, "You perhaps know something?" and she bent down to the Narcissus. And what did it say?

"I can see myself—I can see myself! Oh, how odorous I am! Up in the little garret there stands, half-dressed, a little Dancer. She stands now on one leg, now on both; she despises the whole world; yet she lives only in imagination. She pours water out of the teapot over a piece of stuff which she holds in her hand; it is the bodice; cleanliness is a fine thing. The white dress is hanging on the hook; it was washed in the teapot, and dried on the roof. She puts it on, ties a saffron-colored kerchief round her neck, and then the gown looks whiter. I can see myself—I can see myself!"

"That's nothing to me," said little Gerda. "That does not concern me." And then off she ran to the further end of the garden.

The gate was locked, but she shook the rusted bolt till it was loosened, and the gate opened; and little Gerda ran off barefooted into the wide world. She looked round her thrice, but no one followed her. At last she could run no longer; she sat down on a large stone, and when she looked about her, she saw that the summer had passed; it was late in the autumn, but that one could not remark in the beautiful garden, where there was always sunshine, and where there were flowers the whole year round.

"Dear me, how long I have staid!" said Gerda. "Autumn is come. I must not rest any longer." And she got up to go further.

Oh, how tender and wearied her little feet were! All around it looked so cold and raw: the long willow-leaves were quite yellow, and the fog dripped from them like water; one leaf fell after the other: the sloes only stood full of fruit, which set one's teeth on edge. Oh, how dark and comfortless it was in the dreary world!

FOURTH STORY. *The Prince and Princess*

Gerda was obliged to rest herself again, when, exactly opposite to her, a large Raven came hopping over the white snow. He had long been looking at Gerda and shaking his head; and now he said, "Caw! Caw!" Good day! Good day! He could not say it better; but he felt a sympathy for the little girl, and asked her where she was going all alone. The word "alone" Gerda understood quite well, and felt how much was expressed by it; so she told the Raven her whole history, and asked if he had not seen Kay.

The Raven nodded very gravely, and said, "It may be—it may be!"

"What, do you really think so?" cried the little girl; and she nearly squeezed the Raven to death, so much did she kiss him.

"Gently, gently," said the Raven. "I think I know; I think that it may be little Kay. But now he has forgotten you for the Princess."

"Does he live with a Princess?" asked Gerda.

"Yes—listen," said the Raven; "but it will be difficult for me to speak your language. If you understand the Raven language I can tell you better."

"No, I have not learnt it," said Gerda; "but my grandmother understands it, and she can speak gibberish too. I wish I had learnt it."

"No matter," said the Raven; "I will tell you as well as I can; however, it will be bad enough." And then he told all he knew.

"In the kingdom where we now are there lives a Princess, who is extraordinarily clever; for she has read all the newspapers in the whole world, and has forgotten them again—so clever is she. She was lately, it is said, sitting on her throne—which is not very amusing after all—when she began humming an old tune, and it was just, 'Oh, why should I not be married?' 'That song is not without its meaning,' said she, and so then she was determined to marry; but she would have a husband who knew how to give an answer when he was spoken to—not one who looked only as if he were a great personage, for that is so tiresome. She then had all the ladies of the court drummed together; and when they heard her intention, all were very pleased, and said, 'We are very glad to hear it; it is the very thing we were thinking of.' You may believe every word I say," said the Raven; "for I have a tame sweetheart that hops about in the palace quite free, and it was she who told me all this.

"The newspapers appeared forthwith with a border of hearts and the initials of the Princess; and therein you might read that every good-looking young man was at liberty to come to the palace and speak to the Princess; and he who spoke in such wise as showed he felt himself at home there, that one the Princess would choose for her husband.

"Yes, Yes," said the Raven, "you may believe it; it is as true as I am sitting here. People came in crowds; there was a crush and a hurry, but no one was successful either on the first or second day. They could all talk well enough when they were out in the street; but as soon as they came inside the palace gates, and saw the guard richly dressed in silver, and the lackeys in gold on the staircase, and the large illuminated saloons, then they were abashed; and when they stood before the throne on which the Princess was sitting, all they could do was to repeat the last word they had uttered, and to hear it again did not interest her very much. It was just as if the people within were under a charm, and had fallen into a trance till they came out again into the street; for then—oh, then—they could chatter enough. There was a whole row of them standing from the town-gates to the palace. I was there myself to look," said the Raven. "They grew hungry and thirsty; but from the palace they got nothing whatever, not even a glass of water. Some of the cleverest, it is true, had taken bread and butter with them: but none shared it with his neighbor, for each thought, 'Let him look hungry, and then the Princess won't have him.'"

"But Kay—little Kay," said Gerda, "when did he come? Was he among the number?"

"Patience, patience; we are just come to him. It was on the third day when a little personage without horse or equipage, came marching right boldly up to the palace; his eyes shone like yours, he had beautiful long hair, but his clothes were very shabby."

"That was Kay," cried Gerda, with a voice of delight. "Oh, now I've found him!" and she clapped her hands for joy.

"He had a little knapsack at his back," said the Raven.

"No, that was certainly his sledge," said Gerda; "for when he went away he took his sledge with him."

"That may be," said the Raven; "I did not examine him so minutely; but I know from my tame sweetheart, that when he came into the court-yard of the palace, and saw the body-guard in silver, the lackeys on the staircase, he was not the least abashed; he nodded, and said to them, 'It must be very tiresome to stand on the stairs; for my part, I shall go in.' The saloons were gleaming with lustres—privy councillors and excellencies were walking about barefooted, and wore gold keys; it was enough to make any one feel uncomfortable. His boots creaked, too, so loudly, but still he was not at all afraid."

"That's Kay for certain," said Gerda. "I know he had on new boots; I have heard them creaking in grandmama's room."

"Yes, they creaked," said the Raven. "And on he went boldly up to the Princess, who was sitting on a pearl as large as a spinning-wheel. All the ladies of the court, with their attendants and

attendants' attendants, and all the cavaliers, with their gentlemen and gentlemen's gentlemen, stood round; and the nearer
they stood to the door, the prouder they looked. It was hardly
possible to look at the gentleman's gentleman, so very haughtily
did he stand in the doorway."

"It must have been terrible," said little Gerda. "And did Kay
get the Princess?"

"Were I not a Raven, I should have taken the Princess myself,
although I am promised. It is said he spoke as well as I speak
when I talk Raven language; this I learned from my tame sweetheart. He was bold and nicely behaved; he had not come to woo
the Princess, but only to hear her wisdom. She pleased him, and
he pleased her."

"Yes, yes; for certain that was Kay," said Gerda. "He was so
clever; he could reckon fractions in his head. Oh, won't you take
me to the palace?"

"That is very easily said," answered the Raven. "But how are
we to manage it? I'll speak to my tame sweetheart about it: she
must advise us; for so much I must tell you, such a little girl as you
are will never get permission to enter."

"Oh, yes I shall," said Gerda; "when Kay hears that I am here,
he will come out directly to fetch me."

"Wait for me here on these steps," said the Raven. He moved
his head backwards and forwards and flew away.

The evening was closing in when the Raven returned. "Caw—
caw!" said he. "She sends you her compliments; and here is a
roll for you. She took it out of the kitchen, where there is bread
enough. You are hungry, no doubt. It is not possible for you to
enter the palace, for you are barefooted: the guards in silver, and
the lackeys in gold, would not allow it; but do not cry, you shall
come in still. My sweetheart knows a little back stair that leads to
the bedchamber, and she knows where she can get the key of it."

And they went into the garden in the large avenue, where one
leaf was falling after the other; and when the lights in the palace

had all gradually disappeared, the Raven led little Gerda to the back door, which stood half open.

Oh, how Gerda's heart beat with anxiety and longing! It was just as if she had been about to do something wrong; and yet she only wanted to know if little Kay was there. Yes, he must be there. She called to mind his intelligent eyes, and his long hair, so vividly, she could quite see him as he used to laugh when they were sitting under the roses at home. "He will, no doubt, be glad to see you—to hear what a long way you have come for his sake; to know how unhappy all at home were when he did not come back."

Oh, what a fright and a joy it was!

They were now on the stairs. A single lamp was burning there; and on the floor stood the tame Raven, turning her head on every side and looking at Gerda, who bowed as her grandmother had taught her to do.

"My intended has told me so much good of you, my dear young lady," said the tame Raven. "Your tale is very affecting. If you will take the lamp, I will go before. We will go straight on, for we shall meet no one."

"I think there is somebody just behind us," said Gerda; and something rushed past: it was like shadowy figures on the wall; horses with flowing manes and thin legs, huntsmen, ladies and gentlemen on horseback.

"They are only dreams," said the Raven. "They come to fetch the thoughts of the high personages to the chase; 'tis well, for now you can observe them in bed all the better. But let me find, when you enjoy honor and distinction, that you possess a grateful heart."

"Tut! That's not worth talking about," said the Raven of the woods.

They now entered the first saloon, which was of rose-colored satin, with artificial flowers on the wall. Here the dreams were rushing past, but they hastened by so quickly that Gerda could not see the high personages. One hall was more magnificent than the other; one might indeed well be abashed; and at last they came into the bedchamber. The ceiling of the room resembled a large palm-tree with leaves of glass, of costly glass; and in the middle, from a thick golden stem, hung two beds, each of which resembled a lily. One was white, and in this lay the Princess; the other was red, and it was here that Gerda was to look for little Kay. She bent back one of the red leaves, and saw a brown neck. Oh! that was Kay! She called him quite loud by name, held the lamp towards him—the dreams rushed back again into the chamber—he awoke, turned his head, and—it was not little Kay!

The Prince was only like him about the neck; but he was young and handsome. And out of the white lily leaves the Princess peeped, too, and asked what was the matter. Then little Gerda cried, and told her her whole history, and all that the Ravens had done for her.

"Poor little thing!" said the Prince and the Princess. They praised the Ravens very much, and told them they were not at all angry with them, but they were not to do so again. However, they should have a reward. "Will you fly about here at liberty," asked the Princess; "or would you like to have a fixed appointment as court ravens, with all the broken bits from the kitchen?"

And both the Ravens nodded, and begged for a fixed appointment; for they thought of their old age, and said, "It is a good thing to have a provision for our old days."

And the Prince got up and let Gerda sleep in his bed, and more than this he could not do. She folded her little hands and thought, "How good men and animals are!" and she then fell asleep and slept soundly. All the dreams flew in again, and they now looked like the angels; they drew a little sledge, in which little Kay sat and nodded his head; but the whole was only a dream, and therefore it all vanished as soon as she awoke.

The next day she was dressed from head to foot in silk and velvet. They offered to let her stay at the palace, and lead a happy life; but she begged to have a little carriage with a horse in front, and for a small pair of shoes; then, she said, she would again go forth in the wide world and look for Kay.

Shoes and a muff were given her; she was, too, dressed very nicely; and when she was about to set off, a new carriage stopped before the door. It was of pure gold, and the arms of the Prince and Princess shone like a star upon it; the coachman, the foot-men, and the outriders, for outriders were there, too, all wore golden crowns. The Prince and the Princess assisted her into the carriage themselves, and wished her all success. The Raven of the woods, who was now married, accompanied her for the first three miles. He sat beside Gerda, for he could not bear riding backwards; the other Raven stood in the doorway, and flapped her wings; she could not accompany Gerda, because she suffered from headache since she had had a fixed appointment and ate so much. The carriage was lined inside with sugar-plums, and in the seats were fruits and gingerbread.

"Farewell! Farewell!" cried Prince and Princess; and Gerda wept, and the Raven wept. Thus passed the first miles; and then the Raven bade her farewell, and this was the most painful sepa-ration of all. He flew into a tree, and beat his black wings as long as he could see the carriage, that shone from afar like a sunbeam.

FIFTH STORY. *The Little Robber Maiden*

They drove through the dark wood; but the carriage shone like a torch, and it dazzled the eyes of the robbers, so that they could not bear to look at it.

"'Tis gold! 'Tis gold!" they cried; and they rushed forward, seized the horses, knocked down the little postilion, the coach-man, and the servants, and pulled little Gerda out of the carriage.

"How plump, how beautiful she is! She must have been fed on nut-kernels," said the old female robber, who had a long, scrubby beard, and bushy eyebrows that hung down over her eyes. "She is as good as a fatted lamb! How nice she will be!" And then she drew out a knife, the blade of which shone so that it was quite dreadful to behold.

"Oh!" cried the woman at the same moment. She had been bitten in the ear by her own little daughter, who hung at her back; and who was so wild and unmanageable, that it was quite amusing to see her. "You naughty child!" said the mother: and now she had not time to kill Gerda.

"She shall play with me," said the little robber child. "She shall give me her muff, and her pretty frock; she shall sleep in my bed!" And then she gave her mother another bite, so that she jumped, and ran round with the pain; and the Robbers laughed, and said, "Look, how she is dancing with the little one!"

"I will go into the carriage," said the little robber maiden; and she would have her will, for she was very spoiled and very head-strong. She and Gerda got in; and then away they drove over the stumps of felled trees, deeper and deeper into the woods. The little robber maiden was as tall as Gerda, but stronger, broader-shouldered, and of dark complexion; her eyes were quite black; they looked almost melancholy. She embraced little Gerda, and said, "They shall not kill you as long as I am not displeased with you. You are, doubtless, a Princess?"

"No," said little Gerda; who then related all that had happened to her, and how much she cared about little Kay.

The little robber maiden looked at her with a serious air, nodded her head slightly, and said, "They shall not kill you, even if I am angry with you: then I will do it myself"; and she dried Gerda's eyes, and put both her hands in the handsome muff, which was so soft and warm.

At length the carriage stopped. They were in the midst of the court-yard of a robber's castle. It was full of cracks from top to bottom; and out of the openings magpies and rooks were flying; and the great bull-dogs, each of which looked as if he could swallow a man, jumped up, but they did not bark, for that was forbidden.

In the midst of the large, old, smoking hall burnt a great fire on the stone floor. The smoke disappeared under the stones, and had to seek its own egress. In an immense caldron soup was boiling; and rabbits and hares were being roasted on a spit.

"You shall sleep with me to-night, with all my animals," said the little robber maiden. They had something to eat and drink; and then went into a corner, where straw and carpets were lying. Beside them, on laths and perches, sat nearly a hundred pigeons, all asleep, seemingly; but yet they moved a little when the robber maiden came. "They are all mine," said she, at the same time seizing one that was next to her by the legs and shaking it so that its wings fluttered. "Kiss it," cried the little girl, and flung the pigeon in Gerda's face. "Up there is the rabble of the wood," continued she, pointing to several laths which were fastened before a hole high up in the wall; "that's the rabble; they would all fly away immediately, if they were not well fastened in. And here is my dear old Bac"; and she laid hold of the horns of a reindeer, that had a bright copper ring round its neck, and was tethered to the spot. "We are obliged to lock this fellow in too, or he would make his escape. Every evening I tickle his neck with my sharp knife; he is so frightened at it!" and the little girl drew forth a long knife, from a crack in the wall, and let it glide over the Reindeer's neck. The poor animal kicked; the girl laughed, and pulled Gerda into bed with her.

"Do you intend to keep your knife while you sleep?" asked Gerda; looking at it rather fearfully.

"I always sleep with the knife," said the little robber maiden. "There is no knowing what may happen. But tell me now, once more, all about little Kay; and why you have started off in the wide world alone." And Gerda related all, from the very beginning: the Wood-pigeons cooed above in their cage, and the others slept. The little robber maiden wound her arm round Gerda's neck, held the knife in the other hand, and snored so loud that everybody could hear her; but Gerda could not close her eyes, for she did not know whether she was to live or die. The robbers sat round the fire, sang and drank; and the old female robber jumped about so, that it was quite dreadful for Gerda to see her.

Then the Wood-pigeons said, "Coo! Coo! We have seen little Kay! A white hen carries his sledge; he himself sat in the carriage of the Snow Queen, who passed here, down just over the wood, as we lay in our nest. She blew upon us young ones; and all died except we two. Coo! Coo!"

"What is that you say up there?" cried little Gerda. "Where did the Snow Queen go to? Do you know anything about it?"

"She is no doubt gone to Lapland; for there is always snow and ice there. Only ask the Reindeer, who is tethered there."

"Ice and snow is there! There it is, glorious and beautiful!" said the Reindeer. "One can spring about in the large shining valleys! The Snow Queen has her summer-tent there; but her fixed abode is high up towards the North Pole, on the Island called Spitzbergen."

"Oh, Kay! Poor little Kay!" sighed Gerda.

"Do you choose to be quiet?" said the robber maiden. "If you don't, I shall make you."

In the morning Gerda told her all that the Wood-pigeons had said; and the little maiden looked very serious, but she nodded her head, and said, "That's no matter—that's no matter. Do you know where Lapland lies!" she asked of the Reindeer.

"Who should know better than I?" said the animal; and his eyes rolled in his head. "I was born and bred there—there I leapt about on the fields of snow."

"Listen," said the robber maiden to Gerda. "You see that the men are gone; but my mother is still here, and will remain. However, towards morning she takes a draught out of the large flask,

and then she sleeps a little: then I will do something for you."
She now jumped out of bed, flew to her mother; with her arms
round her neck, and pulling her by the beard, said, "Good morrow, my own sweet nanny-goat of a mother." And her mother
took hold of her nose, and pinched it till it was red and blue; but
this was all done out of pure love.

When the mother had taken a sup at her flask, and was having
a nap, the little robber maiden went to the Reindeer, and said, "I
should very much like to give you still many a tickling with the
sharp knife, for then you are so amusing; however, I will unte-
ther you, and help you out, so that you may go back to Lapland.
But you must make good use of your legs; and take this little girl
for me to the palace of the Snow Queen, where her playfellow
is. You have heard, I suppose, all she said; for she spoke loud
enough, and you were listening."

The Reindeer gave a bound for joy. The robber maiden lifted
up little Gerda, and took the precaution to bind her fast on the
Reindeer's back; she even gave her a small cushion to sit on.
"Here are your worsted leggins, for it will be cold; but the muff I
shall keep for myself, for it is so very pretty. But I do not wish you
to be cold. Here is a pair of lined gloves of my mother's; they just
reach up to your elbow. On with them! Now you look about the
hands just like my ugly old mother!"

And Gerda wept for joy.

"I can't bear to see you fretting," said the little robber maiden.
"This is just the time when you ought to look pleased. Here are
two loaves and a ham for you, so that you won't starve." The
bread and the meat were fastened to the Reindeer's back; the
little maiden opened the door, called in all the dogs, and then
with her knife cut the rope that fastened the animal, and said to
him, "Now, off with you; but take good care of the little girl!"

And Gerda stretched out her hands with the large wadded
gloves towards the robber maiden, and said, "Farewell!" and the

Reindeer flew on over bush and bramble through the great wood, over moor and heath, as fast as he could go.

"Ddsa! Ddsa!" was heard in the sky. It was just as if somebody was sneezing.

"These are my old northern-lights," said the Reindeer, "look how they gleam!" And on he now sped still quicker—day and night on he went: the loaves were consumed, and the ham too; and now they were in Lapland.

SIXTH STORY. *The Lapland Woman and the Finland Woman*

Suddenly they stopped before a little house, which looked very miserable. The roof reached to the ground; and the door was so low, that the family were obliged to creep upon their stomachs when they went in or out. Nobody was at home except an old Lapland woman, who was dressing fish by the light of an oil lamp. And the Reindeer told her the whole of Gerda's history, but first of all his own; for that seemed to him of much greater importance. Gerda was so chilled that she could not speak.

"Poor thing," said the Lapland woman, "you have far to run still. You have more than a hundred miles to go before you get to Finland; there the Snow Queen has her country-house, and burns blue lights every evening. I will give you a few words from me, which I will write on a dried haberdine, for paper I have none; this you can take with you to the Finland woman, and she will be able to give you more information than I can."

When Gerda had warmed herself, and had eaten and drunk, the Lapland woman wrote a few words on a dried haberdine, begged Gerda to take care of them, put her on the Reindeer, bound her fast, and away sprang the animal. "Ddsa! Ddsa!" was again heard in the air; the most charming blue lights burned the whole night in the sky, and at last they came to Finland. They knocked at the chimney of the Finland woman; for as to a door, she had none.

There was such a heat inside that the Finland woman herself went about almost naked. She was diminutive and dirty. She immediately loosened little Gerda's clothes, pulled off her thick gloves and boots; for otherwise the heat would have been too great—and after laying a piece of ice on the Reindeer's head, read what was written on the fish-skin. She read it three times: she then knew it by heart; so she put the fish into the cupboard—for it might very well be eaten, and she never threw anything away.

Then the Reindeer related his own story first, and afterwards that of little Gerda; and the Finland woman winked her eyes, but said nothing.

"You are so clever," said the Reindeer; "you can, I know, twist all the winds of the world together in a knot. If the seaman loosens one knot, then he has a good wind; if a second, then it blows pretty stiffly; if he undoes the third and fourth, then it rages so that the forests are upturned. Will you give the little maiden a potion, that she may possess the strength of twelve men, and vanquish the Snow Queen?"

"The strength of twelve men!" said the Finland woman. "Much good that would be!" Then she went to a cupboard, and drew out a large skin rolled up. When she had unrolled it, strange characters were to be seen written thereon; and the Finland woman read at such a rate that the perspiration trickled down her forehead.

But the Reindeer begged so hard for little Gerda, and Gerda looked so imploringly with tearful eyes at the Finland woman, that she winked, and drew the Reindeer aside into a corner, where they whispered together, while the animal got some fresh ice put on his head.

"'Tis true little Kay is at the Snow Queen's, and finds everything there quite to his taste; and he thinks it the very best place in the world; but the reason of that is, he has a splinter of glass in his eye, and in his heart. These must be got out first; otherwise he will never go back to mankind, and the Snow Queen will retain her power over him."

"But can you give little Gerda nothing to take which will endue her with power over the whole?"

"I can give her no more power than what she has already. Don't you see how great it is? Don't you see how men and animals are forced to serve her; how well she gets through the world barefooted? She must not hear of her power from us; that power lies in her heart, because she is a sweet and innocent child! If she cannot get to the Snow Queen by herself, and rid little Kay of the glass, we cannot help her. Two miles hence the garden of the Snow Queen begins; thither you may carry the little girl. Set her down by the large bush with red berries, standing in the snow; don't stay talking, but hasten back as fast as possible." And now the Finland woman placed little Gerda on the Reindeer's back, and off he ran with all imaginable speed.

"Oh! I have not got my boots! I have not brought my gloves!" cried little Gerda. She remarked she was without them from the cutting frost; but the Reindeer dared not stand still; on he ran till he came to the great bush with the red berries, and there he set Gerda down, kissed her mouth, while large bright tears flowed from the animal's eyes, and then back he went as fast as possible. There stood poor Gerda now, without shoes or gloves, in the very middle of dreadful icy Finland.

She ran on as fast as she could. There then came a whole regiment of snow-flakes, but they did not fall from above, and they were quite bright and shining from the Aurora Borealis. The flakes ran along the ground, and the nearer they came the larger they grew. Gerda well remembered how large and strange the snow-flakes appeared when she once saw them through a magnifying-glass; but now they were large and terrific in another manner—they were all alive. They were the outposts of the Snow Queen. They had the most wondrous shapes; some looked like large ugly porcupines; others like snakes knotted together, with their heads sticking out; and others, again, like small fat bears, with the hair standing on end: all were of dazzling whiteness—all were living snow-flakes.

Little Gerda repeated the Lord's Prayer. The cold was so intense that she could see her own breath, which came like smoke out of her mouth. It grew thicker and thicker, and took the form of little angels, that grew more and more when they touched the earth. All had helms on their heads, and lances and shields in their hands; they increased in numbers; and when Gerda had finished the Lord's Prayer, she was surrounded by a whole legion. They thrust at the horrid snow-flakes with their spears, so that they flew into a thousand pieces; and little Gerda walked on bravely and in security. The angels patted her hands and feet; and then she felt the cold less, and went on quickly towards the palace of the Snow Queen.

But now we shall see how Kay fared. He never thought of Gerda, and least of all that she was standing before the palace.

SEVENTH STORY *What Took Place in the Palace of the Snow Queen, and what Happened Afterward.*

The walls of the palace were of driving snow, and the windows and doors of cutting winds. There were more than a hundred halls there, according as the snow was driven by the winds. The largest was many miles in extent; all were lighted up by the powerful Aurora Borealis, and all were so large, so empty, so icy cold, and so resplendent! Mirth never reigned there; there was never even a little bear-ball, with the storm for music, while the polar bears went on their hind legs and showed off their steps. Never a little tea-party of white young lady foxes; vast, cold, and empty were the halls of the Snow Queen. The northern-lights shone with such precision that one could tell exactly when they were at their highest or lowest degree of brightness. In the middle of the empty, endless hall of snow, was a frozen lake; it was cracked in a thousand pieces, but each piece was so like the other, that it seemed the work of a cunning artificer. In the middle of this lake sat the Snow Queen when she was at home; and then she said she was sitting in the Mirror of Understanding, and that this was the only one and the best thing in the world.

Little Kay was quite blue, yes nearly black with cold; but he did not observe it, for she had kissed away all feeling of cold from his body, and his heart was a lump of ice. He was dragging along some pointed flat pieces of ice, which he laid together in all possible ways, for he wanted to make something with them; just as we have little flat pieces of wood to make geometrical figures with, called the Chinese Puzzle. Kay made all sorts of figures, the most complicated, for it was an ice-puzzle for the understanding. In his eyes the figures were extraordinarily beautiful, and of the utmost importance; for the bit of glass which was in his eye caused this. He found whole figures which represented a written word; but he never could manage to represent just the word he wanted—that word was "eternity"; and the Snow Queen had said, "If you can discover that figure, you shall be your own master, and I will make you a present of the whole world and a pair of new skates." But he could not find it out.

"I am going now to warm lands," said the Snow Queen. "I must have a look down into the black caldrons." It was the volcanoes Vesuvius and Etna that she meant. "I will just give them a coating of white, for that is as it ought to be; besides, it is good for the oranges and the grapes." And then away she flew, and Kay sat quite alone in the empty halls of ice that were miles long, and looked at the blocks of ice, and thought and thought till his skull was almost cracked. There he sat quite benumbed and motionless; one would have imagined he was frozen to death.

Suddenly little Gerda stepped through the great portal into the palace. The gate was formed of cutting winds; but Gerda repeated her evening prayer, and the winds were laid as though they slept; and the little maiden entered the vast, empty, cold halls. There she beheld Kay: she recognised him, flew to embrace him, and cried out, her arms firmly holding him the while, "Kay, sweet little Kay! Have I then found you at last?"

But he sat quite still, benumbed and cold. Then little Gerda shed burning tears; and they fell on his bosom, they penetrated to his heart, they thawed the lumps of ice, and consumed the splinters of the looking-glass; he looked at her, and she sang the hymn:

"The rose in the valley is blooming so sweet, And angels descend there the children to greet."

Hereupon Kay burst into tears; he wept so much that the splinter rolled out of his eye, and he recognised her, and shouted, "Gerda, sweet little Gerda! Where have you been so long? And where have I been?" He looked round him. "How cold it is here!" said he. "How empty and cold!" And he held fast by Gerda, who laughed and wept for joy. It was so beautiful, that even the blocks of ice danced about for joy; and when they were tired and laid themselves down, they formed exactly the letters which the Snow Queen had told him to find out; so now he was his own master, and he would have the whole world and a pair of new skates into the bargain.

Gerda kissed his cheeks, and they grew quite blooming; she kissed his eyes, and they shone like her own; she kissed his hands and feet, and he was again well and merry. The Snow Queen might come back as soon as she liked; there stood his discharge written in resplendent masses of ice.

They took each other by the hand, and wandered forth out of the large hall; they talked of their old grandmother, and of the roses upon the roof; and wherever they went, the winds ceased raging, and the sun burst forth. And when they reached the bush with the red berries, they found the Reindeer waiting for them. He had brought another, a young one, with him, whose udder was filled with milk, which he gave to the little ones, and kissed their lips. They then carried Kay and Gerda—first to the Finland woman, where they warmed themselves in the warm room, and learned what they were to do on their journey home; and they went to the Lapland woman, who made some new clothes for them and repaired their sledges.

The Reindeer and the young hind leaped along beside them, and accompanied them to the boundary of the country. Here the first vegetation peeped forth; here Kay and Gerda took leave of the Lapland woman. "Farewell! Farewell!" they all said. And the first green buds appeared, the first little birds began to chirrup; and out of the wood came, riding on a magnificent horse, which Gerda knew (it was one of the leaders in the golden carriage), a young damsel with a bright-red cap on her head, and armed with pistols. It was the little robber maiden, who, tired of being at home, had determined to make a journey to the north; and afterwards in another direction, if that did not please her. She recognised Gerda immediately, and Gerda knew her too. It was a joyful meeting.

"You are a fine fellow for tramping about," said she to little Kay; "I should like to know, faith, if you deserve that one should run from one end of the world to the other for your sake?"

But Gerda patted her cheeks, and inquired for the Prince and Princess.

"They are gone abroad," said the other.

"But the Raven?" asked little Gerda.

"Oh! The Raven is dead," she answered. "His tame sweetheart is a widow, and wears a bit of black worsted round her leg; she laments most piteously, but it's all mere talk and stuff! Now tell me what you've been doing and how you managed to catch him."

And Gerda and Kay both told their story.

And "Schnipp-schnapp-schnurre-basselurre," said the robber maiden; and she took the hands of each, and promised that if she should some day pass through the town where they lived, she would come and visit them; and then away she rode. Kay and

Gerda took each other's hand: it was lovely spring weather, with abundance of flowers and of verdure. The church-bells rang, and the children recognised the high towers, and the large town; it was that in which they dwelt. They entered and hastened up to their grandmother's room, where everything was standing as formerly. The clock said "tick! tack!" and the finger moved round; but as they entered, they remarked that they were now grown up. The roses on the leads hung blooming in at the open window; there stood the little children's chairs, and Kay and Gerda sat down on them, holding each other by the hand; they both had forgotten the cold empty splendor of the Snow Queen, as though it had been a dream. The grandmother sat in the bright sunshine, and read aloud from the Bible: "Unless ye become as little children, ye cannot enter the kingdom of heaven."

And Kay and Gerda looked in each other's eyes, and all at once they understood the old hymn:

"The rose in the valley is blooming so sweet, And angels descend there the children to greet."

There sat the two grown-up persons; grown-up, and yet children; children at least in heart; and it was summer-time; summer, glorious summer!

The Red Shoes

There was once a little girl who was very pretty and delicate, but in summer she was forced to run about with bare feet, she was so poor, and in winter wear very large wooden shoes, which made her little insteps quite red, and that looked so dangerous!

In the middle of the village lived old Dame Shoemaker; she sat and sewed together, as well as she could, a little pair of shoes out of old red strips of cloth; they were very clumsy, but it was a kind thought. They were meant for the little girl. The little girl was called Karen.

On the very day her mother was buried, Karen received the red shoes, and wore them for the first time. They were certainly not intended for mourning, but she had no others, and with stocking-less feet she followed the poor straw coffin in them.

Suddenly a large old carriage drove up, and a large old lady sat in it: she looked at the little girl, felt compassion for her, and then said to the clergyman:

"Here, give me the little girl. I will adopt her!"

And Karen believed all this happened on account of the red shoes, but the old lady thought they were horrible, and they were burnt. But Karen herself was cleanly and nicely dressed; she must learn to read and sew; and people said she was a nice little thing, but the looking-glass said: "Thou art more than nice, thou art beautiful!"

Now the queen once travelled through the land, and she had her little daughter with her. And this little daughter was a princess, and people streamed to the castle, and Karen was there also, and the little princess stood in her fine white dress, in a window, and let herself be stared at; she had neither a train nor a golden crown, but splendid red morocco shoes. They were certainly far handsomer than those Dame Shoemaker had made for little Karen. Nothing in the world can be compared with red shoes.

Now Karen was old enough to be confirmed; she had new clothes and was to have new shoes also. The rich shoemaker in the city took the measure of her little foot. This took place at his house, in his room; where stood large glass-cases, filled with elegant shoes and brilliant boots. All this looked charming, but the old lady could not see well, and so had no pleasure in them. In the midst of the shoes stood a pair of red ones, just like those the princess had worn. How beautiful they were! The shoemaker said also they had been made for the child of a count, but had not fitted.

"That must be patent leather!" said the old lady. "They shine so!"

"Yes, they shine!" said Karen, and they fitted, and were bought, but the old lady knew nothing about their being red, else she would never have allowed Karen to have gone in red shoes to be confirmed. Yet such was the case.

Everybody looked at her feet; and when she stepped through the chancel door on the church pavement, it seemed to her as if the old figures on the tombs, those portraits of old preachers and preachers' wives, with stiff ruffs, and long black dresses, fixed their eyes on her red shoes. And she thought only of them as the clergyman laid his hand upon her head, and spoke of the holy baptism, of the covenant with God, and how she should be now a matured Christian; and the organ pealed so solemnly; the sweet children's voices sang, and the old music-directors sang, but Karen only thought of her red shoes.

In the afternoon, the old lady heard from everyone that the shoes had been red, and she said that it was very wrong of Karen, that it was not at all becoming, and that in future Karen should only go in black shoes to church, even when she should be older.

The next Sunday there was the sacrament, and Karen looked at the black shoes, looked at the red ones—looked at them again, and put on the red shoes.

The sun shone gloriously; Karen and the old lady walked along the path through the corn; it was rather dusty there.

At the church door stood an old soldier with a crutch, and with a wonderfully long beard, which was more red than white, and he bowed to the ground, and asked the old lady whether he might dust her shoes. And Karen stretched out her little foot.

"See, what beautiful dancing shoes!" said the soldier. "Sit firm when you dance"; and he put his hand out towards the soles.

And the old lady gave the old soldier alms, and went into the church with Karen.

And all the people in the church looked at Karen's red shoes, and all the pictures, and as Karen knelt before the altar, and raised the cup to her lips, she only thought of the red shoes, and they seemed to swim in it; and she forgot to sing her psalm, and she forgot to pray, "Our Father in Heaven!"

Now all the people went out of church, and the old lady got into her carriage. Karen raised her foot to get in after her, when the old soldier said,

"Look, what beautiful dancing shoes!"

And Karen could not help dancing a step or two, and when she began her feet continued to dance; it was just as though the shoes had power over them. She danced round the church corner, she could not leave off; the coachman was obliged to run after and catch hold of her, and he lifted her in the carriage, but her feet continued to dance so that she trod on the old lady dreadfully. At length she took the shoes off, and then her legs had peace.

The shoes were placed in a closet at home, but Karen could not avoid looking at them.

Now the old lady was sick, and it was said she could not recover. She must be nursed and waited upon, and there was no one whose duty it was so much as Karen's. But there was a great ball in the city, to which Karen was invited. She looked at the old lady, who could not recover, she looked at the red shoes, and she thought there could be no sin in it; she put on the red shoes, she might do that also, she thought. But then she went to the ball and began to dance.

When she wanted to dance to the right, the shoes would dance to the left, and when she wanted to dance up the room, the shoes danced back again, down the steps, into the street, and out of the city gate. She danced, and was forced to dance straight out into the gloomy wood.

Then it was suddenly light up among the trees, and she fancied it must be the moon, for there was a face; but it was the old soldier with the red beard; he sat there, nodded his head, and said, "Look, what beautiful dancing shoes!"

Then she was terrified, and wanted to fling off the red shoes, but they clung fast; and she pulled down her stockings, but the shoes seemed to have grown to her feet. And she danced, and must dance, over fields and meadows, in rain and sunshine, by night and day; but at night it was the most fearful.

She danced over the churchyard, but the dead did not dance— they had something better to do than to dance. She wished to seat herself on a poor man's grave, where the bitter tansy grew; but for her there was neither peace nor rest; and when she danced towards the open church door, she saw an angel standing there. He wore long, white garments; he had wings which reached from his shoulders to the earth; his countenance was severe and grave; and in his hand he held a sword, broad and glittering.

"Dance shalt thou!" said he. "Dance in thy red shoes till thou art pale and cold! Till thy skin shrivels up and thou art a skeleton! Dance shalt thou from door to door, and where proud, vain children dwell, thou shalt knock, that they may hear thee and tremble! Dance shalt thou—!"

"Mercy!" cried Karen. But she did not hear the angel's reply, for the shoes carried her through the gate into the fields, across roads and bridges, and she must keep ever dancing.

One morning she danced past a door which she well knew. Within sounded a psalm; a coffin, decked with flowers, was borne forth. Then she knew that the old lady was dead, and felt that she was abandoned by all, and condemned by the angel of God.

She danced, and she was forced to dance through the gloomy night. The shoes carried her over stack and stone; she was torn till she bled; she danced over the heath till she came to a little house. Here, she knew, dwelt the executioner; and she tapped with her fingers at the window, and said, "Come out! Come out! I cannot come in, for I am forced to dance!"

And the executioner said, "Thou dost not know who I am, I fancy? I strike bad people's heads off; and I hear that my axe rings!"

"Don't strike my head off!" said Karen. "Then I can't repent of my sins! But strike off my feet in the red shoes!"

And then she confessed her entire sin, and the executioner struck off her feet with the red shoes, but the shoes danced away with the little feet across the field into the deep wood.

And he carved out little wooden feet for her, and crutches, taught her the psalm criminals always sing; and she kissed the hand which had wielded the axe, and went over the heath.

"Now I have suffered enough for the red shoes!" said she. "Now I will go into the church that people may see me!" And she hastened towards the church door: but when she was near it, the red shoes danced before her, and she was terrified, and turned round. The whole week she was unhappy, and wept many bitter tears; but when Sunday returned, she said, "Well, now I have suffered and struggled enough! I really believe I am as good as many a one who sits in the church, and holds her head so high!"

And away she went boldly; but she had not got farther than the churchyard gate before she saw the red shoes dancing before her; and she was frightened, and turned back, and repented of her sin from her heart.

And she went to the parsonage, and begged that they would take her into service; she would be very industrious, she said, and would do everything she could; she did not care about the wages, only she wished to have a home, and be with good people. And the clergyman's wife was sorry for her and took her into service;

and she was industrious and thoughtful. She sat still and listened when the clergyman read the Bible in the evenings. All the children thought a great deal of her; but when they spoke of dress, and grandeur, and beauty, she shook her head.

The following Sunday, when the family was going to church, they asked her whether she would not go with them; but she glanced sorrowfully, with tears in her eyes, at her crutches. The family went to hear the word of God; but she went alone into her little chamber; there was only room for a bed and chair to stand in it; and here she sat down with her Prayer-Book; and whilst she read with a pious mind, the wind bore the strains of the organ towards her, and she raised her tearful countenance, and said, "O God, help me!"

And the sun shone so clearly, and straight before her stood the angel of God in white garments, the same she had seen that night at the church door; but he no longer carried the sharp sword, but in its stead a splendid green spray, full of roses. And he touched the ceiling with the spray, and the ceiling rose so high, and where he had touched it there gleamed a golden star. And he touched the walls, and they widened out, and she saw the organ which was playing; she saw the old pictures of the preachers and the preachers' wives. The congregation sat in cushioned seats, and sang out of their Prayer-Books. For the church itself had come to the poor girl in her narrow chamber, or else she had come into the church. She sat in the pew with the clergyman's family, and when they had ended the psalm and looked up, they nodded and said, "It is right that thou art come!"

"It was through mercy!" she said.

And the organ pealed, and the children's voices in the choir sounded so sweet and soft! The clear sunshine streamed so warmly through the window into the pew where Karen sat! Her heart was so full of sunshine, peace, and joy, that it broke. Her soul flew on the sunshine to God, and there no one asked after the RED SHOES.

The Snowdrop

It was winter-time; the air was cold, the wind was sharp, but within the closed doors it was warm and comfortable, and within the closed door lay the flower; it lay in the bulb under the snow-covered earth.

One day rain fell. The drops penetrated through the snowy covering down into the earth, and touched the flower-bulb, and talked of the bright world above. Soon the Sunbeam pierced its way through the snow to the root, and within the root there was a stirring.

"Come in," said the flower.

"I cannot," said the Sunbeam. "I am not strong enough to unlock the door! When the summer comes I shall be strong!"

"When will it be summer?" asked the Flower, and she repeated this question each time a new sunbeam made its way down to her. But the summer was yet far distant. The snow still lay upon the ground, and there was a coat of ice on the water every night.

"What a long time it takes! what a long time it takes!" said the Flower. "I feel a stirring and striving within me; I must stretch myself, I must unlock the door, I must get out, and must nod a good morning to the summer, and what a happy time that will be!"

And the Flower stirred and stretched itself within the thin rind which the water had softened from without, and the snow and the earth had warmed, and the Sunbeam had knocked at; and it shot forth under the snow with a greenish-white blossom on a green stalk, with narrow thick leaves, which seemed to want to protect it. The snow was cold, but was pierced by the Sunbeam, therefore it was easy to get through it, and now the Sunbeam came with greater strength than before.

"Welcome, welcome!" sang and sounded every ray, and the

Flower lifted itself up over the snow into the brighter world. The Sunbeams caressed and kissed it, so that it opened altogether, white as snow, and ornamented with green stripes. It bent its head in joy and humility.

"Beautiful Flower!" said the Sunbeams, "how graceful and delicate you are! You are the first, you are the only one! You are our love! You are the bell that rings out for summer, beautiful summer, over country and town. All the snow will melt; the cold winds will be driven away; we shall rule; all will become green, and then you will have companions, syringas, laburnums, and roses; but you are the first, so graceful, so delicate!"

That was a great pleasure. It seemed as if the air were singing and sounding, as if rays of light were piercing through the leaves and the stalks of the Flower. There it stood, so delicate and so easily broken, and yet so strong in its young beauty; it stood there in its white dress with the green stripes, and made a summer. But there was a long time yet to the summer-time. Clouds hid the sun, and bleak winds were blowing.

"You have come too early," said Wind and Weather. "We have still the power, and you shall feel it, and give it up to us. You should have stayed quietly at home and not have run out to make a display of yourself. Your time is not come yet!"

It was a cutting cold! The days which now come brought not a single sunbeam. It was weather that might break such a little Flower in two with cold. But the Flower had more strength than she herself knew of. She was strong in joy and in faith in the summer, which would be sure to come, which had been announced by her deep longing and confirmed by the warm sunlight; and so she remained standing in confidence in the snow in her white garment, bending her head even while the snow-flakes fell thick and heavy, and the icy winds swept over her.

"You'll break!" they said, "and fade, and fade! What did you want out here? Why did you let yourself be tempted? The Sunbeam only made game of you. Now you have what you deserve, you summer gauk."

"Summer gauk!" she repeated in the cold morning hour.

"O summer gauk!" cried some children rejoicingly; "yonder stands one—how beautiful, how beautiful! The first one, the only one!"

These words did the Flower so much good, they seemed to her like warm sunbeams. In her joy the Flower did not even feel when it was broken off. It lay in a child's hand, and was kissed by a child's mouth, and carried into a warm room, and looked on by gentle eyes, and put into water. How strengthening, how invigorating! The Flower thought she had suddenly come upon the summer.

The daughter of the house, a beautiful little girl, was confirmed, and she had a friend who was confirmed, too. He was studying for an examination for an appointment. "He shall be my summer gauk," she said; and she took the delicate Flower and laid it in a piece of scented paper, on which verses were written, beginning with summer gauk and ending with summer gauk. "My friend, be a winter gauk." She had twitted him with the summer. Yes, all this was in the verses, and the paper was folded up like a letter, and the Flower was folded in the letter, too. It was dark around her, dark as in those days when she lay hidden in the bulb. The Flower went forth on her journey, and lay in the post-bag, and was pressed and crushed, which was not at all pleasant; but that soon came to an end.

The journey was over; the letter was opened, and read by the dear friend. How pleased he was! He kissed the letter, and it was laid, with its enclosure of verses, in a box, in which there were many beautiful verses, but all of them without flowers; she was the first, the only one, as the Sunbeams had called her; and it was a pleasant thing to think of that.

She had time enough, moreover, to think about it; she thought of it while the summer passed away, and the long winter went by, and the summer came again, before she appeared once more. But now the young man was not pleased at all. He took hold of the letter very roughly, and threw the verses away, so that the Flower fell on the ground. Flat and faded she certainly was, but why should she be thrown on the ground? Still, it was better to be here than in the fire, where the verses and the paper were being burnt to ashes. What had happened? What happens so often:— the Flower had made a gauk of him, that was a jest; the girl had made a fool of him, that was no jest, she had, during the summer, chosen another friend.

Next morning the sun shone in upon the little flattened Snow-drop, that looked as if it had been painted upon the floor. The servant girl, who was sweeping out the room, picked it up, and laid it in one of the books which were upon the table, in the belief that it must have fallen out while the room was being ar-ranged. Again the flower lay among verses—printed verses—and they are better than written ones—at least, more money has been spent upon them.

And after this years went by. The book stood upon the book-shelf, and then it was taken up and somebody read out of it. It was a good book; verses and songs by the old Danish poet, Ambrosius Stub, which are well worth reading. The man who was now read-ing the book turned over a page.

"Why, there's a flower!" he said; "a snowdrop, a summer gauk, a poet gauk! That flower must have been put in there with a mean-ing! Poor Ambrosius Stub! he was a summer fool too, a poet fool; he came too early, before his time, and therefore he had to taste the sharp winds, and wander about as a guest from one noble landed proprietor to another, like a flower in a glass of water, a flower in rhymed verses! Summer fool, winter fool, fun and fol-ly—but the first, the only, the fresh young Danish poet of those days. Yes, thou shalt remain as a token in the book, thou little snowdrop: thou hast been put there with a meaning."

And so the Snowdrop was put back into the book, and felt

equally honored and pleased to know that it was a token in the glorious book of songs, and that he who was the first to sing and to write had been also a snowdrop, had been a summer gauk, and had been looked upon in the winter-time as a fool. The Flower understood this, in her way, as we interpret everything in our way.

That is the story of the Snowdrop.

The Ugly Duckling

It was lovely summer weather in the country, and the golden corn, the green oats, and the haystacks piled up in the meadows looked beautiful. The stork walking about on his long red legs chattered in the Egyptian language, which he had learnt from his mother. The corn-fields and meadows were surrounded by large forests, in the midst of which were deep pools. It was, indeed, delightful to walk about in the country. In a sunny spot stood a pleasant old farm-house close by a deep river, and from the house down to the water side grew great burdock leaves, so high, that under the tallest of them a little child could stand upright. The spot was as wild as the centre of a thick wood. In this snug retreat sat a duck on her nest, watching for her young brood to hatch; she was beginning to get tired of her task, for the little ones were a long time coming out of their shells, and she seldom had any visitors. The other ducks liked much better to swim about in the river than to climb the slippery banks, and sit under a burdock leaf, to have a gossip with her. At length one shell cracked, and then another, and from each egg came a living creature that lifted its head and cried, "Peep, peep." "Quack, quack," said the mother, and then they all quacked as well as they could, and looked about them on every side at the large green leaves. Their mother allowed them to look as much as they liked, because green is good for the eyes. "How large the world is," said the young ducks, when they found how much more room they now had than while they were inside the egg-shell. "Do you imagine this is the whole world?" asked the mother; "Wait till you have seen the garden; it stretches far beyond that to the parson's field, but I have never ventured to such a distance. Are you all out?" she continued, rising; "No, I declare, the largest egg lies there still. I wonder how long this is to last, I am quite tired of it;" and she seated herself again on the nest.

"Well, how are you getting on?" asked an old duck, who paid her a visit.

"One egg is not hatched yet," said the duck, "it will not break. But just look at all the others, are they not the prettiest little ducklings you ever saw? They are the image of their father, who is so unkind, he never comes to see."

"Let me see the egg that will not break," said the duck; "I have no doubt it is a turkey's egg. I was persuaded to hatch some once, and after all my care and trouble with the young ones, they were afraid of the water. I quacked and clucked, but all to no purpose. I could not get them to venture in. Let me look at the egg. Yes, that is a turkey's egg; take my advice, leave it where it is and teach the other children to swim."

"I think I will sit on it a little while longer," said the duck; "as I have sat so long already, a few days will be nothing."

"Please yourself," said the old duck, and she went away.

At last the large egg broke, and a young one crept forth crying, "Peep, peep." It was very large and ugly. The duck stared at it and exclaimed, "It is very large and not at all like the others. I wonder if it really is a turkey. We shall soon find it out, however when we go to the water. It must go in, if I have to push it myself."

On the next day the weather was delightful, and the sun shone brightly on the green burdock leaves, so the mother duck took her young brood down to the water, and jumped in with a splash. "Quack, quack," cried she, and one after another the little ducklings jumped in. The water closed over their heads, but they came up again in an instant, and swam about quite prettily with their legs paddling under them as easily as possible, and the ugly duckling was also in the water swimming with them.

"Oh," said the mother, "that is not a turkey; how well he uses his legs, and how upright he holds himself! He is my own child, and he is not so very ugly after all if you look at him properly. Quack, quack! come with me now, I will take you into grand society, and introduce you to the farmyard, but you must keep close to me or you may be trodden upon; and, above all, beware of the cat."

When they reached the farmyard, there was a great disturbance, two families were fighting for an eel's head, which, after all, was carried off by the cat. "See, children, that is the way of the world," said the mother duck, whetting her beak, for she would have liked the eel's head herself. "Come, now, use your legs, and let me see how well you can behave. You must bow your heads prettily to that old duck yonder; she is the highest born of them all, and has Spanish blood, therefore, she is well off. Don't you see she has a red flag tied to her leg, which is something very grand, and a great honor for a duck; it shows that every one is anxious not to lose her, as she can be recognized both by man and beast. Come, now, don't turn your toes, a well-bred duckling spreads his feet wide apart, just like his father and mother, in this way; now bend your neck, and say 'quack.'"

The ducklings did as they were bid, but the other duck stared, and said, "Look, here comes another brood, as if there were not enough of us already! and what a queer looking object one of them is; we don't want him here," and then one flew out and bit him in the neck.

"Let him alone," said the mother; "he is not doing any harm."

"Yes, but he is so big and ugly," said the spiteful duck "and therefore he must be turned out."

"The others are very pretty children," said the old duck, with the rag on her leg, "all but that one; I wish his mother could improve him a little."

"That is impossible, your grace," replied the mother; "he is not pretty; but he has a very good disposition, and swims as well or even better than the others. I think he will grow up pretty, and perhaps be smaller; he has remained too long in the egg, and therefore his figure is not properly formed;" and then she stroked his neck and smoothed the feathers, saying, "It is a drake, and therefore not of so much consequence. I think he will grow up strong, and able to take care of himself."

"The other ducklings are graceful enough," said the old duck. "Now make yourself at home, and if you can find an eel's head, you can bring it to me."

And so they made themselves comfortable; but the poor duckling, who had crept out of his shell last of all, and looked so ugly, was bitten and pushed and made fun of, not only by the ducks, but by all the poultry. "He is too big," they all said, and the turkey cock, who had been born into the world with spurs, and fancied himself really an emperor, puffed himself out like a vessel in full sail, and flew at the duckling, and became quite red in the head with passion, so that the poor little thing did not know where to go, and was quite miserable because he was so ugly and laughed at by the whole farmyard. So it went on from day to day till it got worse and worse. The poor duckling was driven about by every one; even his brothers and sisters were unkind to him, and would say, "Ah, you ugly creature, I wish the cat would get you," and his mother said she wished he had never been born. The ducks pecked him, the chickens beat him, and the girl who fed the poultry kicked him with her feet. So at last he ran away, frightening the little birds in the hedge as he flew over the palings.

"They are afraid of me because I am ugly," he said. So he closed his eyes, and flew still farther, until he came out on a large moor, inhabited by wild ducks. Here he remained the whole night, feeling very tired and sorrowful.

In the morning, when the wild ducks rose in the air, they stared at their new comrade. "What sort of a duck are you?" they all said, coming round him.

He bowed to them, and was as polite as he could be, but he did not reply to their question. "You are exceedingly ugly," said the wild ducks, "but that will not matter if you do not want to marry one of our family."

Poor thing! he had no thoughts of marriage; all he wanted was permission to lie among the rushes, and drink some of the water on the moor. After he had been on the moor two days, there came two wild geese, or rather goslings, for they had not been out of the egg long, and were very saucy. "Listen, friend," said one of them to the duckling, "you are so ugly, that we like you very well. Will you go with us, and become a bird of passage? Not far from here is another moor, in which there are some pretty wild geese, all unmarried. It is a chance for you to get a wife; you may be lucky, ugly as you are."

"Pop, pop," sounded in the air, and the two wild geese fell dead among the rushes, and the water was tinged with blood. "Pop, pop," echoed far and wide in the distance, and whole flocks of wild geese rose up from the rushes. The sound continued from every direction, for the sportsmen surrounded the moor, and some were even seated on branches of trees, overlooking the rushes. The blue smoke from the guns rose like clouds over the dark trees, and as it floated away across the water, a number of sporting dogs bounded in among the rushes, which bent beneath them wherever they went. How they terrified the poor duckling! He turned away his head to hide it under his wing, and at the same moment a large terrible dog passed quite near him. His jaws were open, his tongue hung from his mouth, and his eyes glared fearfully. He thrust his nose close to the duckling, showing his sharp teeth, and then, "splash, splash," he went into the water without touching him, "Oh," sighed the duckling, "how thankful I am for being so ugly; even a dog will not bite me." And so he lay quite still, while the shot rattled through the rushes, and gun after gun was fired over him. It was late in the day before all became quiet, but even then the poor young thing did not dare to move. He waited quietly for several hours, and then, after looking carefully around him, hastened away from the moor as fast as he could. He ran over field and meadow till a storm arose, and he could hardly struggle against it. Towards evening, he reached a poor little cottage that seemed ready to fall, and only remained standing because it could not decide on which side to fall first. The storm continued so violent, that the duckling could go no farther; he sat down by the cottage, and then he noticed that the door was not quite closed in consequence of one of the hinges having given way. There was therefore a narrow opening near the bottom large enough for him to slip through, which he did very quietly, and got a shelter for the night. A woman, a tom cat, and a hen lived in this cottage. The tom cat, whom the mistress called, "My little son," was a great favorite; he could raise his back, and purr, and could even throw out sparks from his fur if it were stroked the wrong way. The hen had very short legs, so she was called "Chickie short legs." She laid good eggs, and her mistress loved her as if she had been her own child. In the morning, the strange visitor was discovered, and the tom cat began to purr, and the hen to cluck.

"What is that noise about?" said the old woman, looking round the room, but her sight was not very good; therefore, when she saw the duckling she thought it must be a fat duck, that had strayed from home. "Oh what a prize!" she exclaimed, "I hope it is not a drake, for then I shall have some duck's eggs. I must wait and see." So the duckling was allowed to remain on trial for three weeks, but there were no eggs. Now the tom cat was the master of the house, and the hen was mistress, and they always said, "We and the world," for they believed themselves to be half the world, and the better half too. The duckling thought that others might hold a different opinion on the subject, but the hen would not listen to such doubts. "Can you lay eggs?" she asked. "No." "Then have the goodness to hold your tongue." "Can you raise your back, or purr, or throw out sparks?" said the tom cat. "No." "Then you have no right to express an opinion when sensible people are speaking." So the duckling sat in a corner, feeling very low spirited, till the sunshine and the fresh air came into the room through the open door, and then he began to feel such a great longing for a swim on the water, that he could not help telling the hen.

"What an absurd idea," said the hen. "You have nothing else to do, therefore you have foolish fancies. If you could purr or lay eggs, they would pass away."

"But it is so delightful to swim about on the water," said the duckling, "and so refreshing to feel it close over your head, while you dive down to the bottom."

"Delightful, indeed!" said the hen, "why you must be crazy! Ask the cat, he is the cleverest animal I know, ask him how he would like to swim about on the water, or to dive under it, for I will not speak of my own opinion; ask our mistress, the old woman—there is no one in the world more clever than she is. Do you think she would like to swim, or to let the water close over her head?"

"You don't understand me," said the duckling.

"We don't understand you? Who can understand you, I wonder? Do you consider yourself more clever than the cat, or the old woman? I will say nothing of myself. Don't imagine such nonsense, child, and thank your good fortune that you have been received here. Are you not in a warm room, and in society from which you may learn something. But you are a chatterer, and your company is not very agreeable. Believe me, I speak only for your own good. I may tell you unpleasant truths, but that is a proof of my friendship. I advise you, therefore, to lay eggs, and learn to purr as quickly as possible."

"I believe I must go out into the world again," said the duckling.

"Yes, do," said the hen. So the duckling left the cottage, and soon found water on which it could swim and dive, but was avoided by all other animals, because of its ugly appearance. Autumn came, and the leaves in the forest turned to orange and gold. Then, as winter approached, the wind caught them as they fell and whirled them in the cold air. The clouds, heavy with hail and snow-flakes, hung low in the sky, and the raven stood on the ferns crying, "Croak, croak." It made one shiver with cold to look at him. All this was very sad for the poor little duckling. One evening, just as the sun set amid radiant clouds, there came a large flock of beautiful birds out of the bushes. The duckling had never seen any like them before. They were swans, and they curved their graceful necks, while their soft plumage shown with dazzling whiteness. They uttered a singular cry, as they spread their glorious wings and flew away from those cold regions to warmer countries across the sea. As they mounted higher and higher in the air, the ugly little duckling felt quite a strange sensation as he watched them. He whirled himself in the water like a wheel, stretched out his neck towards them, and uttered a cry so strange that it frightened himself. Could he ever forget those beautiful, happy birds; and when at last they were out of his sight, he dived under the water, and rose again almost beside himself with excitement. He knew not the names of these birds, nor where they had flown, but he felt towards them as he had never felt for any other bird in the world. He was not envious of these beautiful creatures, but wished to be as lovely as they. Poor ugly creature, how gladly he would have lived even with the ducks had they only given him encouragement. The winter grew colder and colder; he was obliged to swim about on the water to keep it from freezing, but every night the space on which he swam became smaller and smaller. At length it froze so hard that the ice in the water crackled as he moved, and the duckling had to paddle with his legs as well as he could, to keep the space from closing up. He became exhausted at last, and lay still and helpless, frozen fast in the ice.

Early in the morning, a peasant, who was passing by, saw what had happened. He broke the ice in pieces with his wooden shoe, and carried the duckling home to his wife. The warmth revived the poor little creature; but when the children wanted to play with him, the duckling thought they would do him some harm; so he started up in terror, fluttered into the milk-pan, and splashed the milk about the room. Then the woman clapped her hands, which frightened him still more. He flew first into the butter-cask, then into the meal-tub, and out again. What a condition he was in! The woman screamed, and struck at him with the tongs; the children laughed and screamed, and tumbled over each other, in their efforts to catch him; but luckily he escaped. The door stood open; the poor creature could just manage to slip out among the bushes, and lie down quite exhausted in the newly fallen snow.

It would be very sad, were I to relate all the misery and privations which the poor little duckling endured during the hard winter; but when it had passed, he found himself lying one morning in a moor, amongst the rushes. He felt the warm sun shining, and heard the lark singing, and saw that all around was beautiful spring. Then the young bird felt that his wings were strong, as he flapped them against his sides, and rose high into the air. They bore him onwards, until he found himself in a large garden, before he well knew how it had happened. The apple-trees were in full blossom, and the fragrant elders bent their long green branches down to the stream which wound round a smooth lawn. Everything looked beautiful, in the freshness of early spring. From a thicket close by came three beautiful white swans, rustling their feathers, and swimming lightly over the smooth water. The duckling remembered the lovely birds, and felt more strangely unhappy than ever.

"I will fly to those royal birds," he exclaimed, "and they will kill me, because I am so ugly, and dare to approach them; but it does not matter: better be killed by them than pecked by the ducks, beaten by the hens, pushed about by the maiden who feeds the poultry, or starved with hunger in the winter."

Then he flew to the water, and swam towards the beautiful

swans. The moment they espied the stranger, they rushed to meet him with outstretched wings.

"Kill me," said the poor bird; and he bent his head down to the surface of the water, and awaited death.

But what did he see in the clear stream below? His own image; no longer a dark, gray bird, ugly and disagreeable to look at, but a graceful and beautiful swan. To be born in a duck's nest, in a farm-yard, is of no consequence to a bird, if it is hatched from a swan's egg. He now felt glad at having suffered sorrow and trouble, be-cause it enabled him to enjoy so much better all the pleasure and happiness around him; for the great swans swam round the new-comer, and stroked his neck with their beaks, as a welcome.

Into the garden presently came some little children, and threw bread and cake into the water.

"See," cried the youngest, "there is a new one;" and the rest were delighted, and ran to their father and mother, dancing and clapping their hands, and shouting joyously, "There is another swan come; a new one has arrived."

Then they threw more bread and cake into the water, and said, "The new one is the most beautiful of all; he is so young and pretty." And the old swans bowed their heads before him.

Then he felt quite ashamed, and hid his head under his wing; for he did not know what to do, he was so happy, and yet not at all proud. He had been persecuted and despised for his ugliness, and now he heard them say he was the most beautiful of all the birds. Even the elder-tree bent down its bows into the water before him, and the sun shone warm and bright. Then he rustled his feathers, curved his slender neck, and cried joyfully, from the depths of his heart, "I never dreamed of such happiness as this, while I was an ugly duckling."

The Swineherd

There was once a poor Prince, who had a kingdom. His kingdom was very small, but still quite large enough to marry upon; and he wished to marry.

It was certainly rather cool of him to say to the Emperor's daughter, "Will you have me?" But so he did; for his name was renowned far and wide; and there were a hundred princesses who would have answered, "Yes!" and "Thank you kindly." We shall see what this princess said.

Listen!

It happened that where the Prince's father lay buried, there grew a rose tree—a most beautiful rose tree, which blossomed only once in every five years, and even then bore only one flower, but that was a rose! It smelt so sweet that all cares and sorrows were forgotten by him who inhaled its fragrance.

And furthermore, the Prince had a nightingale, who could sing in such a manner that it seemed as though all sweet melodies dwelt in her little throat. So the Princess was to have the rose, and the nightingale; and they were accordingly put into large silver caskets, and sent to her.

The Emperor had them brought into a large hall, where the Princess was playing at "Visiting," with the ladies of the court; and when she saw the caskets with the presents, she clapped her hands for joy.

"Ah, if it were but a little pussy-cat!" said she; but the rose tree, with its beautiful rose came to view.

"Oh, how prettily it is made!" said all the court ladies.

"It is more than pretty," said the Emperor, "it is charming!"

But the Princess touched it, and was almost ready to cry.

"Fie, papa!" said she. "It is not made at all, it is natural!"

"Let us see what is in the other casket, before we get into a bad humor," said the Emperor. So the nightingale came forth and sang so delightfully that at first no one could say anything ill-humored of her.

"Superbe! Charmant!" exclaimed the ladies; for they all used to chatter French, each one worse than her neighbor.

"How much the bird reminds me of the musical box that belonged to our blessed Empress," said an old knight. "Oh yes! These are the same tones, the same execution."

"Yes! yes!" said the Emperor, and he wept like a child at the remembrance.

"I will still hope that it is not a real bird," said the Princess.

"Yes, it is a real bird," said those who had brought it. "Well then let the bird fly," said the Princess; and she positively refused to see the Prince.

However, he was not to be discouraged; he daubed his face over brown and black; pulled his cap over his ears, and knocked at the door.

"Good day to my lord, the Emperor!" said he. "Can I have employment at the palace?"

"Why, yes," said the Emperor. "I want some one to take care of the pigs, for we have a great many of them."

So the Prince was appointed "Imperial Swineherd." He had a dirty little room close by the pigsty; and there he sat the whole day, and worked. By the evening he had made a pretty little kitchen-pot. Little bells were hung all round it; and when the pot was boiling, these bells tinkled in the most charming manner, and played the old melody,

"Ach! du lieber Augustin,   Alles ist weg, weg, weg!"*   *
"Ah! dear Augustine!   All is gone, gone, gone!"

But what was still more curious, whoever held his finger in the smoke of the kitchen-pot, immediately smelt all the dishes that were cooking on every hearth in the city—this, you see, was something quite different from the rose.

Now the Princess happened to walk that way; and when she

heard the tune, she stood quite still, and seemed pleased; for she could play "Lieber Augustine"; it was the only piece she knew; and she played it with one finger.

"Why there is my piece," said the Princess. "That swineherd must certainly have been well educated! Go in and ask him the price of the instrument."

So one of the court-ladies must run in; however, she drew on wooden slippers first.

"What will you take for the kitchen-pot?" said the lady.

"I will have ten kisses from the Princess," said the swineherd.

"Yes, indeed!" said the lady.

"I cannot sell it for less," rejoined the swineherd.

"He is an impudent fellow!" said the Princess, and she walked on; but when she had gone a little way, the bells tinkled so prettily

"Ach! du lieber Augustin,   Alles ist weg, weg, weg!"

"Stay," said the Princess. "Ask him if he will have ten kisses from the ladies of my court."

"No, thank you!" said the swineherd. "Ten kisses from the Princess, or I keep the kitchen-pot myself."

"That must not be, either!" said the Princess. "But do you all stand before me that no one may see us."

And the court-ladies placed themselves in front of her, and spread out their dresses—the swineherd got ten kisses, and the Princess—the kitchen-pot.

That was delightful! The pot was boiling the whole evening, and the whole of the following day. They knew perfectly well what was cooking at every fire throughout the city, from the chamberlain's to the cobbler's; the court-ladies danced and clapped their hands.

"We know who has soup, and who has pancakes for dinner to-day, who has cutlets, and who has eggs. How interesting!"

"Yes, but keep my secret, for I am an Emperor's daughter."

The swineherd—that is to say—the Prince, for no one knew

that he was other than an ill-favored swineherd, let not a day pass without working at something; he at last constructed a rattle, which, when it was swung round, played all the waltzes and jig tunes, which have ever been heard since the creation of the world.

"Ah, that is superbe!" said the Princess when she passed by. "I have never heard prettier compositions! Go in and ask him the price of the instrument; but mind, he shall have no more kisses!"

"He will have a hundred kisses from the Princess!" said the lady who had been to ask.

"I think he is not in his right senses!" said the Princess, and walked on, but when she had gone a little way, she stopped again. "One must encourage art," said she, "I am the Emperor's daughter. Tell him he shall, as on yesterday, have ten kisses from me, and may take the rest from the ladies of the court."

"Oh—but we should not like that at all!" said they. "What are you muttering?" asked the Princess. "If I can kiss him, surely you can. Remember that you owe everything to me." So the ladies were obliged to go to him again.

"A hundred kisses from the Princess," said he, "or else let everyone keep his own!"

"Stand round!" said she; and all the ladies stood round her whilst the kissing was going on.

"What can be the reason for such a crowd close by the pigsty?" said the Emperor, who happened just then to step out on the balcony; he rubbed his eyes, and put on his spectacles. "They are the ladies of the court; I must go down and see what they are about!" So he pulled up his slippers at the heel, for he had trodden them down.

As soon as he had got into the court-yard, he moved very softly, and the ladies were so much engrossed with counting the kisses, that all might go on fairly, that they did not perceive the Emperor. He rose on his tiptoes.

"What is all this?" said he, when he saw what was going on, and he boxed the Princess's ears with his slipper, just as the swineherd was taking the eighty-sixth kiss.

"March out!" said the Emperor, for he was very angry; and both Princess and swineherd were thrust out of the city.

The Princess now stood and wept, the swineherd scolded, and the rain poured down.

"Alas! Unhappy creature that I am!" said the Princess. "If I had but married the handsome young Prince! Ah! how unfortunate I am!"

And the swineherd went behind a tree, washed the black and brown color from his face, threw off his dirty clothes, and stepped forth in his princely robes; he looked so noble that the Princess could not help bowing before him.

"I am come to despise thee," said he. "Thou would'st not have an honorable Prince! Thou could'st not prize the rose and the nightingale, but thou wast ready to kiss the swineherd for the sake of a trumpery plaything. Thou art rightly served."

He then went back to his own little kingdom, and shut the door of his palace in her face. Now she might well sing,

"Ach! du lieber Augustin,   Alles ist weg, weg, weg!"

The Ice Maiden

I. Little Rudy~

We will pay a visit to Switzerland, and wander through that country of mountains, whose steep and rocky sides are overgrown with forest trees. Let us climb to the dazzling snow-fields at their summits, and descend again to the green meadows beneath, through which rivers and brooks rush along as if they could not quickly enough reach the sea and vanish. Fiercely shines the sun over those deep valleys, as well as upon the heavy masses of snow which lie on the mountains.

During the year these accumulations thaw or fall in the rolling avalance, or are piled up in shining glaciers. Two of these glaciers lie in the broad, rocky cliffs, between the Schreckhorn and the Wetterhorn, near the little town of Grindelwald. They are wonderful to behold, and therefore in the summer time strangers come here from all parts of the world to see them. They cross snow-covered mountains, and travel through the deep valleys, or ascend for hours, higher and still higher, the valleys appearing to sink lower and lower as they proceed, and become as small as if seen from an air balloon. Over the lofty summits of these mountains the clouds often hang like a dark veil; while beneath in the valley, where many brown, wooden houses are scattered about, the bright rays of the sun may be shining upon a little brilliant patch of green, making it appear almost transparent. The waters foam and dash along in the valleys beneath; the streams from above trickle and murmur as they fall down the rocky mountain's side, looking like glittering silver bands.

On both sides of the mountain-path stand these little wooden houses; and, as within, there are many children and many mouths to feed, each house has its own little potato garden. These children rush out in swarms, and surround travellers, whether on foot or in carriages. They are all clever at making a bargain. They offer for sale the sweetest little toy-houses, models of the mountain cottages in Switzerland. Whether it be rain or sunshine, these crowds of children are always to be seen with their wares.

About twenty years ago, there might be seen occasionally, standing at a short distance from the other children, a little boy, who was also anxious to sell his curious wares. He had an earnest, expressive countenance, and held the box containing his carved toys tightly with both hands, as if unwilling to part with it. His earnest look, and being also a very little boy, made him noticed by the strangers; so that he often sold the most, without knowing why. An hour's walk farther up the ascent lived his grandfather, who cut and carved the pretty little toy-houses; and in the old man's room stood a large press, full of all sorts of carved things—nut-crackers, knives and forks, boxes with beautifully carved foliage, leaping chamois. It contained everything that could delight the eyes of a child. But the boy, who was named Rudy, looked with still greater pleasure and longing at some old fire-arms which hung upon the rafters, under the ceiling of the room. His grandfather promised him that he should have them some day, but that he must first grow big and strong, and learn how to use them. Small as he was, the goats were placed in his care, and a good goat-keeper should also be a good climber, and such Rudy was; he sometimes, indeed, climbed higher than the goats, for he was fond of seeking for birds'-nests at the top of high trees; he was bold and daring, but was seldom seen to smile, excepting when he stood by the roaring cataract, or heard the descending roll of the avalanche. He never played with the other children, and was not seen with them, unless his grandfather sent him down to sell his curious workmanship. Rudy did not much like trade; he loved to climb the mountains, or to sit by his grandfather and listen to his tales of olden times, or of the people in Meyringen, the place of his birth.

"In the early ages of the world," said the old man, "these people could not be found in Switzerland. They are a colony from the north, where their ancestors still dwell, and are called Swedes."

This was something for Rudy to know, but he learnt more from other sources, particularly from the domestic animals who belonged to the house. One was a large dog, called Ajola, which had belonged to his father; and the other was a tom-cat. This cat stood very high in Rudy's favor, for he had taught him to climb.

"Come out on the roof with me," said the cat; and Rudy quite understood him, for the language of fowls, ducks, cats, and dogs, is as easily understood by a young child as his own native tongue. But it must be at the age when grandfather's stick becomes a neighing horse, with head, legs, and tail. Some children retain these ideas later than others, and they are considered backwards and childish for their age. People say so; but is it so?

"Come out on the roof with me, little Rudy," was the first thing he heard the cat say, and Rudy understood him. "What people say about falling down is all nonsense," continued the cat; "you will not fall, unless you are afraid. Come, now, set one foot here and another there, and feel your way with your fore-feet. Keep your eyes wide open, and move softly, and if you come to a hole jump over it, and cling fast as I do." And this was just what Rudy did. He was often on the sloping roof with the cat, or on the tops of high trees. But, more frequently, higher still on the ridges of the rocks where puss never came.

"Higher, higher!" cried the trees and the bushes, "see to what height we have grown, and how fast we hold, even to the narrow edges of the rocks."

Rudy often reached the top of the mountain before the sunrise, and there inhaled his morning draught of the fresh, invigorating mountain air,—God's own gift, which men call the sweet fragrance of plant and herb on the mountain-side, and the mint and wild thyme in the valleys. The overhanging clouds absorb all heaviness from the air, and the winds convey them away over the pine-tree summits. The spirit of fragrance, light and fresh, remained behind, and this was Rudy's morning draught. The sunbeams—those blessing-bringing daughters of the sun—kissed his cheeks. Vertigo might be lurking on the watch, but he dared not approach him. The swallows, who had not less than seven nests in his grandfather's house, flew up to him and his goats, singing, "We and you, you and we." They brought him greetings from his grandfather's house, even from two hens, the only birds of the household; but Rudy was not intimate with them.

Although so young and such a little fellow, Rudy had travelled a great deal. He was born in the canton of Valais, and brought to his grandfather over the mountains. He had walked to Staubbach—a little town that seems to flutter in the air like a silver veil—the glittering, snow-clad mountain Jungfrau. He had also been to the great glaciers; but this is connected with a sad story, for here his mother met her death, and his grandfather used to say that all Rudy's childish merriment was lost from that time. His mother had written in a letter, that before he was a year old he had laughed more than he cried; but after his fall into the snow-covered crevasse, his disposition had completely changed. The grandfather seldom spoke of this, but the fact was generally known. Rudy's father had been a postilion, and the large dog which now lived in his grandfather's cottage had always followed him on his journeys over the Simplon to the lake of Geneva. Rudy's relations, on his father's side, lived in the canton of Valais, in the valley of the Rhone. His uncle was a chamois hunter, and a well-known guide. Rudy was only a year old when his father died, and his mother was anxious to return with her child to her own relations, who lived in the Bernese Oberland. Her father dwelt at a few hours' distance from Grindelwald; he was a carver in wood, and gained so much by it that he had plenty to live upon. She set out homewards in the month of June, carrying her infant in her arms, and, accompanied by two chamois hunters, crossed the Gemmi on her way to Grindelwald. They had already left more than half the journey behind them. They had crossed high ridges, and traversed snow-fields; they could even see her native valley, with its familiar wooden cottages. They had only one more glacier to climb. Some newly fallen snow concealed a cleft which, though it did not extend to the foaming waters in the depths beneath, was still much deeper than the height of a man. The young woman, with the child in her arms, slipped upon it, sank in, and disappeared. Not a shriek, not a groan was heard; nothing but the whining of a little child. More than an hour elapsed before her two companions could obtain from the nearest house ropes and poles to assist in raising them; and it was with much exertion that they at last succeeded in raising from the crevasse what appeared to be two dead bodies. Every means was used to restore them to life. With the child they were successful, but not with the mother; so the old grandfather received his daughter's little son into his house an orphan,—a little boy who laughed more than he cried; but it seemed as if laughter had left him in the cold ice-world into which he had fallen, where, as the Swiss peasants say, the souls of the lost are confined till the judgment-day.

The glaciers appear as if a rushing stream had been frozen in its course, and pressed into blocks of green crystal, which, balanced one upon another, form a wondrous palace of crystal for the Ice Maiden—the queen of the glaciers. It is she whose mighty power can crush the traveller to death, and arrest the flowing river in its course. She is also a child of the air, and with the swiftness of the chamois she can reach the snow-covered mountain tops, where the boldest mountaineer has to cut footsteps in the ice to ascend. She will sail on a frail pine-twig over the raging torrents beneath, and spring lightly from one iceberg to another, with her long, snow-white hair flowing around her, and her dark-green robe glittering like the waters of the deep Swiss lakes. "Mine is the power to seize and crush," she cried. "Once a beautiful boy was stolen from me by man,—a boy whom I had kissed, but had not kissed to death. He is again among mankind, and tends the goats on the mountains. He is always climbing higher and higher, far away from all others, but not from me. He is mine; I will send for him." And she gave Vertigo the commission.

It was summer, and the Ice Maiden was melting amidst the green verdure, when Vertigo swung himself up and down. Vertigo has many brothers, quite a troop of them, and the Ice Maiden chose the strongest among them. They exercise their power in different ways, and everywhere. Some sit on the banisters of steep stairs, others on the outer rails of lofty towers, or spring like squirrels along the ridges of the mountains. Others tread the air as a swimmer treads the water, and lure their victims here and there till they fall into the deep abyss. Vertigo and the Ice Maiden clutch at human beings, as the polypus seizes upon all that comes within its reach. And now Vertigo was to seize Rudy.

"Seize him, indeed," cried Vertigo; "I cannot do it. That monster of a cat has taught him her tricks. That child of the human race has a power within him which keeps me at a distance; I cannot possibly reach the boy when he hangs from the branches of trees, over the precipice; or I would gladly tickle his feet, and send him heels over head through the air; but I cannot accomplish it."

"We must accomplish it," said the Ice Maiden; "either you or I must; and I will—I will!"

"No, no!" sounded through the air, like an echo on the mountain church bells chime. It was an answer in song, in the melting tones of a chorus from others of nature's spirits—good and loving spirits, the daughters of the sunbeam. They who place themselves in a circle every evening on the mountain peaks; there they spread out their rose-colored wings, which, as the sun sinks, become more flaming red, until the lofty Alps seem to burn with fire. Men call this the Alpine glow. After the sun has set, they disappear within the white snow on the mountain-tops, and slumber there till sunrise, when they again come forth. They have great love for flowers, for butterflies, and for mankind; and from among the latter they had chosen little Rudy. "You shall not catch him; you shall not seize him!" they sang.

"Greater and stronger than he have I seized!" said the Ice Maiden.

Then the daughters of the sun sang a song of the traveller, whose cloak had been carried away by the wind. "The wind took the covering, but not the man; it could even seize upon him, but not hold him fast. The children of strength are more powerful, more ethereal, even than we are. They can rise higher than our parent, the sun. They have the magic words that rule the wind and the waves, and compel them to serve and obey; and they can, at last, cast off the heavy, oppressive weight of mortality, and soar upwards." Thus sweetly sounded the bell-like tones of the chorus.

And each morning the sun's rays shone through the one little window of the grandfather's house upon the quiet child. The daughters of the sunbeam kissed him; they wished to thaw, and melt, and obliterate the ice kiss which the queenly maiden of the glaciers had given him as he lay in the lap of his dead mother, in the deep crevasse of ice from which he had been so wonderfully rescued.

II. The Journey To The New Home ~

Rudy was just eight years old, when his uncle, who lived on the other side of the mountain, wished to have the boy, as he thought he might obtain a better education with him, and learn something more. His grandfather thought the same, so he consented to let him go. Rudy had many to say farewell to, as well as his grandfather. First, there was Ajola, the old dog.

"Your father was the postilion, and I was the postilion's dog," said Ajola. "We have often travelled the same journey together; I knew all the dogs and men on this side of the mountain. It is not my habit to talk much; but now that we have so little time to converse together, I will say something more than usual. I will relate to you a story, which I have reflected upon for a long time. I do not understand it, and very likely you will not, but that is of no consequence. I have, however, learnt from it that in this world things are not equally divided, neither for dogs nor for men. All are not born to lie on the lap and to drink milk: I have never been petted in this way, but I have seen a little dog seated in the place of a gentleman or lady, and travelling inside a post-chaise. The lady, who was his mistress, or of whom he was master, carried a bottle of milk, of which the little dog now and then drank; she also offered him pieces of sugar to crunch. He sniffed at them proudly, but would not eat one, so she ate them herself. I was running along the dirty road by the side of the carriage as hungry as a dog could be, chewing the cud of my own thoughts, which were rather in confusion. But many other things seemed in confusion also. Why was not I lying on a lap and travelling in a coach? I could not tell; yet I knew I could not alter my own condition, either by barking or growling."

This was Ajola's farewell speech, and Rudy threw his arms round the dog's neck and kissed his cold nose. Then he took the cat in his arms, but he struggled to get free.

"You are getting too strong for me," he said; "but I will not use my claws against you. Clamber away over the mountains; it was I who taught you to climb. Do not fancy you are going to fall, and you will be quite safe." Then the cat jumped down and ran away; he did not wish Rudy to see that there were tears in his eyes.

The hens were hopping about the floor; one of them had no tail; a traveller, who fancied himself a sportsman, had shot off her tail, he had mistaken her for a bird of prey.

"Rudy is going away over the mountains," said one of the hens.

"He is always in such a hurry," said the other; "and I don't like taking leave," so they both hopped out.

But the goats said farewell; they bleated and wanted to go with him, they were so very sorry.

Just at this time two clever guides were going to cross the mountains to the other side of the Gemmi, and Rudy was to go with them on foot. It was a long walk for such a little boy, but he had plenty of strength and invincible courage. The swallows flew with him a little way, singing, "We and you—you and we." The way led across the rushing Lutschine, which falls in numerous streams from the dark clefts of the Grindelwald glaciers. Trunks of fallen trees and blocks of stone form bridges over these streams. After passing a forest of alders, they began to ascend, passing by some blocks of ice that had loosened themselves from the side of the mountain and lay across their path; they had to step over these ice-blocks or walk round them. Rudy crept here and ran there, his eyes sparkling with joy, and he stepped so firmly with his iron-tipped mountain shoe, that he left a mark behind him wherever he placed his foot.

The earth was black where the mountain torrents or the melted ice had poured upon it, but the bluish green, glassy ice sparkled and glittered. They had to go round little pools, like lakes, enclosed between large masses of ice; and, while thus wandering out of their path, they came near an immense stone, which lay balanced on the edge of an icy peak. The stone lost its balance just as they reached it, and rolled over into the abyss beneath, while the noise of its fall was echoed back from every hollow cliff of the glaciers.

They were always going upwards. The glaciers seemed to spread above them like a continued chain of masses of ice, piled up in wild confusion between bare and rugged rocks. Rudy thought for a moment of what had been told him, that he and his mother had once lain buried in one of these cold, heart-chilling fissures; but he soon banished such thoughts, and looked upon the story as fabulous, like many other stories which had been told him. Once or twice, when the men thought the way was rather difficult for such a little boy, they held out their hands to assist him; but he would not accept their assistance, for he stood on the slippery ice as firmly as if he had been a chamois. They came at length to rocky ground; sometimes stepping upon moss-covered stones, sometimes passing beneath stunted fir-trees, and again through green meadows. The landscape was always changing, but ever above them towered the lofty snow-clad mountains, whose names not only Rudy but every other child knew—"The Jungfrau," "The Monk and the Eiger."

Rudy had never been so far away before; he had never trodden on the wide-spreading ocean of snow that lay here with its immovable billows, from which the wind blows off the snowflake now and then, as it cuts the foam from the waves of the sea. The glaciers stand here so close together it might almost be said they are hand-in-hand; and each is a crystal palace for the Ice Maiden, whose power and will it is to seize and imprison the unwary traveller.

The sun shone warmly, and the snow sparkled as if covered with glittering diamonds. Numerous insects, especially butterflies and bees, lay dead in heaps on the snow. They had ventured too high, or the wind had carried them here and left them to die of cold.

Around the Wetterhorn hung a feathery cloud, like a woolbag, and a threatening cloud too, for as it sunk lower it increased in size, and concealed within was a "fohn," fearful in its violence should it break loose. This journey, with its varied incidents,—the wild paths, the night passed on the mountain, the steep rocky precipices, the hollow clefts, in which the rustling waters from time immemorial had worn away passages for themselves through blocks of stone,—all these were firmly impressed on Rudy's memory.

In a forsaken stone building, which stood just beyond the seas of snow, they one night took shelter. Here they found some charcoal and pine branches, so that they soon made a fire. They arranged couches to lie on as well as they could, and then the men seated themselves by the fire, took out their pipes, and began to smoke. They also prepared a warm, spiced drink, of which they partook and Rudy was not forgotten—he had his share. Then they began to talk of those mysterious beings with which the land of the Alps abounds; the hosts of apparitions which come in the night, and carry off the sleepers through the air, to the wonderful floating town of Venice; of the wild herds-man, who drives the black sheep across the meadows. These flocks are never seen, yet the tinkle of their little bells has often been heard, as well as their unearthly bleating. Rudy listened eagerly, but without fear, for he knew not what fear meant; and while he listened, he fancied he could hear the roaring of the spectral herd. It seemed to come nearer and roar louder, till the men heard it also and listened in silence, till, at length, they told Rudy that he must not dare to sleep. It was a "fohn," that violent storm-wind which rushes from the mountain to the valley beneath, and in its fury snaps asunder the trunks of large trees as if they were but slender reeds, and carries the wooden houses from one side of a river to the other as easily as we could move the pieces on a chess-board. After an hour had passed, they told Rudy that it was all over, and he might go to sleep; and, fatigued with his long walk, he readily slept at the word of command.

Very early the following morning they again set out. The sun on this day lighted up for Rudy new mountains, new glaciers, and new snow-fields. They had entered the Canton Valais, and found themselves on the ridge of the hills which can be seen from Grindelwald; but he was still far from his new home. They pointed out to him other clefts, other meadows, other woods and rocky paths, and other houses. Strange men made their appearance before him, and what men! They were misshapen, wretched-looking creatures, with yellow complexions; and on their necks were dark, ugly lumps of flesh, hanging down like bags. They were called cretins. They dragged themselves along painfully, and stared at the strangers with vacant eyes. The women looked more dreadful than the men. Poor Rudy! were these the sort of people he should see at his new home?

III. The Uncle

Rudy arrived at last at his uncle's house, and was thankful to find the people like those he had been accustomed to see. There was only one cretin amongst them, a poor idiot boy, one of those unfortunate beings who, in their neglected conditions, go from house to house, and are received and taken care of in different families, for a month or two at a time.

Poor Saperli had just arrived at his uncle's house when Rudy came. The uncle was an experienced hunter; he also followed the trade of a cooper; his wife was a lively little person, with a face like a bird, eyes like those of an eagle, and a long, hairy throat. Everything was new to Rudy—the fashion of the dress, the manners, the employments, and even the language; but the latter his childish ear would soon learn. He saw also that there was more wealth here, when compared with his former home at his grandfather's. The rooms were larger, the walls were adorned with the horns of the chamois, and brightly polished guns. Over the door hung a painting of the Virgin Mary, fresh alpine roses and a burning lamp stood near it. Rudy's uncle was, as we have said, one of the most noted chamois hunters in the whole district, and also one of the best guides. Rudy soon became the pet of the house; but there was another pet, an old hound, blind and lazy, who would never more follow the hunt, well as he had once done so. But his former good qualities were not forgotten, and therefore the animal was kept in the family and treated with every indulgence. Rudy stroked the old hound, but he did not like strangers, and Rudy was as yet a stranger; he did not, however, long remain so, he soon endeared himself to every heart, and became like one of the family.

"We are not very badly off, here in the canton Valais," said his uncle one day; "we have the chamois, they do not die so fast as the wild goats, and it is certainly much better here now than in former times. How highly the old times have been spoken of, but ours is better. The bag has been opened, and a current of air now blows through our once confined valley. Something better always makes its appearance when old, worn-out things fail."

When his uncle became communicative, he would relate stories of his youthful days, and farther back still of the warlike times in which his father had lived. Valais was then, as he expressed it, only a closed-up bag, quite full of sick people, miserable cretins; but the French soldiers came, and they were capital doctors, they soon killed the disease and the sick people, too. The French people knew how to fight in more ways than one, and the girls knew how to conquer too; and when he said this the uncle nodded at his wife, who was a French woman by birth, and laughed. The French could also do battle on the stones. "It was they who cut a road out of the solid rock over the Simplon—such a road, that I need only say to a child of three years old, 'Go down to Italy, you have only to keep in the high road,' and the child will soon arrive in Italy, if he followed my directions."

Then the uncle sang a French song, and cried, "Hurrah! long live Napoleon Buonaparte." This was the first time Rudy had ever heard of France, or of Lyons, that great city on the Rhone where his uncle had once lived. His uncle said that Rudy, in a very few years, would become a clever hunter, he had quite a talent for it; he taught the boy to hold a gun properly, and to load and fire it. In the hunting season he took him to the hills, and made him drink the warm blood of the chamois, which is said to prevent the hunter from becoming giddy; he taught him to know the time when, from the different mountains, the avalanche is likely to fall, namely, at noontide or in the evening, from the effects of the sun's rays; he made him observe the movements of the chamois when he gave a leap, so that he might fall firmly and lightly on his feet. He told him that when on the fissures of the rocks he could find no place for his feet, he must support himself on his elbows, and cling with his legs, and even lean firmly with his back, for this could be done when necessary. He told him also that the chamois are very cunning, they place lookers-out on the watch; but the hunter must be more cunning than they are, and find them out by the scent.

One day, when Rudy went out hunting with his uncle, he hung a coat and hat on an alpine staff, and the chamois mistook it for a man, as they generally do. The mountain path was narrow here; indeed it was scarcely a path at all, only a kind of shelf, close to the yawning abyss. The snow that lay upon it was partially thawed, and the stones crumbled beneath the feet. Every fragment of stone broken off struck the sides of the rock in its fall, till it rolled into the depths beneath, and sunk to rest. Upon this shelf Rudy's uncle laid himself down, and crept forward. At about a hundred paces behind him stood Rudy, upon the highest point of the rock, watching a great vulture hovering in the air; with a single stroke of his wing the bird might easily cast the creeping hunter into the abyss beneath, and make him his prey. Rudy's uncle had eyes for nothing but the chamois, who, with its young kid, had just appeared round the edge of the rock. So Rudy kept his eyes fixed on the bird, he knew well what the great creature wanted; therefore he stood in readiness to discharge his gun at the proper moment. Suddenly the chamois made a spring, and his uncle fired and struck the animal with the deadly bullet; while the young kid rushed away, as if for a long life he had been accustomed to danger and practised flight. The large bird, alarmed at the report of the gun, wheeled off in another direction, and Rudy's uncle was saved from danger, of which he knew nothing till he was told of it by the boy.

While they were both in pleasant mood, wending their way

homewards, and the uncle whistling the tune of a song he had learnt in his young days, they suddenly heard a peculiar sound which seemed to come from the top of the mountain. They looked up, and saw above them, on the over-hanging rock, the snow-covering heave and lift itself as a piece of linen stretched on the ground to dry raises itself when the wind creeps under it. Smooth as polished marble slabs, the waves of snow cracked and loosened themselves, and then suddenly, with the rumbling noise of distant thunder, fell like a foaming cataract into the abyss. An avalanche had fallen, not upon Rudy and his uncle, but very near them. Alas, a great deal too near!

"Hold fast, Rudy!" cried his uncle; "hold fast, with all your might."

Then Rudy clung with his arms to the trunk of the nearest tree, while his uncle climbed above him, and held fast by the branches. The avalanche rolled past them at some distance; but the gust of wind that followed, like the storm-wings of the avalanche, snapped asunder the trees and bushes over which it swept, as if they had been but dry rushes, and threw them about in every direction. The tree to which Rudy clung was thus overthrown, and Rudy dashed to the ground. The higher branches were snapped off, and carried away to a great distance; and among these shattered branches lay Rudy's uncle, with his skull fractured. When they found him, his hand was still warm; but it would have been impossible to recognize his face. Rudy stood by, pale and trembling; it was the first shock of his life, the first time he had ever felt fear. Late in the evening he returned home with the fatal news,—to that home which was now to be so full of sorrow. His uncle's wife uttered not a word, nor shed a tear, till the corpse was brought in; then her agony burst forth. The poor cretin crept away to his bed, and nothing was seen of him during the whole of the following day. Towards evening, however, he came to Rudy, and said, "Will you write a letter for me? Saperli cannot write; Saperli can only take the letters to the post."

"A letter for you!" said Rudy; "who do you wish to write to?"

"To the Lord Christ," he replied.

"What do you mean?" asked Rudy.

Then the poor idiot, as the cretin was often called, looked at Rudy with a most touching expression in his eyes, clasped his hands, and said, solemnly and devoutly, "Saperli wants to send a letter to Jesus Christ, to pray Him to let Saperli die, and not the master of the house here."

Rudy pressed his hand, and replied, "A letter would not reach Him up above; it would not give him back whom we have lost."

It was not, however, easy for Rudy to convince Saperli of the impossibility of doing what he wished.

"Now you must work for us," said his foster-mother; and Rudy very soon became the entire support of the house.

IV. Babette~

Who was the best marksman in the canton Valais? The chamois knew well. "Save yourselves from Rudy," they might well say. And who is the handsomest marksman? "Oh, it is Rudy," said the maidens; but they did not say, "Save yourselves from Rudy." Neither did anxious mothers say so; for he bowed to them as pleasantly as to the young girls. He was so brave and cheerful. His cheeks were brown, his teeth white, and his eyes dark and sparkling. He was now a handsome young man of twenty years. The most icy water could not deter him from swimming; he could twist and turn like a fish. None could climb like he, and he clung as firmly to the edges of the rocks as a limpet. He had strong muscular power, as could be seen when he leapt from rock to rock. He had learnt this first from the cat, and more lately from the chamois. Rudy was considered the best guide over the mountains; every one had great confidence in him. He might have made a great deal of money as guide. His uncle had also taught him the trade of a cooper; but he had no inclination for either; his delight was in chamois-hunting, which also brought him plenty of money. Rudy would be a very good match, as people said, if he would not look above his own station. He was also such a famous partner in dancing, that the girls often dreamt about him, and one and another thought of him even when awake.

"He kissed me in the dance," said Annette, the schoolmaster's daughter, to her dearest friend; but she ought not to have told this, even to her dearest friend. It is not easy to keep such secrets; they are like sand in a sieve; they slip out. It was therefore soon known that Rudy, so brave and so good as he was, had kissed some one while dancing, and yet he had never kissed her who was dearest to him.

"Ah, ah," said an old hunter, "he has kissed Annette, has he? he has begun with A, and I suppose he will kiss through the whole alphabet."

But a kiss in the dance was all the busy tongues could accuse him of. He certainly had kissed Annette, but she was not the flower of his heart.

Down in the valley, near Bex, among the great walnut-trees, by the side of a little rushing mountain-stream, lived a rich miller. His dwelling-house was a large building, three storeys high, with little turrets. The roof was covered with chips, bound together with tin plates, that glittered in sunshine and in the moonlight. The largest of the turrets had a weather-cock, representing an apple pierced by a glittering arrow, in memory of William Tell. The mill was a neat and well-ordered place, that allowed itself to be sketched and written about; but the miller's daughter did not permit any to sketch or write about her. So, at least, Rudy would have said, for her image was pictured in his heart; her eyes shone in it so brightly, that quite a flame had been kindled there; and, like all other fires, it had burst forth so suddenly, that the miller's daughter, the beautiful Babette, was quite unaware of it. Rudy had never spoken a word to her on the subject. The miller was rich, and, on that account, Babette stood very high, and was rather difficult to aspire to. But said Rudy to himself, "Nothing is too high for a man to reach: he must climb with confidence in himself, and he will not fail." He had learnt this lesson in his youthful home.

It happened once that Rudy had some business to settle at Bex. It was a long journey at that time, for the railway had not been opened. From the glaciers of the Rhone, at the foot of the Simplon, between its ever-changing mountain summits, stretches the valley of the canton Valais. Through it runs the noble river of the Rhone, which often overflows its banks, covering fields and highways, and destroying everything in its course. Near the towns of Sion and St. Maurice, the valley takes a turn, and bends like an elbow, and behind St. Maurice becomes so narrow that there is only space enough for the bed of the river and a narrow carriage-road. An old tower stands here, as if it were guardian to the canton Valais, which ends at this point; and from it we can look across the stone bridge to the toll-house on the other side, where the canton Vaud commences. Not far from this spot stands the town of Bex, and at every step can be seen an increase of fruitfulness and verdure. It is like entering a grove of chestnut and walnut-trees. Here and there the cypress and pomegranate blossoms peep forth; and it is almost as warm as an Italian climate. Rudy arrived at Bex, and soon finished the business which had brought him there, and then walked about the town; but not even the miller's boy could be seen, nor any one belonging to the mill, not to mention Babette. This did not please him at all. Evening came on. The air was filled with the perfume of the wild thyme and the blossoms of the lime-trees, and the green woods on the mountains seemed to be covered with a shining veil, blue as the sky. Over everything reigned a stillness, not of sleep or of death, but as if Nature were holding her breath, that her image might be photographed on the blue vault of heaven. Here and

there, amidst the trees of the silent valley, stood poles which supported the wires of the electric telegraph. Against one of these
poles leaned an object so motionless that it might have been mistaken for the trunk of a tree; but it was Rudy, standing there as
still as at that moment was everything around him. He was not
asleep, neither was he dead; but just as the various events in the
world—matters of momentous importance to individuals—were
flying through the telegraph wires, without the quiver of a wire
or the slightest tone, so, through the mind of Rudy, thoughts of
overwhelming importance were passing, without an outward sign
of emotion. The happiness of his future life depended upon the
decision of his present reflections. His eyes were fixed on one spot
in the distance—a light that twinkled through the foliage from
the parlor of the miller's house, where Babette dwelt. Rudy stood
so still, that it might have been supposed he was watching for a
chamois; but he was in reality like a chamois, who will stand for a
moment, looking as if it were chiselled out of the rock, and then,
if only a stone rolled by, would suddenly bound forward with a
spring, far away from the hunter. And so with Rudy: a sudden
roll of his thoughts roused him from his stillness, and made him
bound forward with determination to act.

"Never despair!" cried he. "A visit to the mill, to say good evening to the miller, and good evening to little Babette, can do no
harm. No one ever fails who has confidence in himself. If I am to
be Babette's husband, I must see her some time or other."

Then Rudy laughed joyously, and took courage to go to the
mill. He knew what he wanted; he wanted to marry Babette. The
clear water of the river rolled over its yellow bed, and willows and
lime-trees were reflected in it, as Rudy stepped along the path to
the miller's house. But, as the children sing—

"There was no one at home in the house,
Only a kitten at play."

The cat standing on the steps put up its back and cried "mew."

But Rudy had no inclination for this sort of conversation; he passed on, and knocked at the door. No one heard him, no one opened the door. "Mew," said the cat again; and had Rudy been still a child, he would have understood this language, and known that the cat wished to tell him there was no one at home. So he was obliged to go to the mill and make inquiries, and there he heard that the miller had gone on a journey to Interlachen, and taken Babette with him, to the great shooting festival, which began that morning, and would continue for eight days, and that people from all the German settlements would be there.

Poor Rudy! we may well say. It was not a fortunate day for his visit to Bex. He had just to return the way he came, through St. Maurice and Sion, to his home in the valley. But he did not despair. When the sun rose the next morning, his good spirits had returned; indeed he had never really lost them. "Babette is at Interlachen," said Rudy to himself, "many days' journey from here. It is certainly a long way for any one who takes the high-road, but not so far if he takes a short cut across the mountain, and that just suits a chamois-hunter. I have been that way before, for it leads to the home of my childhood, where, as a little boy, I lived with my grandfather. And there are shooting matches at Interlachen. I will go, and try to stand first in the match. Babette will be there, and I shall be able to make her acquaintance."

Carrying his light knapsack, which contained his Sunday clothes, on his back, and with his musket and his game-bag over his shoulder, Rudy started to take the shortest way across the mountain. Still it was a great distance. The shooting matches were to commence on that day, and to continue for a whole week. He had been told also that the miller and Babette would remain that time with some relatives at Interlachen. So over the Gemmi Rudy climbed bravely, and determined to descend the side of the Grindelwald. Bright and joyous were his feelings as he stepped lightly onwards, inhaling the invigorating mountain air. The valley sunk as he ascended, the circle of the horizon expanded. One snow-capped peak after another rose before him, till the whole of the glittering Alpine range became visible. Rudy knew each ice-clad peak, and he continued his course towards the Schreckhorn, with its white powdered stone finger raised high in the air. At length he had crossed the highest ridges, and before him lay the green pasture lands sloping down towards the valley, which was once his home. The buoyancy of the air made his heart light. Hill and valley were blooming in luxuriant beauty, and his thoughts were youthful dreams, in which old age or death were out of the question. Life, power, and enjoyment were in the future, and he felt free and light as a bird. And the swallows flew round him, as in the days of his childhood, singing "We and you—you and we." All was overflowing with joy. Beneath him lay the meadows, covered with velvety green, with the murmuring river flowing through them, and dotted here and there were small wooden houses. He could see the edges of the glaciers, looking like green glass against the soiled snow, and the deep chasms beneath the loftiest glacier. The church bells were ringing, as if to welcome him to his home with their sweet tones. His heart beat quickly, and for a moment he seemed to have foregotten Babette, so full were his thoughts of old recollections. He was, in imagination, once more wandering on the road where, when a little boy, he, with other children, came to sell their curiously carved toy houses. Yonder, behind the fir-trees, still stood his grandfather's house, his mother's father, but strangers dwelt in it now. Children came running to him, as he had once done, and wished to sell their wares. One of them offered him an Alpine rose. Rudy took the rose as a good omen, and thought of Babette. He quickly crossed the bridge where the two rivers flow into each other. Here he found a walk over-shadowed with large walnut-trees, and their thick foliage formed a pleasant shade. Very soon he perceived in the distance, waving flags, on which glittered a white cross on a red ground—the standard of the Danes as well as of the Swiss—and before him lay Interlachen.

"It is really a splendid town, like none other that I have ever seen," said Rudy to himself. It was indeed a Swiss town in its holiday dress. Not like the many other towns, crowded with heavy stone houses, stiff and foreign looking. No; here it seemed as if the wooden houses on the hills had run into the valley, and placed themselves in rows and ranks by the side of the clear river, which rushes like an arrow in its course. The streets were rather irregular, it is true, but still this added to their picturesque appearance. There was one street which Rudy thought the prettiest of them all; it had been built since he had visited the town when a little boy. It seemed to him as if all the neatest and most curiously carved toy houses which his grandfather once kept in the large cupboard at home, had been brought out and placed in this spot, and that they had increased in size since then, as the old chestnut trees had done. The houses were called hotels; the woodwork on the windows and balconies was curiously carved. The roofs were gayly painted, and before each house was a flower garden, which separated it from the macadamized high-road. These houses all stood on the same side of the road, so that the fresh, green meadows, in which were cows grazing, with bells on their necks, were not hidden. The sound of these bells is often heard amidst Alpine scenery. These meadows were encircled by lofty hills, which receded a little in the centre, so that the most beautifully formed of Swiss mountains—the snow-crowned Jungfrau—could be distinctly seen glittering in the distance. A number of elegantly dressed gentlemen and ladies from foreign lands, and crowds of country people from the neighboring cantons, were assembled in the town. Each marksman wore the number of hits he had made twisted in a garland round his hat. Here were music and singing of all descriptions: hand-organs, trumpets, shouting, and noise. The houses and bridges were adorned with verses and inscriptions. Flags and banners were waving. Shot after shot was fired, which was the best music to Rudy's ears. And amidst all this excitement he quite forgot Babette, on whose account only he had come. The shooters were thronging round the target, and Rudy was soon amongst them. But when he took his turn to fire, he proved himself the best shot, for he always struck the bull's-eye.

"Who may that young stranger be?" was the inquiry on all sides. "He speaks French as it is spoken in the Swiss cantons."

"And makes himself understood very well when he speaks German," said some.

"He lived here, when a child, with his grandfather, in a house on the road to Grindelwald," remarked one of the sportsmen.

And full of life was this young stranger; his eyes sparkled, his glance was steady, and his arm sure, therefore he always hit the mark. Good fortune gives courage, and Rudy was always courageous. He soon had a circle of friends gathered round him. Every one noticed him, and did him homage. Babette had quite vanished from his thoughts, when he was struck on the shoulder by a heavy hand, and a deep voice said to him in French, "You are from the canton Valais."

Rudy turned round, and beheld a man with a ruddy, pleasant face, and a stout figure. It was the rich miller from Bex. His broad, portly person, hid the slender, lovely Babette; but she came forward and glanced at him with her bright, dark eyes. The rich miller was very much flattered at the thought that the young man, who was acknowledged to be the best shot, and was so praised by every one, should be from his own canton. Now was Rudy really fortunate: he had travelled all this way to this place, and those he had forgotten were now come to seek him. When country people go far from home, they often meet with those they know, and improve their acquaintance. Rudy, by his shooting, had gained the first place in the shooting-match, just as the miller at home at Bex stood first, because of his money and his mill. So the two men shook hands, which they had never done before. Babette, too, held out her hand to Rudy frankly, and he pressed it in his, and looked at her so earnestly, that she blushed deeply. The miller talked of the long journey they had travelled, and of the many towns they had seen. It was his opinion that he had really made as great a journey as if he had travelled in a steamship, a railway carriage, or a post-chaise.

"I came by a much shorter way," said Rudy; "I came over the mountains. There is no road so high that a man may not venture upon it."

"Ah, yes; and break your neck," said the miller; "and you look like one who will break his neck some day, you are so daring."

"Oh, nothing ever happens to a man if he has confidence in himself," replied Rudy.

The miller's relations at Interlachen, with whom the miller and Babette were staying, invited Rudy to visit them, when they found he came from the same canton as the miller. It was a most pleasant visit. Good fortune seemed to follow him, as it does those who think and act for themselves, and who remember the proverb, "Nuts are given to us, but they are not cracked for us." And Rudy was treated by the miller's relations almost like one of the family, and glasses of wine were poured out to drink to the welfare of the best shooter. Babette clinked glasses with Rudy, and he returned thanks for the toast. In the evening they all took a delightful walk under the walnut-trees, in front of the stately hotels; there were so many people, and such crowding, that Rudy was obliged to offer his arm to Babette. Then he told her how happy it made him to meet people from the canton Vaud,—for Vaud and Valais were neighboring cantons. He spoke of this pleasure so heartily that Babette could not resist giving his arm a slight squeeze; and so they walked on together, and talked and chatted like old acquaintances. Rudy felt inclined to laugh sometimes at the absurd dress and walk of the foreign ladies; but Babette did not wish to make fun of them, for she knew there must be some good, excellent people amongst them; she, herself, had a godmother, who was a high-born English lady. Eighteen years before, when Babette was christened, this lady was staying at Bex, and she stood godmother for her, and gave her the valuable brooch she now wore in her bosom.

Her godmother had twice written to her, and this year she was expected to visit Interlachen with her two daughters; "but they are old-maids," added Babette, who was only eighteen: "they are nearly thirty." Her sweet little mouth was never still a moment, and all that she said sounded in Rudy's ears as matters of the greatest importance, and at last he told her what he was longing to tell. How often he had been at Bex, how well he knew the mill, and how often he had seen Babette, when most likely she had not noticed him; and lastly, that full of many thoughts which he could not tell her, he had been to the mill on the evening when she and her father has started on their long journey, but not too far for him to find a way to overtake them. He told her all this, and a great deal more; he told her how much he could endure for her; and that it was to see her, and not the shooting-match, which had brought him to Interlachen. Babette became quite silent after hearing all this; it was almost too much, and it troubled her.

And while they thus wandered on, the sun sunk behind the lofty mountains. The Jungfrau stood out in brightness and splendor, as a back-ground to the green woods of the surrounding hills. Every one stood still to look at the beautiful sight, Rudy and Babette among them.

"Nothing can be more beautiful than this," said Babette.

"Nothing!" replied Rudy, looking at Babette.

"To-morrow I must return home," remarked Rudy a few minutes afterwards.

"Come and visit us at Bex," whispered Babette; "my father will be pleased to see you."

V. *On The Way Home~*

Oh, what a number of things Rudy had to carry over the mountains, when he set out to return home! He had three silver cups, two handsome pistols, and a silver coffee-pot. This latter would be useful when he began housekeeping. But all these were not the heaviest weight he had to bear; something mightier and more important he carried with him in his heart, over the high mountains, as he journeyed homeward.

The weather was dismally dark, and inclined to rain; the clouds hung low, like a mourning veil on the tops of the mountains, and shrouded their glittering peaks. In the woods could be heard the sound of the axe and the heavy fall of the trunks of the trees, as they rolled down the slopes of the mountains. When seen from the heights, the trunks of these trees looked like slender stems; but on a nearer inspection they were found to be large and strong enough for the masts of a ship. The river murmured monotonously, the wind whistled, and the clouds sailed along hurriedly.

Suddenly there appeared, close by Rudy's side, a young maiden; he had not noticed her till she came quite near to him. She was also going to ascend the mountain. The maiden's eyes shone with an unearthly power, which obliged you to look into them; they were strange eyes,—clear, deep, and unfathomable.

"Hast thou a lover?" asked Rudy; all his thoughts were naturally on love just then.

"I have none," answered the maiden, with a laugh; it was as if she had not spoken the truth.

"Do not let us go such a long way round," said she. "We must keep to the left; it is much shorter."

"Ah, yes," he replied; "and fall into some crevasse. Do you pretend to be a guide, and not know the road better than that?"

"I know every step of the way," said she; "and my thoughts are collected, while yours are down in the valley yonder. We should think of the Ice Maiden while we are up here; men say she is not kind to their race."

"I fear her not," said Rudy. "She could not keep me when I was a child; I will not give myself up to her now I am a man."

Darkness came on, the rain fell, and then it began to snow, and the whiteness dazzled the eyes.

"Give me your hand," said the maiden; "I will help you to mount." And he felt the touch of her icy fingers.

"You help me," cried Rudy; "I do not yet require a woman to help me to climb." And he stepped quickly forwards away from her.

The drifting snow-shower fell like a veil between them, the wind whistled, and behind him he could hear the maiden laughing and singing, and the sound was most strange to hear.

"It certainly must be a spectre or a servant of the Ice Maiden," thought Rudy, who had heard such things talked about when he was a little boy, and had stayed all night on the mountain with the guides.

The snow fell thicker than ever, the clouds lay beneath him; he looked back, there was no one to be seen, but he heard sounds of mocking laughter, which were not those of a human voice.

When Rudy at length reached the highest part of the mountain, where the path led down to the valley of the Rhone, the snow had ceased, and in the clear heavens he saw two bright stars twinkling. They reminded him of Babette and of himself, and of his future happiness, and his heart glowed at the thought.

VI. The Visit to the Mill~

"What beautiful things you have brought home!" said his

old foster-mother; and her strange-looking eagle-eyes sparkled, while she wriggled and twisted her skinny neck more quickly and strangely than ever. "You have brought good luck with you, Rudy. I must give you a kiss, my dear boy."

Rudy allowed himself to be kissed; but it could be seen by his countenance that he only endured the infliction as a homely duty.

"How handsome you are, Rudy!" said the old woman.

"Don't flatter," said Rudy, with a laugh; but still he was pleased.

"I must say once more," said the old woman, "that you are very lucky."

"Well, in that I believe you are right," said he, as he thought of Babette. Never had he felt such a longing for that deep valley as he now had. "They must have returned home by this time," said he to himself, "it is already two days over the time which they fixed upon. I must go to Bex."

So Rudy set out to go to Bex; and when he arrived there, he found the miller and his daughter at home. They received him kindly, and brought him many greetings from their friends at Interlachen. Babette did not say much. She seemed to have become quite silent; but her eyes spoke, and that was quite enough for Rudy. The miller had generally a great deal to talk about, and seemed to expect that every one should listen to his jokes, and laugh at them; for was not he the rich miller? But now he was more inclined to hear Rudy's adventures while hunting and travelling, and to listen to his descriptions of the difficulties the chamois-hunter has to overcome on the mountain-tops, or of the dangerous snow-drifts which the wind and weather cause to cling to the edges of the rocks, or to lie in the form of a frail bridge over the abyss beneath. The eyes of the brave Rudy sparkled as he described the life of a hunter, or spoke of the cunning of the chamois and their wonderful leaps; also of the powerful fohn and the rolling avalanche. He noticed that the more he described, the more interested the miller became, especially when he spoke of the fierce vulture and of the royal eagle. Not far from Bex, in the canton Valais, was an eagle's nest, more curiously built under a high, over-hanging rock. In this nest was a young eagle; but who would venture to take it? A young Englishman had offered Rudy a whole handful of gold, if he would bring him the young eagle alive.

"There is a limit to everything," was Rudy's reply. "The eagle could not be taken; it would be folly to attempt it."

The wine was passed round freely, and the conversation kept up pleasantly; but the evening seemed too short for Rudy, although it was midnight when he left the miller's house, after this his first visit.

While the lights in the windows of the miller's house still twinkled through the green foliage, out through the open skylight came the parlor-cat on to the roof, and along the water-pipe walked the kitchen-cat to meet her.

"What is the news at the mill?" asked the parlor-cat. "Here in the house there is secret love-making going on, which the father knows nothing about. Rudy and Babette have been treading on each other's paws, under the table, all the evening. They trod on my tail twice, but I did not mew; that would have attracted notice."

"Well, I should have mewed," said the kitchen-cat.

"What might suit the kitchen would not suit the parlor," said the other. "I am quite curious to know what the miller will say when he finds out this engagement."

Yes, indeed; what would the miller say? Rudy himself was anxious to know that; but to wait till the miller heard of it from others was out of the question. Therefore, not many days after this visit, he was riding in the omnibus that runs between the two cantons, Valais and Vaud. These cantons are separated by the Rhone, over which is a bridge that unites them. Rudy, as usual, had plenty of courage, and indulged in pleasant thoughts of the favorable answer he should receive that evening. And when the omnibus returned, Rudy was again seated in it, going homewards; and at the same time the parlor-cat at the miller's house ran out quickly, crying,—

"Here, you from the kitchen, what do you think? The miller knows all now. Everything has come to a delightful end. Rudy came here this evening, and he and Babette had much whispering and secret conversation together. They stood in the path near the miller's room. I lay at their feet; but they had no eyes or thoughts for me.

"'I will go to your father at once,' said he; 'it is the most honorable way.'

"'Shall I go with you?' asked Babette; 'it will give you courage.'

"'I have plenty of courage,' said Rudy; 'but if you are with me, he must be friendly, whether he says Yes or No.'

"So they turned to go in, and Rudy trod heavily on my tail; he certainly is very clumsy. I mewed; but neither he nor Babette had any ears for me. They opened the door, and entered together. I was before them, and jumped on the back of a chair. I hardly know what Rudy said; but the miller flew into a rage, and threatened to kick him out of the house. He told him he might go to the mountains, and look after the chamois, but not after our little Babette."

"And what did they say? Did they speak?" asked the kitchen-cat.

"What did they say! why, all that people generally do say when they go a-wooing—'I love her, and she loves me; and when there is milk in the can for one, there is milk in the can for two.'

"'But she is so far above you,' said the miller; 'she has heaps of gold, as you know. You should not attempt to reach her.'

"'There is nothing so high that a man cannot reach, if he will,' answered Rudy; for he is a brave youth.

"'Yet you could not reach the young eagle,' said the miller, laughing. 'Babette is higher than the eagle's nest.'

"'I will have them both,' said Rudy.

"'Very well; I will give her to you when you bring me the young eaglet alive,' said the miller; and he laughed till the tears stood in his eyes. 'But now I thank you for this visit, Rudy; and if you come to-morrow, you will find nobody at home. Good-bye, Rudy.'

"Babette also wished him farewell; but her voice sounded as mournful as the mew of a little kitten that has lost its mother.

"'A promise is a promise between man and man,' said Rudy. 'Do not weep, Babette; I shall bring the young eagle.'

"'You will break your neck, I hope,' said the miller, 'and we shall be relieved from your company.'

"I call that kicking him out of the house," said the parlor-cat. "And now Rudy is gone, and Babette sits and weeps, while the miller sings German songs that he learnt on his journey; but I do not trouble myself on the matter,—it would be of no use."

"Yet, for all that, it is a very strange affair," said the kitchen-cat.

VII. *The Eagle's Nest~*

From the mountain-path came a joyous sound of some person whistling, and it betokened good humor and undaunted courage. It was Rudy, going to meet his friend Vesinaud. "You must come and help," said he. "I want to carry off the young eaglet from the top of the rock. We will take young Ragli with us."

"Had you not better first try to take down the moon? That would be quite as easy a task," said Vesinaud. "You seem to be in good spirits."

"Yes, indeed I am. I am thinking of my wedding. But to be serious, I will tell you all about it, and how I am situated."

Then he explained to Vesinaud and Ragli what he wished to do, and why.

"You are a daring fellow," said they; "but it is no use; you will break your neck."

"No one falls, unless he is afraid," said Rudy.

So at midnight they set out, carrying with them poles, ladders, and ropes. The road lay amidst brushwood and underwood, over rolling stones, always upwards higher and higher in the dark night. Waters roared beneath them, or fell in cascades from above. Humid clouds were driving through the air as the hunters reached the precipitous ledge of the rock. It was even darker here, for the sides of the rocks almost met, and the light penetrated only through a small opening at the top. At a little distance from the edge could be heard the sound of the roaring, foaming waters in the yawning abyss beneath them. The three seated themselves on a stone, to await in stillness the dawn of day, when the parent eagle would fly out, as it would be necessary to shoot the old bird before they could think of gaining possession of the young one. Rudy sat motionless, as if he had been part of the stone on which he sat. He held his gun ready to fire, with his eyes fixed steadily on the highest point of the cliff, where the eagle's nest lay concealed beneath the overhanging rock.

The three hunters had a long time to wait. At last they heard a rustling, whirring sound above them, and a large hovering object darkened the air. Two guns were ready to aim at the dark body of the eagle as it rose from the nest. Then a shot was fired; for an instant the bird fluttered its wide-spreading wings, and seemed as if it would fill up the whole of the chasm, and drag down the hunters in its fall. But it was not so; the eagle sunk gradually into the abyss beneath, and the branches of trees and bushes were broken by its weight. Then the hunters roused themselves: three of the longest ladders were brought and bound together; the topmost ring of these ladders would just reach the edge of the rock which hung over the abyss, but no farther. The point beneath which the eagle's nest lay sheltered was much higher, and the sides of the rock were as smooth as a wall. After consulting together, they determined to bind together two more ladders, and to hoist them over the cavity, and so form a communication with the three beneath them, by binding the upper ones to the lower. With great difficulty they contrived to drag the two ladders over the rock, and there they hung for some moments, swaying over the abyss; but no sooner had they fastened them together, than Rudy placed his foot on the lowest step.

It was a bitterly cold morning; clouds of mist were rising from beneath, and Rudy stood on the lower step of the ladder as a fly rests on a piece of swinging straw, which a bird may have dropped from the edge of the nest it was building on some tall factory chimney; but the fly could fly away if the straw were shaken, Rudy could only break his neck. The wind whistled around him, and beneath him the waters of the abyss, swelled by the thawing of the glaciers, those palaces of the Ice Maiden, foamed and roared in their rapid course. When Rudy began to ascend, the ladder trembled like the web of the spider, when it draws out the long, delicate threads; but as soon as he reached the fourth of the ladders, which had been bound together, he felt more confidence,—he knew that they had been fastened securely by skilful hands. The fifth ladder, that appeared to reach the nest, was supported by the sides of the rock, yet it swung to and fro, and flapped about like a slender reed, and as if it had been bound by fishing lines. It seemed a most dangerous undertaking to ascend it, but Rudy knew how to climb; he had learnt that from the cat, and he had no fear. He did not observe Vertigo, who stood in the air behind him, trying to lay hold of him with his outstretched polypous arms.

When at length he stood on the topmost step of the ladder, he found that he was still some distance below the nest, and not even able to see into it. Only by using his hands and climbing could he possibly reach it. He tried the strength of the stunted trees, and the thick underwood upon which the nest rested, and of which it was formed, and finding they would support his weight, he grasped them firmly, and swung himself up from the ladder till his head and breast were above the nest, and then what an overpowering stench came from it, for in it lay the putrid remains of lambs, chamois, and birds. Vertigo, although he could not reach him, blew the poisonous vapor in his face, to make him giddy and faint; and beneath, in the dark, yawning deep, on the rushing waters, sat the Ice Maiden, with her long, pale, green hair falling around her, and her death-like eyes fixed upon him, like the two barrels of a gun. "I have thee now," she cried.

In a corner of the eagle's nest sat the young eaglet, a large and powerful bird, though still unable to fly. Rudy fixed his eyes upon it, held on by one hand with all his strength, and with the other threw a noose round the young eagle. The string slipped to its legs. Rudy tightened it, and thus secured the bird alive. Then flinging the sling over his shoulder, so that the creature hung a good way down behind him, he prepared to descend with the help of a rope, and his foot soon touched safely the highest step of the ladder. Then Rudy, remembering his early lesson in climbing, "Hold fast, and do not fear," descended carefully down the ladders, and at last stood safely on the ground with the young living eaglet, where he was received with loud shouts of joy and congratulations.

VIII. *What Fresh News the Parlor-Cat Had to Tell~*

"There is what you asked for," said Rudy, as he entered the miller's house at Bex, and placed on the floor a large basket. He removed the lid as he spoke, and a pair of yellow eyes, encircled by a black ring, stared forth with a wild, fiery glance, that seemed ready to burn and destroy all that came in its way. Its short, strong beak was open, ready to bite, and on its red throat were short feathers, like stubble.

"The young eaglet!" cried the miller.

Babette screamed, and started back, while her eyes wandered from Rudy to the bird in astonishment.

"You are not to be discouraged by difficulties, I see," said the miller.

"And you will keep your word," replied Rudy. "Each has his own characteristic, whether it is honor or courage."

"But how is it you did not break your neck?" asked the miller.

"Because I held fast," answered Rudy; "and I mean to hold fast to Babette."

"You must get her first," said the miller, laughing; and Babette thought this a very good sign.

"We must take the bird out of the basket," said she. "It is getting into a rage; how its eyes glare. How did you manage to conquer it?"

Then Rudy had to describe his adventure, and the miller's eyes opened wide as he listened.

"With your courage and your good fortune you might win three wives," said the miller.

"Oh, thank you," cried Rudy.

"But you have not won Babette yet," said the miller, slapping the young Alpine hunter on the shoulder playfully.

"Have you heard the fresh news at the mill?" asked the parlor-cat of the kitchen-cat. "Rudy has brought us the young eagle, and he is to take Babette in exchange. They kissed each other in the presence of the old man, which is as good as an engagement. He was quite civil about it; drew in his claws, and took his afternoon nap, so that the two were left to sit and wag their tails as much as they pleased. They have so much to talk about that it will not be finished till Christmas." Neither was it finished till Christmas.

The wind whirled the faded, fallen leaves; the snow drifted in the valleys, as well as upon the mountains, and the Ice Maiden sat in the stately palace which, in winter time, she generally occupied. The perpendicular rocks were covered with slippery ice, and where in summer the stream from the rocks had left a watery veil, icicles large and heavy hung from the trees, while the snow-powdered fir-trees were decorated with fantastic garlands of crystal. The Ice Maiden rode on the howling wind across the deep valleys, the country, as far as Bex, was covered with a carpet of snow, so that the Ice Maiden could follow Rudy, and see him, when he visited the mill; and while in the room at the miller's house, where he was accustomed to spend so much of his time with Babette. The wedding was to take place in the following summer, and they heard enough of it, for so many of their friends spoke of the matter.

Then came sunshine to the mill. The beautiful Alpine roses bloomed, and joyous, laughing Babette, was like the early spring, which makes all the birds sing of summer time and bridal days.

"How those two do sit and chatter together," said the parlor-cat; "I have had enough of their mewing."

IX. The Ice Maiden~

The walnut and chestnut trees, which extend from the bridge of St. Maurice, by the river Rhone, to the shores of the lake of Geneva, were already covered with the delicate green garlands of early spring, just bursting into bloom, while the Rhone rushed wildly from its source among the green glaciers which form the ice palace of the Ice Maiden. She sometimes allows herself to be carried by the keen wind to the lofty snow-fields, where she stretches herself in the sunshine on the soft snowy-cushions. From thence she throws her far-seeing glance into the deep valley beneath, where human beings are busily moving about like ants on a stone in the sun. "Spirits of strength, as the children of the sun call you," cried the Ice Maiden, "ye are but worms! Let but a snow-ball roll, and you and your houses and your towns are crushed and swept away." And she raised her proud head, and looked around her with eyes that flashed death from their glance. From the valley came a rumbling sound; men were busily at work blasting the rocks to form tunnels, and laying down roads for the railway. "They are playing at work underground, like moles," said she. "They are digging passages beneath the earth, and the noise is like the reports of cannons. I shall throw down my palaces, for the clamor is louder than the roar of thunder." Then there ascended from the valley a thick vapor, which waved itself in the air like a fluttering veil. It rose, as a plume of feathers, from a steam engine, to which, on the lately-opened railway, a string of carriages was linked, carriage to carriage, looking like a winding serpent. The train shot past with the speed of an arrow. "They play at being masters down there, those spirits of strength!" exclaimed the Ice Maiden; "but the powers of nature are still the rulers." And she laughed and sang till her voice sounded through the valley, and people said it was the rolling of an avalanche. But the children of the sun sang in louder strains in praise of the mind of man, which can span the sea as with a yoke, can level mountains, and fill up valleys. It is the power of thought which gives man the mastery over nature.

Just at this moment there came across the snow-field, where the Ice Maiden sat, a party of travellers. They had bound themselves fast to each other, so that they looked like one large body on the slippery plains of ice encircling the deep abyss.

"Worms!" exclaimed the Ice Maiden. "You, the lords of the powers of nature!" And she turned away and looked maliciously at the deep valley where the railway train was rushing by. "There they sit, these thoughts!" she exclaimed. "There they sit in their power over nature's strength. I see them all. One sits proudly apart, like a king; others sit together in a group; yonder, half of them are asleep; and when the steam dragon stops, they will get out and go their way. The thoughts go forth into the world," and she laughed.

"There goes another avalanche," said those in the valley beneath.

"It will not reach us," said two who sat together behind the steam dragon. "Two hearts and one beat," as people say. They were Rudy and Babette, and the miller was with them. "I am like the luggage," said he; "I am here as a necessary appendage."

"There sit those two," said the Ice Maiden. "Many a chamois have I crushed. Millions of Alpine roses have I snapped and broken off; not a root have I spared. I know them all, and their thoughts, those spirits of strength!" and again she laughed.

"There rolls another avalanche," said those in the valley.

X. *The Godmother~*

At Montreux, one of the towns which encircle the northeast part of the lake of Geneva, lived Babette's godmother, the noble English lady, with her daughters and a young relative. They had only lately arrived, yet the miller had paid them a visit, and informed them of Babette's engagement to Rudy. The whole story of their meeting at Interlachen, and his brave adventure with the eaglet, were related to them, and they were all very much interested, and as pleased about Rudy and Babette as the miller himself. The three were invited to come to Montreux; it was but right for Babette to become acquainted with her godmother, who wished to see her very much. A steam-boat started from the town of Villeneuve, at one end of the lake of Geneva, and arrived at Bernex, a little town beyond Montreux, in about half an hour. And in this boat, the miller, with his daughter and Rudy, set out to visit her godmother. They passed the coast which has been so celebrated in song. Here, under the walnut-trees, by the deep blue lake, sat Byron, and wrote his melodious verses about the prisoner confined in the gloomy castle of Chillon. Here, where Clarens, with its weeping-willows, is reflected in the clear water, wandered Rousseau, dreaming of Heloise. The river Rhone glides gently by beneath the lofty snow-capped hills of Savoy, and not far from its mouth lies a little island in the lake, so small that, seen from the shore, it looks like a ship. The surface of the island is rocky; and about a hundred years ago, a lady caused the ground to be covered with earth, in which three acacia-trees were planted, and the whole enclosed with stone walls. The acacia-trees now overshadow every part of the island. Babette was enchanted with the spot; it seemed to her the most beautiful object in the whole voyage, and she thought how much she should like to land there. But the steam-ship passed it by, and did not stop till it reached Bernex. The little party walked slowly from this place to Montreux, passing the sun-lit walls with which the vineyards of the little mountain town of Montreux are surrounded, and peasants' houses, overshadowed by fig-trees, with gardens in which grow the laurel and the cypress.

Halfway up the hill stood the boarding-house in which Babette's godmother resided. She was received most cordially; her godmother was a very friendly woman, with a round, smiling countenance. When a child, her head must have resembled one of Raphael's cherubs; it was still an angelic face, with its white locks of silvery hair. The daughters were tall, elegant, slender maidens.

The young cousin, whom they had brought with them, was dressed in white from head to foot; he had golden hair and golden whiskers, large enough to be divided amongst three gentlemen; and he began immediately to pay the greatest attention to Babette.

Richly bound books, note-paper, and drawings, lay on the large table. The balcony window stood open, and from it could be seen the beautiful wide extended lake, the water so clear and still, that the mountains of Savoy, with their villages, woods, and snow-crowned peaks, were clearly reflected in it.

Rudy, who was usually so lively and brave, did not in the least feel himself at home; he acted as if he were walking on peas, over a slippery floor. How long and wearisome the time appeared; it was like being in a treadmill. And then they went out for a walk, which was very slow and tedious. Two steps forward and one backwards had Rudy to take to keep pace with the others. They walked down to Chillon, and went over the old castle on the rocky island. They saw the implements of torture, the deadly dungeons, the rusty fetters in the rocky walls, the stone benches for those condemned to death, the trap-doors through which the unhappy creatures were hurled upon iron spikes, and impaled alive. They called looking at all these a pleasure. It certainly was the right place to visit. Byron's poetry had made it celebrated in the world. Rudy could only feel that it was a place of execution. He leaned against the stone framework of the window, and gazed down into the deep, blue water, and over to the little island with the three acacias, and wished himself there, away and free from the whole chattering party. But Babette was most unusually lively and good-tempered.

"I have been so amused," she said.

The cousin had found her quite perfect.

"He is a perfect fop," said Rudy; and this was the first time Rudy had said anything that did not please Babette.

The Englishman had made her a present of a little book, in remembrance of their visit to Chillon. It was Byron's poem, "The Prisoner of Chillon," translated into French, so that Babette could read it.

"The book may be very good," said Rudy; "but that finely combed fellow who gave it to you is not worth much."

"He looks something like a flour-sack without any flour," said the miller, laughing at his own wit. Rudy laughed, too, for so had he appeared to him.

XI. The Cousin~

When Rudy went a few days after to pay a visit to the mill, he found the young Englishman there. Babette was just thinking of preparing some trout to set before him. She understood well how to garnish the dish with parsley, and make it look quite tempting. Rudy thought all this quite unnecessary. What did the Englishman want there? What was he about? Why should he be entertained, and waited upon by Babette? Rudy was jealous, and that made Babette happy. It amused her to discover all the feelings of his heart; the strong points and weak ones. Love was to her as yet only a pastime, and she played with Rudy's whole heart. At the same time it must be acknowledged that her fortune, her whole life, her inmost thoughts, her best and most noble feelings in this world were all for him. Still the more gloomy he looked, the more her eyes laughed. She could almost have kissed the fair Englishman, with the golden whiskers, if by so doing she could have put Rudy in a rage, and made him run out of the house. That would have proved how much he loved her. All this was not right in Babette, but she was only nineteen years of age, and she did not reflect on what she did, neither did she think that her conduct would appear to the young Englishman as light, and not even becoming the modest and much-loved daughter of the miller.

The mill at Bex stood in the highway, which passed under the snow-clad mountains, and not far from a rapid mountain-stream, whose waters seemed to have been lashed into a foam like soap-suds. This stream, however, did not pass near enough to the mill, and therefore the mill-wheel was turned by a smaller stream which tumbled down the rocks on the opposite side, where it was opposed by a stone mill-dam, and obtained greater strength and speed, till it fell into a large basin, and from thence through a channel to the mill-wheel. This channel sometimes overflowed, and made the path so slippery that any one passing that way might easily fall in, and be carried towards the mill wheel with frightful rapidity. Such a catastrophe nearly happened to the young Englishman. He had dressed himself in white clothes, like a miller's man, and was climbing the path to the miller's house, but he had never been taught to climb, and therefore slipped, and nearly went in head-foremost. He managed, however, to scramble out with wet sleeves and bespattered trousers. Still, wet and splashed with mud, he contrived to reach Babette's window, to which he had been guided by the light that shone from it. Here he climbed the old linden-tree that stood near it, and began to imitate the voice of an owl, the only bird he could venture to mimic. Babette heard the noise, and glanced through the thin window curtain; but when she saw the man in white, and guessed who he was, her little heart beat with terror as well as anger. She quickly put out the light, felt if the fastening of the window was secure, and then left him to howl as long as he liked. How dreadful it would be, thought Babette, if Rudy were here in the house. But Rudy was not in the house. No, it was much worse, he was outside, standing just under the linden-tree. He was speaking loud, angry words. He could fight, and there might be murder! Babette opened the window in alarm, and called Rudy's name; she told him to go away, she did not wish him to remain there.

"You do not wish me to stay," cried he; "then this is an appointment you expected—this good friend whom you prefer to me. Shame on you, Babette!"

"You are detestable!" exclaimed Babette, bursting into tears. "Go away. I hate you."

"I have not deserved this," said Rudy, as he turned away, his cheeks burning, and his heart like fire.

Babette threw herself on the bed, and wept bitterly. "So much as I loved thee, Rudy, and yet thou canst think ill of me."

Thus her anger broke forth; it relieved her, however: otherwise she would have been more deeply grieved; but now she could sleep soundly, as youth only can sleep.

XII. Evil Powers~

Rudy left Bex, and took his way home along the mountain path. The air was fresh, but cold; for here amidst the deep snow, the Ice Maiden reigned. He was so high up that the large trees beneath him, with their thick foliage, appeared like garden plants, and the pines and bushes even less. The Alpine roses grew near the snow, which lay in detached stripes, and looked like linen laid out to bleach. A blue gentian grew in his path, and he crushed it with the butt end of his gun. A little higher up, he espied two chamois. Rudy's eyes glistened, and his thoughts flew at once in a different direction; but he was not near enough to take a sure aim. He ascended still higher, to a spot where a few rough blades of grass grew between the blocks of stone and the chamois passed quietly on over the snow-fields. Rudy walked hurriedly, while the clouds of mist gathered round him. Suddenly he found himself on the brink of a precipitous rock. The rain was falling in torrents. He felt a burning thirst, his head was hot, and his limbs trembled with cold. He seized his hunting-flask, but it was empty; he had not thought of filling it before ascending the mountain. He had never been ill in his life, nor ever experienced such sensations as those he now felt. He was so tired that he could scarcely resist lying down at his full length to sleep, although the ground was flooded with the rain. Yet when he tried to rouse himself a little, every object around him danced and trembled before his eyes.

Suddenly he observed in the doorway of a hut newly built under the rock, a young maiden. He did not remember having seen this hut before, yet there it stood; and he thought, at first, that the young maiden was Annette, the schoolmaster's daughter, whom he had once kissed in the dance. The maiden was not Annette; yet it seemed as if he had seen her somewhere before, perhaps near Grindelwald, on the evening of his return home from Interlachen, after the shooting-match.

"How did you come here?" he asked.

"I am at home," she replied; "I am watching my flocks."

"Your flocks!" he exclaimed; "where do they find pasture? There is nothing here but snow and rocks."

"Much you know of what grows here," she replied, laughing. "Not far beneath us there is beautiful pasture-land. My goats go there. I tend them carefully; I never miss one. What is once mine remains mine."

"You are bold," said Rudy.

"And so are you," she answered.

"Have you any milk in the house?" he asked; "if so, give me some to drink; my thirst is intolerable."

"I have something better than milk," she replied, "which I will give you. Some travellers who were here yesterday with their guide left behind them a half a flask of wine, such as you have never tasted. They will not come back to fetch it, I know, and I shall not drink it; so you shall have it."

Then the maiden went to fetch the wine, poured some into a wooden cup, and offered it to Rudy.

"How good it is!" said he; "I have never before tasted such warm, invigorating wine." And his eyes sparkled with new life; a glow diffused itself over his frame; it seemed as if every sorrow, every oppression were banished from his mind, and a fresh, free nature were stirring within him. "You are surely Annette, the schoolmaster's daughter," cried he; "will you give me a kiss?"

"Yes, if you will give me that beautiful ring which you wear on your finger."

"My betrothal ring?" he replied.

"Yes, just so," said the maiden, as she poured out some more wine, and held it to his lips. Again he drank, and a living joy streamed through every vein.

"The whole world is mine, why therefore should I grieve?" thought he. "Everything is created for our enjoyment and happiness. The stream of life is a stream of happiness; let us flow on with it to joy and felicity."

Rudy gazed on the young maiden; it was Annette, and yet it was not Annette; still less did he suppose it was the spectral phantom, whom he had met near Grindelwald. The maiden up here on the mountain was fresh as the new fallen snow, blooming as an Alpine rose, and as nimble-footed as a young kid. Still, she was one of Adam's race, like Rudy. He flung his arms round the beautiful being, and gazed into her wonderfully clear eyes,—only for a moment; but in that moment words cannot express the effect of his gaze. Was it the spirit of life or of death that overpowered him? Was he rising higher, or sinking lower and lower into the deep, deadly abyss? He knew not; but the walls of ice shone like blue-green glass; innumerable clefts yawned around him, and the water-drops tinkled like the chiming of church bells, and shone clearly as pearls in the light of a pale-blue flame. The Ice Maiden, for she it was, kissed him, and her kiss sent a chill as of ice through his whole frame. A cry of agony escaped from him; he struggled to get free, and tottered from her. For a moment all was dark before his eyes, but when he opened them again it was light, and the Alpine maiden had vanished. The powers of evil had played their game; the sheltering hut was no more to be seen. The water trickled down the naked sides of the rocks, and snow lay thickly all around. Rudy shivered with cold; he was wet through to the skin; and his ring was gone,—the betrothal ring that Babette had given him. His gun lay near him in the snow; he took it up and tried to discharge it, but it missed fire. Heavy clouds lay on the mountain clefts, like firm masses of snow. Upon one of these Vertigo sat, lurking after his powerless prey, and from beneath came a sound as if a piece of rock had fallen from the cleft, and was crushing everything that stood in its way or opposed its course.

But, at the miller's, Babette sat alone and wept. Rudy had not been to see her for six days. He who was in the wrong, and who ought to ask her forgiveness; for did she not love him with her whole heart?

XIII. At the Mill~

"What strange creatures human beings are," said the parlor-cat to the kitchen-cat; "Babette and Rudy have fallen out with each other. She sits and cries, and he thinks no more about her."

"That does not please me to hear," said the kitchen-cat.

"Nor me either," replied the parlor-cat; "but I do not take it to heart. Babette may fall in love with the red whiskers, if she likes, but he has not been here since he tried to get on the roof."

The powers of evil carry on their game both around us and within us. Rudy knew this, and thought a great deal about it. What was it that had happened to him on the mountain? Was it really a ghostly apparition, or a fever dream? Rudy knew nothing of fever, or any other ailment. But, while he judged Babette, he began to examine his own conduct. He had allowed wild thoughts to chase each other in his heart, and a fierce tornado to break loose. Could he confess to Babette, indeed, every thought which in the hour of temptation might have led him to wrong doing? He had lost her ring, and that very loss had won him back to her. Could she expect him to confess? He felt as if his heart would break while he thought of it, and while so many memories lingered on his mind. He saw her again, as she once stood before him, a laughing, spirited child; many loving words, which she had spoken to him out of the fulness of her love, came like a ray of sunshine into his heart, and soon it was all sunshine as he thought of Babette. But she must also confess she was wrong; that she should do.

He went to the mill—he went to confession. It began with a kiss, and ended with Rudy being considered the offender. It was such a great fault to doubt Babette's truth—it was most abominable of him. Such mistrust, such violence, would cause them both great unhappiness. This certainly was very true, she knew that; and therefore Babette preached him a little sermon, with which she was herself much amused, and during the preaching of which she looked quite lovely. She acknowledged, however, that on one point Rudy was right. Her godmother's nephew was a fop: she intended to burn the book which he had given her, so that not the slightest thing should remain to remind her of him.

"Well, that quarrel is all over," said the kitchen-cat. "Rudy is come back, and they are friends again, which they say is the greatest of all pleasures."

"I heard the rats say one night," said the kitchen-cat, "that the greatest pleasure in the world was to eat tallow candles and to feast on rancid bacon. Which are we to believe, the rats or the lovers?"

"Neither of them," said the parlor-cat; "it is always the safest plan to believe nothing you hear."

The greatest happiness was coming for Rudy and Babette. The happy day, as it is called, that is, their wedding-day, was near at hand. They were not to be married at the church at Bex, nor at the miller's house; Babette's godmother wished the nuptials to be solemnized at Montreux, in the pretty little church in that town. The miller was very anxious that this arrangement should be agreed to. He alone knew what the newly-married couple would receive from Babette's godmother, and he knew also that it was a wedding present well worth a concession. The day was fixed, and they were to travel as far as Villeneuve the evening before, to be in time for the steamer which sailed in the morning for Montreux, and the godmother's daughters were to dress and adorn the bride.

"Here in this house there ought to be a wedding-day kept," said the parlor-cat, "or else I would not give a mew for the whole affair."

"There is going to be great feasting," replied the kitchen-cat. "Ducks and pigeons have been killed, and a whole roebuck hangs on the wall. It makes me lick my lips when I think of it."

"To-morrow morning they will begin the journey."

Yes, to-morrow! And this evening, for the last time, Rudy and Babette sat in the miller's house as an engaged couple. Outside, the Alps glowed in the evening sunset, the evening bells chimed, and the children of the sunbeam sang, "Whatever happens is best."

XIV. Night Visions~

The sun had gone down, and the clouds lay low on the valley of the Rhone. The wind blew from the south across the mountains; it was an African wind, a wind which scattered the clouds for a moment, and then suddenly fell. The broken clouds hung in fantastic forms upon the wood-covered hills by the rapid Rhone. They assumed the shapes of antediluvian animals, of eagles hovering in the air, of frogs leaping over a marsh, and then sunk down upon the rushing stream and appeared to sail upon it, although floating in the air. An uprooted fir-tree was being carried away by the current, and marking out its path by eddying circles on the water. Vertigo and his sisters were dancing upon it, and raising these circles on the foaming river. The moon lighted up the snow on the mountain-tops, shone on the dark woods, and on the drifting clouds those fantastic forms which at night might be taken for spirits of the powers of nature. The mountain-dweller saw them through the panes of his little window. They sailed in hosts before the Ice Maiden as she came out of her palace of ice. Then she seated herself on the trunk of the fir-tree as on a broken skiff, and the water from the glaciers carried her down the river to the open lake.

"The wedding guests are coming," sounded from air and sea. These were the sights and sounds without; within there were visions, for Babette had a wonderful dream. She dreamt that she had been married to Rudy for many years, and that, one day when he was out chamois hunting, and she alone in their dwelling at home, the young Englishman with the golden whiskers sat with her. His eyes were quite eloquent, and his words possessed a magic power; he offered her his hand, and she was obliged to follow him. They went out of the house and stepped downwards, always downwards, and it seemed to Babette as if she had a weight on her heart which continually grew heavier. She felt she was committing a sin against Rudy, a sin against God. Suddenly she found herself forsaken, her clothes torn by the thorns, and her hair gray; she looked upwards in her agony, and there, on the edge of the rock, she espied Rudy. She stretched out her arms to him, but she did not venture to call him or to pray; and had she called him, it would have been useless, for it was not Rudy, only his hunting coat and hat hanging on an alpenstock, as the hunters sometimes arrange them to deceive the chamois. "Oh!" she exclaimed in her agony; "oh, that I had died on the happiest day of my life, my wedding-day. O my God, it would have been a mercy and a blessing had Rudy travelled far away from me, and I had never known him. None know what will happen in the future." And then, in ungodly despair, she cast herself down into the deep rocky gulf. The spell was broken; a cry of terror escaped her, and she awoke.

The dream was over; it had vanished. But she knew she had dreamt something frightful about the young Englishman, yet months had passed since she had seen him or even thought of him. Was he still at Montreux, and should she meet him there on her wedding day? A slight shadow passed over her pretty mouth as she thought of this, and she knit her brows; but the smile soon returned to her lip, and joy sparkled in her eyes, for this was the morning of the day on which she and Rudy were to be married, and the sun was shining brightly. Rudy was already in the parlor when she entered it, and they very soon started for Villeneuve. Both of them were overflowing with happiness, and the miller was in the best of tempers, laughing and merry; he was a good, honest soul, and a kind father.

"Now we are masters of the house," said the parlor-cat.

XV. The Conclusion~

It was early in the afternoon, and just at dinner-time, when the three joyous travellers reached Villeneuve. After dinner, the miller placed himself in the arm-chair, smoked his pipe, and had a little nap. The bridal pair went arm-in-arm out through the town and along the high road, at the foot of the wood-covered rocks, and by the deep, blue lake.

The gray walls, and the heavy clumsy-looking towers of the gloomy castle of Chillon, were reflected in the clear flood. The little island, on which grew the three acacias, lay at a short distance, looking like a bouquet rising from the lake. "How delightful it must be to live there," said Babette, who again felt the greatest wish to visit the island; and an opportunity offered to gratify her wish at once, for on the shore lay a boat, and the rope by which it was moored could be very easily loosened. They saw no one near, so they took possession of it without asking permission of any one, and Rudy could row very well. The oars divided the pliant water like the fins of a fish—that water which, with all its yielding softness, is so strong to bear and to carry, so mild and smiling when at rest, and yet so terrible in its destroying power. A white streak of foam followed in the wake of the boat, which, in a few minutes, carried them both to the little island, where they went on shore; but there was only just room enough for two to dance. Rudy swung Babette round two or three times; and then, hand-in-hand, they sat down on a little bench under the drooping acacia-tree, and looked into each other's eyes, while everything around them glowed in the rays of the setting sun.

The fir-tree forests on the mountains were covered with a purple hue like the heather bloom; and where the woods terminated, and the rocks became prominent, they looked almost transparent in the rich crimson glow of the evening sky. The surface of the lake was like a bed of pink rose-leaves.

As the evening advanced, the shadows fell upon the snow-capped mountains of Savoy painting them in colors of deep blue, while their topmost peaks glowed like red lava; and for a moment this light was reflected on the cultivated parts of the mountains, making them appear as if newly risen from the lap of earth, and giving to the snow-crested peak of the Dent du Midi the appearance of the full moon as it rises above the horizon.

Rudy and Babette felt that they had never seen the Alpine glow in such perfection before. "How very beautiful it is, and what happiness to be here!" exclaimed Babette.

"Earth has nothing more to bestow upon me," said Rudy; "an evening like this is worth a whole life. Often have I realized my good fortune, but never more than in this moment. I feel that if my existence were to end now, I should still have lived a happy life. What a glorious world this is; one day ends, and another begins even more beautiful than the last. How infinitely good God is, Babette!"

"I have such complete happiness in my heart," said she.

"Earth has no more to bestow," answered Rudy. And then came the sound of the evening bells, borne upon the breeze over the mountains of Switzerland and Savoy, while still, in the golden splendor of the west, stood the dark blue mountains of Jura.

"God grant you all that is brightest and best!" exclaimed Babette.

"He will," said Rudy. "He will to-morrow. To-morrow you will be wholly mine, my own sweet wife."

"The boat!" cried Babette, suddenly. The boat in which they were to return had broken loose, and was floating away from the island.

"I will fetch it back," said Rudy; throwing off his coat and boots, he sprang into the lake, and swam with strong efforts towards it.

The dark-blue water, from the glaciers of the mountains, was icy cold and very deep. Rudy gave but one glance into the water beneath; but in that one glance he saw a gold ring rolling, glittering, and sparkling before him. His engaged ring came into his mind; but this was larger, and spread into a glittering circle, in which appeared a clear glacier. Deep chasms yawned around it, the water-drops glittered as if lighted with blue flame, and tinkled like the chiming of church bells. In one moment he saw what would require many words to describe. Young hunters, and young maidens—men and women who had sunk in the deep chasms of the glaciers—stood before him here in lifelike forms, with eyes open and smiles on their lips; and far beneath them could be heard the chiming of the church bells of buried villages, where the villagers knelt beneath the vaulted arches of churches in which ice-blocks formed the organ pipes, and the mountain stream the music.

On the clear, transparent ground sat the Ice Maiden. She raised herself towards Rudy, and kissed his feet; and instantly a cold, deathly chill, like an electric shock, passed through his limbs. Ice or fire! It was impossible to tell, the shock was so instantaneous.

"Mine! mine!" sounded around him, and within him; "I kissed thee when thou wert a little child. I once kissed thee on the mouth, and now I have kissed thee from heel to toe; thou art wholly mine." And then he disappeared in the clear, blue water.

All was still. The church bells were silent; the last tone floated away with the last red glimmer on the evening clouds. "Thou art mine," sounded from the depths below: but from the heights above, from the eternal world, also sounded the words, "Thou art mine!" Happy was he thus to pass from life to life, from earth to heaven. A chord was loosened, and tones of sorrow burst forth. The icy kiss of death had overcome the perishable body; it was but the prelude before life's real drama could begin, the discord which was quickly lost in harmony. Do you think this a sad story? Poor Babette! for her it was unspeakable anguish.

The boat drifted farther and farther away. No one on the opposite shore knew that the betrothed pair had gone over to the little island. The clouds sunk as the evening drew on, and it became dark. Alone, in despair, she waited and trembled. The weather became fearful; flash after flash lighted up the mountains of Jura, Savoy, and Switzerland, while peals of thunder, that lasted for many minutes, rolled over her head. The lightning was so vivid that every single vine stem could be seen for a moment as distinctly as in the sunlight at noon-day; and then all was veiled in darkness. It flashed across the lake in winding, zigzag lines, lighting it up on all sides; while the echoes of the thunder grew louder and stronger. On land, the boats were all carefully drawn up on the beach, every living thing sought shelter, and at length the rain poured down in torrents.

"Where can Rudy and Babette be in this awful weather?" said the miller.

Poor Babette sat with her hands clasped, and her head bowed down, dumb with grief; she had ceased to weep and cry for help.

"In the deep water!" she said to herself; "far down he lies, as if beneath a glacier."

Deep in her heart rested the memory of what Rudy had told her of the death of his mother, and of his own recovery, even after he had been taken up as dead from the cleft in the glacier.

"Ah," she thought, "the Ice Maiden has him at last."

Suddenly there came a flash of lightning, as dazzling as the rays of the sun on the white snow. The lake rose for a moment like a shining glacier; and before Babette stood the pallid, glittering, majestic form of the Ice Maiden, and at her feet lay Rudy's corpse.

"Mine!" she cried, and again all was darkness around the heaving water.

"How cruel," murmured Babette; "why should he die just as the day of happiness drew near? Merciful God, enlighten my understanding, shed light upon my heart; for I cannot comprehend the arrangements of Thy providence, even while I bow to the decree of Thy almighty wisdom and power." And God did enlighten her heart.

A sudden flash of thought, like a ray of mercy, recalled her dream of the preceding night; all was vividly represented before her. She remembered the words and wishes she had then expressed, that what was best for her and for Rudy she might piously submit to.

"Woe is me," she said; "was the germ of sin really in my heart? was my dream a glimpse into the course of my future life, whose thread must be violently broken to rescue me from sin? Oh, miserable creature that I am!"

Thus she sat lamenting in the dark night, while through the deep stillness the last words of Rudy seemed to ring in her ears. "This earth has nothing more to bestow." Words, uttered in the fulness of joy, were again heard amid the depths of sorrow.

Years have passed since this sad event happened. The shores of the peaceful lake still smile in beauty. The vines are full of luscious grapes. Steamboats, with waving flags, pass swiftly by. Pleasure-boats, with their swelling sails, skim lightly over the watery mirror, like white butterflies. The railway is opened beyond Chillon, and goes far into the deep valley of the Rhone. At every station strangers alight with red-bound guide-books in their hands, in which they read of every place worth seeing. They visit Chillon, and observe on the lake the little island with the three acacias, and then read in their guide-book the story of the bridal pair who, in the year 1856, rowed over to it. They read that the two were missing till the next morning, when some people on the shore heard the despairing cries of the bride, and went to her assistance, and by her were told of the bridegroom's fate.

But the guide-book does not speak of Babette's quiet life afterwards with her father, not at the mill—strangers dwell there now—but in a pretty house in a row near the station. On many an evening she sits at her window, and looks out over the chestnut-trees to the snow-capped mountains on which Rudy once roamed. She looks at the Alpine glow in the evening sky, which is caused by the children of the sun retiring to rest on the mountain-tops; and again they breathe their song of the traveller whom the whirlwind could deprive of his cloak but not of his life. There is a rosy tint on the mountain snow, and there are rosy gleams in each heart in which dwells the thought, "God permits nothing to happen, which is not the best for us." But this is not often revealed to all, as it was revealed to Babette in her wonderful dream.

Little Tiny or Thumbelina

There was once a woman who wished very much to have a little child, but she could not obtain her wish. At last she went to a fairy, and said, "I should so very much like to have a little child; can you tell me where I can find one?"

"Oh, that can be easily managed," said the fairy. "Here is a barleycorn of a different kind to those which grow in the farmer's fields, and which the chickens eat; put it into a flower-pot, and see what will happen."

"Thank you," said the woman, and she gave the fairy twelve shillings, which was the price of the barleycorn. Then she went home and planted it, and immediately there grew up a large handsome flower, something like a tulip in appearance, but with its leaves tightly closed as if it were still a bud. "It is a beautiful flower," said the woman, and she kissed the red and golden-colored leaves, and while she did so the flower opened, and she could see that it was a real tulip. Within the flower, upon the green velvet stamens, sat a very delicate and graceful little maiden. She was scarcely half as long as a thumb, and they gave her the name of "Thumbelina," or Tiny, because she was so small. A walnut-shell, elegantly polished, served her for a cradle; her bed was formed of blue violet-leaves, with a rose-leaf for a counterpane. Here she slept at night, but during the day she amused herself on a table, where the woman had placed a plateful of water. Round this plate were wreaths of flowers with their stems in the water, and upon it floated a large tulip-leaf, which served Tiny for a boat. Here the little maiden sat and rowed herself from side to side, with two oars made of white horse-hair. It really was a very pretty sight. Tiny could, also, sing so softly and sweetly that nothing like her singing had ever before been heard. One night, while she lay in her pretty bed, a large, ugly, wet toad crept through a broken pane of glass in the window, and leaped right upon the table where Tiny lay sleeping under her rose-leaf quilt.

"What a pretty little wife this would make for my son," said the toad, and she took up the walnut-shell in which little Tiny lay asleep, and jumped through the window with it into the garden.

In the swampy margin of a broad stream in the garden lived the toad, with her son. He was uglier even than his mother, and when he saw the pretty little maiden in her elegant bed, he could only cry, "Croak, croak, croak."

"Don't speak so loud, or she will wake," said the toad, "and then she might run away, for she is as light as swan's down. We will place her on one of the water-lily leaves out in the stream; it will be like an island to her, she is so light and small, and then she cannot escape; and, while she is away, we will make haste and prepare the state-room under the marsh, in which you are to live when you are married."

Far out in the stream grew a number of water-lilies, with broad green leaves, which seemed to float on the top of the water. The largest of these leaves appeared farther off than the rest, and the old toad swam out to it with the walnut-shell, in which little Tiny lay still asleep. The tiny little creature woke very early in the morning, and began to cry bitterly when she found where she was, for she could see nothing but water on every side of the large green leaf, and no way of reaching the land. Meanwhile the old toad was very busy under the marsh, decking her room with rushes and wild yellow flowers, to make it look pretty for her new daughter-in-law. Then she swam out with her ugly son to the leaf on which she had placed poor little Tiny. She wanted to fetch the pretty bed, that she might put it in the bridal chamber to be ready for her. The old toad bowed low to her in the water, and said, "Here is my son, he will be your husband, and you will live happily in the marsh by the stream."

"Croak, croak, croak," was all her son could say for himself; so the toad took up the elegant little bed, and swam away with it, leaving Tiny all alone on the green leaf, where she sat and wept. She could not bear to think of living with the old toad, and having her ugly son for a husband. The little fishes, who swam about in the water beneath, had seen the toad, and heard what she said, so they lifted their heads above the water to look at the little maiden. As soon as they caught sight of her, they saw she was very pretty, and it made them very sorry to think that she must go and live with the ugly toads. "No, it must never be!" so they assembled together in the water, round the green stalk which held the leaf on which the little maiden stood, and gnawed it away at the root with their teeth. Then the leaf floated down the stream, carrying Tiny far away out of reach of land.

Tiny sailed past many towns, and the little birds in the bushes saw her, and sang, "What a lovely little creature;" so the leaf swam away with her farther and farther, till it brought her to other lands. A graceful little white butterfly constantly fluttered round her, and at last alighted on the leaf. Tiny pleased him, and she was glad of it, for now the toad could not possibly reach her, and the country through which she sailed was beautiful, and the sun shone upon the water, till it glittered like liquid gold. She took off her girdle and tied one end of it round the butterfly, and the other end of the ribbon she fastened to the leaf, which now glided on much faster than ever, taking little Tiny with it as she stood. Presently a large cockchafer flew by; the moment he caught sight of her, he seized her round her delicate waist with his claws, and flew with her into a tree. The green leaf floated away on the brook, and the butterfly flew with it, for he was fastened to it, and could not get away.

Oh, how frightened little Tiny felt when the cockchafer flew with her to the tree! But especially was she sorry for the beautiful white butterfly which she had fastened to the leaf, for if he could not free himself he would die of hunger. But the cockchafer did not trouble himself at all about the matter. He seated himself by her side on a large green leaf, gave her some honey from the flowers to eat, and told her she was very pretty, though not in the least like a cockchafer. After a time, all the cockchafers turned up their feelers, and said, "She has only two legs! how ugly that looks." "She has no feelers," said another. "Her waist is quite slim. Pooh! she is like a human being."

"Oh! she is ugly," said all the lady cockchafers, although Tiny was very pretty. Then the cockchafer who had run away with her, believed all the others when they said she was ugly, and would have nothing more to say to her, and told her she might go where she liked. Then he flew down with her from the tree, and placed her on a daisy, and she wept at the thought that she was so ugly that even the cockchafers would have nothing to say to her. And all the while she was really the loveliest creature that one could imagine, and as tender and delicate as a beautiful rose-leaf. During the whole summer poor little Tiny lived quite alone in the wide forest. She wove herself a bed with blades of grass, and hung it up under a broad leaf, to protect herself from the rain. She sucked the honey from the flowers for food, and drank the dew from their leaves every morning. So passed away the summer and the autumn, and then came the winter,—the long, cold winter. All the birds who had sung to her so sweetly were flown away, and the trees and the flowers had withered. The large clover leaf under the shelter of which she had lived, was now rolled together and shrivelled up, nothing remained but a yellow withered stalk. She felt dreadfully cold, for her clothes were torn, and she was herself so frail and delicate, that poor little Tiny was nearly frozen to death. It began to snow too; and the snow-flakes, as they fell upon her, were like a whole shovelful falling upon one of us, for we are tall, but she was only an inch high. Then she wrapped herself up in a dry leaf, but it cracked in the middle and could not keep her warm, and she shivered with cold. Near the wood in which she had been living lay a corn-field, but the corn had been cut a long time; nothing remained but the bare dry stubble standing up out of the frozen ground. It was to her like struggling through a large wood. Oh! how she shivered with the cold. She came at last to the door of a field-mouse, who had a little den under the corn-stubble. There dwelt the field-mouse in warmth and comfort, with a whole roomful of corn, a kitchen, and a beautiful dining room. Poor little Tiny stood before the door just like a little beggar-girl, and begged for a small piece of barley-corn, for she had been without a morsel to eat for two days.

"You poor little creature," said the field-mouse, who was really a good old field-mouse, "come into my warm room and dine with me." She was very pleased with Tiny, so she said, "You are quite welcome to stay with me all the winter, if you like; but you must keep my rooms clean and neat, and tell me stories, for I shall like to hear them very much." And Tiny did all the field-mouse asked her, and found herself very comfortable.

"We shall have a visitor soon," said the field-mouse one day; "my neighbor pays me a visit once a week. He is better off than I am; he has large rooms, and wears a beautiful black velvet coat. If you could only have him for a husband, you would be well provided for indeed. But he is blind, so you must tell him some of your prettiest stories."

But Tiny did not feel at all interested about this neighbor, for he was a mole. However, he came and paid his visit dressed in his black velvet coat.

"He is very rich and learned, and his house is twenty times larger than mine," said the field-mouse.

He was rich and learned, no doubt, but he always spoke slightingly of the sun and the pretty flowers, because he had never seen them. Tiny was obliged to sing to him, "Lady-bird, lady-bird, fly away home," and many other pretty songs. And the mole fell in love with her because she had such a sweet voice; but he said nothing yet, for he was very cautious. A short time before, the mole had dug a long passage under the earth, which led from the dwelling of the field-mouse to his own, and here she had permission to walk with Tiny whenever she liked. But he warned them not to be alarmed at the sight of a dead bird which lay in the passage. It was a perfect bird, with a beak and feathers, and could not have been dead long, and was lying just where the mole had made his passage. The mole took a piece of phosphorescent wood in his mouth, and it glittered like fire in the dark; then he went before them to light them through the long, dark passage. When they came to the spot where lay the dead bird, the mole pushed his broad nose through the ceiling, the earth gave way, so that there was a large hole, and the daylight shone into the passage. In the middle of the floor lay a dead swallow, his beautiful wings pulled close to his sides, his feet and his head drawn up under his feathers; the poor bird had evidently died of the cold. It made little Tiny very sad to see it, she did so love the little birds; all the summer they had sung and twittered for her so beautifully. But the mole pushed it aside with his crooked legs, and said, "He will sing no more now. How miserable it must be to be born a little bird! I am thankful that none of my children will ever be birds, for they can do nothing but cry, 'Tweet, tweet,' and always die of hunger in the winter."

"Yes, you may well say that, as a clever man!" exclaimed the field-mouse, "What is the use of his twittering, for when winter comes he must either starve or be frozen to death. Still birds are very high bred."

Tiny said nothing; but when the two others had turned their backs on the bird, she stooped down and stroked aside the soft feathers which covered the head, and kissed the closed eyelids. "Perhaps this was the one who sang to me so sweetly in the summer," she said; "and how much pleasure it gave me, you dear, pretty bird."

The mole now stopped up the hole through which the daylight shone, and then accompanied the lady home. But during the night Tiny could not sleep; so she got out of bed and wove a large, beautiful carpet of hay; then she carried it to the dead bird, and spread it over him; with some down from the flowers which she had found in the field-mouse's room. It was as soft as wool, and she spread some of it on each side of the bird, so that he might lie warmly in the cold earth. "Farewell, you pretty little bird," said she, "farewell; thank you for your delightful singing during the summer, when all the trees were green, and the warm sun shone upon us." Then she laid her head on the bird's breast, but she was alarmed immediately, for it seemed as if something inside the bird went "thump, thump." It was the bird's heart; he was not really dead, only benumbed with the cold, and the warmth had restored him to life. In autumn, all the swallows fly away into warm countries, but if one happens to linger, the cold seizes it, it becomes frozen, and falls down as if dead; it remains where it fell, and the cold snow covers it. Tiny trembled very much; she was quite frightened, for the bird was large, a great deal larger than herself,—she was only an inch high. But she took courage, laid the wool more thickly over the poor swallow, and then took a leaf which she had used for her own counterpane, and laid it over the head of the poor bird. The next morning she again stole out to see him. He was alive but very weak; he could only open his eyes for a moment to look at Tiny, who stood by holding a piece of decayed wood in her hand, for she had no other lantern. "Thank you, pretty little maiden," said the sick swallow; "I have been so nicely warmed, that I shall soon regain my strength, and be able to fly about again in the warm sunshine."

"Oh," said she, "it is cold out of doors now; it snows and freezes. Stay in your warm bed; I will take care of you."

Then she brought the swallow some water in a flower-leaf, and after he had drank, he told her that he had wounded one of his wings in a thorn-bush, and could not fly as fast as the others, who were soon far away on their journey to warm countries. Then at last he had fallen to the earth, and could remember no more, nor how he came to be where she had found him. The whole winter the swallow remained underground, and Tiny nursed him with care and love. Neither the mole nor the field-mouse knew anything about it, for they did not like swallows. Very soon the spring time came, and the sun warmed the earth. Then the swallow bade farewell to Tiny, and she opened the hole in the ceiling which the mole had made. The sun shone in upon them so beautifully, that the swallow asked her if she would go with him; she could sit on his back, he said, and he would fly away with her into the green woods. But Tiny knew it would make the field-mouse very grieved if she left her in that manner, so she said, "No, I cannot."

"Farewell, then, farewell, you good, pretty little maiden," said the swallow; and he flew out into the sunshine.

Tiny looked after him, and the tears rose in her eyes. She was very fond of the poor swallow.

"Tweet, tweet," sang the bird, as he flew out into the green woods, and Tiny felt very sad. She was not allowed to go out into the warm sunshine. The corn which had been sown in the field over the house of the field-mouse had grown up high into the air, and formed a thick wood to Tiny, who was only an inch in height.

"You are going to be married, Tiny," said the field-mouse. "My neighbor has asked for you. What good fortune for a poor child like you. Now we will prepare your wedding clothes. They must be both woollen and linen. Nothing must be wanting when you are the mole's wife."

Tiny had to turn the spindle, and the field-mouse hired four spiders, who were to weave day and night. Every evening the mole visited her, and was continually speaking of the time when the summer would be over. Then he would keep his wedding-day with Tiny; but now the heat of the sun was so great that it burned the earth, and made it quite hard, like a stone. As soon, as the summer was over, the wedding should take place. But Tiny was not at all pleased; for she did not like the tiresome mole. Every morning when the sun rose, and every evening when it went down, she would creep out at the door, and as the wind blew aside the ears of corn, so that she could see the blue sky, she thought how beautiful and bright it seemed out there, and wished so much to see her dear swallow again. But he never returned; for by this time he had flown far away into the lovely green forest.

When autumn arrived, Tiny had her outfit quite ready; and the field-mouse said to her, "In four weeks the wedding must take place."

Then Tiny wept, and said she would not marry the disagreeable mole.

"Nonsense," replied the field-mouse. "Now don't be obstinate, or I shall bite you with my white teeth. He is a very handsome mole; the queen herself does not wear more beautiful velvets and furs. His kitchen and cellars are quite full. You ought to be very thankful for such good fortune."

So the wedding-day was fixed, on which the mole was to fetch Tiny away to live with him, deep under the earth, and never again to see the warm sun, because he did not like it. The poor child was very unhappy at the thought of saying farewell to the beautiful sun, and as the field-mouse had given her permission to stand at the door, she went to look at it once more.

"Farewell bright sun," she cried, stretching out her arm towards it; and then she walked a short distance from the house; for the corn had been cut, and only the dry stubble remained in the fields. "Farewell, farewell," she repeated, twining her arm round a little red flower that grew just by her side. "Greet the little swallow from me, if you should see him again."

"Tweet, tweet," sounded over her head suddenly. She looked up, and there was the swallow himself flying close by. As soon as he spied Tiny, he was delighted; and then she told him how un-willing she felt to marry the ugly mole, and to live always beneath the earth, and never to see the bright sun any more. And as she told him she wept.

"Cold winter is coming," said the swallow, "and I am going to fly away into warmer countries. Will you go with me? You can sit on my back, and fasten yourself on with your sash. Then we can fly away from the ugly mole and his gloomy rooms,—far away, over the mountains, into warmer countries, where the sun shines more brightly—than here; where it is always summer, and the flowers bloom in greater beauty. Fly now with me, dear little Tiny; you saved my life when I lay frozen in that dark passage."

"Yes, I will go with you," said Tiny; and she seated herself on the bird's back, with her feet on his outstretched wings, and tied her girdle to one of his strongest feathers.

Then the swallow rose in the air, and flew over forest and over sea, high above the highest mountains, covered with eternal snow. Tiny would have been frozen in the cold air, but she crept under the bird's warm feathers, keeping her little head uncovered, so that she might admire the beautiful lands over which they passed. At length they reached the warm countries, where the sun shines brightly, and the sky seems so much higher above the earth. Here, on the hedges, and by the wayside, grew purple, green, and white grapes; lemons and oranges hung from trees in the woods; and the air was fragrant with myrtles and orange blossoms. Beautiful children ran along the country lanes, playing with large gay but-terflies; and as the swallow flew farther and farther, every place appeared still more lovely.

At last they came to a blue lake, and by the side of it, shaded by trees of the deepest green, stood a palace of dazzling white marble, built in the olden times. Vines clustered round its lofty pillars, and at the top were many swallows' nests, and one of these was the home of the swallow who carried Tiny.

"This is my house," said the swallow; "but it would not do for you to live there—you would not be comfortable. You must choose for yourself one of those lovely flowers, and I will put you down upon it, and then you shall have everything that you can wish to make you happy."

"That will be delightful," she said, and clapped her little hands for joy.

A large marble pillar lay on the ground, which, in falling, had been broken into three pieces. Between these pieces grew the most beautiful large white flowers; so the swallow flew down with Tiny, and placed her on one of the broad leaves. But how surprised she was to see in the middle of the flower, a tiny little man, as white and transparent as if he had been made of crystal! He had a gold crown on his head, and delicate wings at his shoulders, and was not much larger than Tiny herself. He was the angel of the flower; for a tiny man and a tiny woman dwell in every flower; and this was the king of them all.

"Oh, how beautiful he is!" whispered Tiny to the swallow.

The little prince was at first quite frightened at the bird, who was like a giant, compared to such a delicate little creature as himself; but when he saw Tiny, he was delighted, and thought her the prettiest little maiden he had ever seen. He took the gold crown from his head, and placed it on hers, and asked her name, and if she would be his wife, and queen over all the flowers.

This certainly was a very different sort of husband to the son of a toad, or the mole, with my black velvet and fur; so she said, "Yes," to the handsome prince. Then all the flowers opened, and out of each came a little lady or a tiny lord, all so pretty it was quite a pleasure to look at them. Each of them brought Tiny a present; but the best gift was a pair of beautiful wings, which had belonged to a large white fly and they fastened them to Tiny's shoulders, so that she might fly from flower to flower. Then there was much rejoicing, and the little swallow who sat above them, in his nest, was asked to sing a wedding song, which he did as well as he could; but in his heart he felt sad for he was very fond of Tiny, and would have liked never to part from her again.

"You must not be called Tiny any more," said the spirit of the flowers to her. "It is an ugly name, and you are so very pretty. We will call you Maia."

"Farewell, farewell," said the swallow, with a heavy heart as he left the warm countries to fly back into Denmark. There he had a nest over the window of a house in which dwelt the writer of fairy tales. The swallow sang, "Tweet, tweet," and from his song came the whole story.

The Fir Tree

Out in the woods stood a nice little Fir Tree. The place he had was a very good one: the sun shone on him: as to fresh air, there was enough of that, and round him grew many large-sized comrades, pines as well as firs. But the little Fir wanted so very much to be a grown-up tree.

He did not think of the warm sun and of the fresh air; he did not care for the little cottage children that ran about and prattled when they were in the woods looking for wild-strawberries. The children often came with a whole pitcher full of berries, or a long row of them threaded on a straw, and sat down near the young tree and said, "Oh, how pretty he is! What a nice little fir!" But this was what the Tree could not bear to hear.

At the end of a year he had shot up a good deal, and after another year he was another long bit taller; for with fir trees one can always tell by the shoots how many years old they are.

"Oh! Were I but such a high tree as the others are," sighed he. "Then I should be able to spread out my branches, and with the tops to look into the wide world! Then would the birds build nests among my branches: and when there was a breeze, I could bend with as much stateliness as the others!"

Neither the sunbeams, nor the birds, nor the red clouds which morning and evening sailed above him, gave the little Tree any pleasure.

In winter, when the snow lay glittering on the ground, a hare would often come leaping along, and jump right over the little Tree. Oh, that made him so angry! But two winters were past, and in the third the Tree was so large that the hare was obliged to go round it. "To grow and grow, to get older and be tall," thought the Tree—"that, after all, is the most delightful thing in the world!"

In autumn the wood-cutters always came and felled some of

the largest trees. This happened every year; and the young Fir Tree, that had now grown to a very comely size, trembled at the sight; for the magnificent great trees fell to the earth with noise and cracking, the branches were lopped off, and the trees looked long and bare; they were hardly to be recognised; and then they were laid in carts, and the horses dragged them out of the wood.

Where did they go to? What became of them?

In spring, when the swallows and the storks came, the Tree asked them, "Don't you know where they have been taken? Have you not met them anywhere?"

The swallows did not know anything about it; but the Stork looked musing, nodded his head, and said, "Yes; I think I know; I met many ships as I was flying hither from Egypt; on the ships were magnificent masts, and I venture to assert that it was they that smelt so of fir. I may congratulate you, for they lifted themselves on high most majestically!"

"Oh, were I but old enough to fly across the sea! But how does the sea look in reality? What is it like?"

"That would take a long time to explain," said the Stork, and with these words off he went.

"Rejoice in thy growth!" said the Sunbeams. "Rejoice in thy vigorous growth, and in the fresh life that moveth within thee!"

And the Wind kissed the Tree, and the Dew wept tears over him; but the Fir understood it not.

When Christmas came, quite young trees were cut down: trees which often were not even as large or of the same age as this Fir Tree, who could never rest, but always wanted to be off. These young trees, and they were always the finest looking, retained their branches; they were laid on carts, and the horses drew them out of the wood.

"Where are they going to?" asked the Fir. "They are not taller than I; there was one indeed that was considerably shorter; and why do they retain all their branches? Whither are they taken?"

"We know! We know!" chirped the Sparrows. "We have peeped

in at the windows in the town below! We know whither they are taken! The greatest splendor and the greatest magnificence one can imagine await them. We peeped through the windows, and saw them planted in the middle of the warm room and ornamented with the most splendid things, with gilded apples, with gingerbread, with toys, and many hundred lights!"

"And then?" asked the Fir Tree, trembling in every bough. "And then? What happens then?"

"We did not see anything more: it was incomparably beautiful."

"I would fain know if I am destined for so glorious a career," cried the Tree, rejoicing. "That is still better than to cross the sea! What a longing do I suffer! Were Christmas but come! I am now tall, and my branches spread like the others that were carried off last year! Oh! were I but already on the cart! Were I in the warm room with all the splendor and magnificence! Yes; then something better, something still grander, will surely follow, or wherefore should they thus ornament me? Something better, something still grander must follow—but what? Oh, how I long, how I suffer! I do not know myself what is the matter with me!"

"Rejoice in our presence!" said the Air and the Sunlight. "Rejoice in thy own fresh youth!"

But the Tree did not rejoice at all; he grew and grew, and was green both winter and summer. People that saw him said, "What a fine tree!" and towards Christmas he was one of the first that was cut down. The axe struck deep into the very pith; the Tree fell to the earth with a sigh; he felt a pang—it was like a swoon; he could not think of happiness, for he was sorrowful at being separated from his home, from the place where he had sprung up. He well knew that he should never see his dear old comrades, the little bushes and flowers around him, anymore; perhaps not even the birds! The departure was not at all agreeable.

The Tree only came to himself when he was unloaded in a court-yard with the other trees, and heard a man say, "That one is splendid! We don't want the others." Then two servants came in rich livery and carried the Fir Tree into a large and splendid drawing-room. Portraits were hanging on the walls, and near the white porcelain stove stood two large Chinese vases with lions on the covers. There, too, were large easy-chairs, silken sofas, large tables full of picture-books and full of toys, worth hundreds and hundreds of crowns—at least the children said so. And the Fir Tree was stuck upright in a cask that was filled with sand; but no one could see that it was a cask, for green cloth was hung all round it, and it stood on a large gaily-colored carpet. Oh! how the Tree quivered! What was to happen? The servants, as well as the young ladies, decorated it. On one branch there hung little nets cut out of colored paper, and each net was filled with sugarplums; and among the other boughs gilded apples and walnuts were suspended, looking as though they had grown there, and little blue and white tapers were placed among the leaves. Dolls that looked for all the world like men—the Tree had never beheld such before—were seen among the foliage, and at the very top a large star of gold tinsel was fixed. It was really splendid—beyond description splendid.

"This evening!" they all said. "How it will shine this evening!"

"Oh!" thought the Tree. "If the evening were but come! If the tapers were but lighted! And then I wonder what will happen! Perhaps the other trees from the forest will come to look at me! Perhaps the sparrows will beat against the windowpanes! I wonder if I shall take root here, and winter and summer stand covered with ornaments!"

He knew very much about the matter—but he was so impatient that for sheer longing he got a pain in his back, and this with trees is the same thing as a headache with us.

The candles were now lighted—what brightness! What splendor! The Tree trembled so in every bough that one of the tapers set fire to the foliage. It blazed up famously.

"Help! Help!" cried the young ladies, and they quickly put out the fire.

Now the Tree did not even dare tremble. What a state he was in! He was so uneasy lest he should lose something of his splendor, that he was quite bewildered amidst the glare and brightness; when suddenly both folding-doors opened and a troop of children rushed in as if they would upset the Tree. The older persons followed quietly; the little ones stood quite still. But it was only for a moment; then they shouted that the whole place re-echoed with their rejoicing; they danced round the Tree, and one present after the other was pulled off.

"What are they about?" thought the Tree. "What is to happen now!" And the lights burned down to the very branches, and as they burned down they were put out one after the other, and then the children had permission to plunder the Tree. So they fell upon it with such violence that all its branches cracked; if it had not been fixed firmly in the ground, it would certainly have tumbled down.

The children danced about with their beautiful playthings; no one looked at the Tree except the old nurse, who peeped between the branches; but it was only to see if there was a fig or an apple left that had been forgotten.

"A story! A story!" cried the children, drawing a little fat man towards the Tree. He seated himself under it and said, "Now we are in the shade, and the Tree can listen too. But I shall tell only one story. Now which will you have; that about Ivedy-Avedy, or about Humpy-Dumpy, who tumbled downstairs, and yet after all came to the throne and married the princess?"

"Ivedy-Avedy," cried some; "Humpy-Dumpy," cried the others. There was such a bawling and screaming—the Fir Tree alone was silent, and he thought to himself, "Am I not to bawl with the rest? Am I to do nothing whatever?" for he was one of the company, and had done what he had to do.

And the man told about Humpy-Dumpy that tumbled down, who notwithstanding came to the throne, and at last married the princess. And the children clapped their hands, and cried. "Oh, go on! Do go on!" They wanted to hear about Ivedy-Avedy too, but the little man only told them about Humpy-Dumpy. The Fir Tree stood quite still and absorbed in thought; the birds in the wood had never related the like of this. "Humpy-Dumpy fell downstairs, and yet he married the princess! Yes, yes! That's the way of the world!" thought the Fir Tree, and believed it all, because the man who told the story was so good-looking. "Well, well! who knows, perhaps I may fall downstairs, too, and get a princess as wife!" And he looked forward with joy to the morrow, when he hoped to be decked out again with lights, playthings, fruits, and tinsel.

"I won't tremble to-morrow!" thought the Fir Tree. "I will enjoy to the full all my splendor! To-morrow I shall hear again the story of Humpy-Dumpy, and perhaps that of Ivedy-Avedy too." And the whole night the Tree stood still and in deep thought.

In the morning the servant and the housemaid came in.

"Now then the splendor will begin again," thought the Fir. But they dragged him out of the room, and up the stairs into the loft: and here, in a dark corner, where no daylight could enter, they left him. "What's the meaning of this?" thought the Tree. "What am I to do here? What shall I hear now, I wonder?" And he leaned against the wall lost in reverie. Time enough had he too for his reflections; for days and nights passed on, and nobody came up; and when at last somebody did come, it was only to put some great trunks in a corner, out of the way. There stood the Tree quite hidden; it seemed as if he had been entirely forgotten.

"'Tis now winter out-of-doors!" thought the Tree. "The earth is hard and covered with snow; men cannot plant me now, and therefore I have been put up here under shelter till the spring-time comes! How thoughtful that is! How kind man is, after all!

If it only were not so dark here, and so terribly lonely! Not even a hare! And out in the woods it was so pleasant, when the snow was on the ground, and the hare leaped by; yes—even when he jumped over me; but I did not like it then! It is really terribly lonely here!"

"Squeak! Squeak!" said a little Mouse, at the same moment, peeping out of his hole. And then another little one came. They snuffed about the Fir Tree, and rustled among the branches.

"It is dreadfully cold," said the Mouse. "But for that, it would be delightful here, old Fir, wouldn't it?"

"I am by no means old," said the Fir Tree. "There's many a one considerably older than I am."

"Where do you come from," asked the Mice; "and what can you do?" They were so extremely curious. "Tell us about the most beautiful spot on the earth. Have you never been there? Were you never in the larder, where cheeses lie on the shelves, and hams hang from above; where one dances about on tallow candles: that place where one enters lean, and comes out again fat and portly?"

"I know no such place," said the Tree. "But I know the wood, where the sun shines and where the little birds sing." And then he told all about his youth; and the little Mice had never heard the like before; and they listened and said,

"Well, to be sure! How much you have seen! How happy you must have been!"

"I!" said the Fir Tree, thinking over what he had himself related. "Yes, in reality those were happy times." And then he told about Christmas-eve, when he was decked out with cakes and candles.

"Oh," said the little Mice, "how fortunate you have been, old Fir Tree!"

"I am by no means old," said he. "I came from the wood this winter; I am in my prime, and am only rather short for my age."

"What delightful stories you know," said the Mice: and the

next night they came with four other little Mice, who were to
hear what the Tree recounted: and the more he related, the more
he remembered himself; and it appeared as if those times had really been happy times. "But they may still come—they may still
come! Humpy-Dumpy fell downstairs, and yet he got a princess!"
and he thought at the moment of a nice little Birch Tree growing out in the woods: to the Fir, that would be a real charming
princess.

"Who is Humpy-Dumpy?" asked the Mice. So then the Fir Tree
told the whole fairy tale, for he could remember every single word
of it; and the little Mice jumped for joy up to the very top of the
Tree. Next night two more Mice came, and on Sunday two Rats
even; but they said the stories were not interesting, which vexed
the little Mice; and they, too, now began to think them not so
very amusing either.

"Do you know only one story?" asked the Rats.

"Only that one," answered the Tree. "I heard it on my happiest
evening; but I did not then know how happy I was."

"It is a very stupid story! Don't you know one about bacon and
tallow candles? Can't you tell any larder stories?"

"No," said the Tree.

"Then good-bye," said the Rats; and they went home.

At last the little Mice stayed away also; and the Tree sighed:
"After all, it was very pleasant when the sleek little Mice sat
round me, and listened to what I told them. Now that too is over.
But I will take good care to enjoy myself when I am brought out
again."

But when was that to be? Why, one morning there came a
quantity of people and set to work in the loft. The trunks were
moved, the tree was pulled out and thrown—rather hard, it is
true—down on the floor, but a man drew him towards the stairs,
where the daylight shone.

"Now a merry life will begin again," thought the Tree. He felt
the fresh air, the first sunbeam—and now he was out in the court-

yard. All passed so quickly, there was so much going on around him, the Tree quite forgot to look to himself. The court adjoined a garden, and all was in flower; the roses hung so fresh and odorous over the balustrade, the lindens were in blossom, the Swallows flew by, and said, "Quirre-vit! My husband is come!" but it was not the Fir Tree that they meant.

"Now, then, I shall really enjoy life," said he exultingly, and spread out his branches; but, alas, they were all withered and yellow! It was in a corner that he lay, among weeds and nettles. The golden star of tinsel was still on the top of the Tree, and glittered in the sunshine.

In the court-yard some of the merry children were playing who had danced at Christmas round the Fir Tree, and were so glad at the sight of him. One of the youngest ran and tore off the golden star.

"Only look what is still on the ugly old Christmas tree!" said he, trampling on the branches, so that they all cracked beneath his feet.

And the Tree beheld all the beauty of the flowers, and the freshness in the garden; he beheld himself, and wished he had remained in his dark corner in the loft; he thought of his first youth in the wood, of the merry Christmas-eve, and of the little Mice who had listened with so much pleasure to the story of Humpy-Dumpy.

"'Tis over—'tis past!" said the poor Tree. "Had I but rejoiced when I had reason to do so! But now 'tis past, 'tis past!"

And the gardener's boy chopped the Tree into small pieces; there was a whole heap lying there. The wood flamed up splendidly under the large brewing copper, and it sighed so deeply! Each sigh was like a shot.

The boys played about in the court, and the youngest wore the gold star on his breast which the Tree had had on the happiest evening of his life. However, that was over now—the Tree gone, the story at an end. All, all was over—every tale must end at last.

The Little Match Girl

Most terribly cold it was; it snowed, and was nearly quite dark, and evening—the last evening of the year. In this cold and darkness there went along the street a poor little girl, bareheaded, and with naked feet. When she left home she had slippers on, it is true; but what was the good of that? They were very large slippers, which her mother had hitherto worn; so large were they; and the poor little thing lost them as she scuffled away across the street, because of two carriages that rolled by dreadfully fast.

One slipper was nowhere to be found; the other had been laid hold of by an urchin, and off he ran with it; he thought it would do capitally for a cradle when he some day or other should have children himself. So the little maiden walked on with her tiny naked feet, that were quite red and blue from cold. She carried a quantity of matches in an old apron, and she held a bundle of them in her hand. Nobody had bought anything of her the whole livelong day; no one had given her a single farthing.

She crept along trembling with cold and hunger—a very picture of sorrow, the poor little thing!

The flakes of snow covered her long fair hair, which fell in beautiful curls around her neck; but of that, of course, she never once now thought. From all the windows the candles were gleaming, and it smelt so deliciously of roast goose, for you know it was New Year's Eve; yes, of that she thought.

In a corner formed by two houses, of which one advanced more than the other, she seated herself down and cowered together. Her little feet she had drawn close up to her, but she grew colder and colder, and to go home she did not venture, for she had not sold any matches and could not bring a farthing of money: from her father she would certainly get blows, and at home it was cold too, for above her she had only the roof, through which the wind whistled, even though the largest cracks were stopped up with straw and rags.

Her little hands were almost numbed with cold. Oh! a match might afford her a world of comfort, if she only dared take a single one out of the bundle, draw it against the wall, and warm her fingers by it. She drew one out. "Rischt!" how it blazed, how it burnt! It was a warm, bright flame, like a candle, as she held her hands over it: it was a wonderful light. It seemed really to the little maiden as though she were sitting before a large iron stove, with burnished brass feet and a brass ornament at top. The fire burned with such blessed influence; it warmed so delightfully. The little girl had already stretched out her feet to warm them too; but—the small flame went out, the stove vanished: she had only the remains of the burnt-out match in her hand.

She rubbed another against the wall: it burned brightly, and where the light fell on the wall, there the wall became transparent like a veil, so that she could see into the room. On the table was spread a snow-white tablecloth; upon it was a splendid porcelain service, and the roast goose was steaming famously with its stuffing of apple and dried plums. And what was still more capital to behold was, the goose hopped down from the dish, reeled about on the floor with knife and fork in its breast, till it came up to the poor little girl; when—the match went out and nothing but the thick, cold, damp wall was left behind. She lighted another match. Now there she was sitting under the most magnificent Christmas tree: it was still larger, and more decorated than the one which she had seen through the glass door in the rich merchant's house.

Thousands of lights were burning on the green branches, and gaily-colored pictures, such as she had seen in the shop-windows, looked down upon her. The little maiden stretched out her hands towards them when—the match went out. The lights of the Christmas tree rose higher and higher, she saw them now as stars in heaven; one fell down and formed a long trail of fire.

"Someone is just dead!" said the little girl; for her old grand-mother, the only person who had loved her, and who was now no more, had told her, that when a star falls, a soul ascends to God.

She drew another match against the wall: it was again light, and in the lustre there stood the old grandmother, so bright and radiant, so mild, and with such an expression of love.

"Grandmother!" cried the little one. "Oh, take me with you! You go away when the match burns out; you vanish like the warm stove, like the delicious roast goose, and like the magnificent Christmas tree!" And she rubbed the whole bundle of matches quickly against the wall, for she wanted to be quite sure of keep-ing her grandmother near her. And the matches gave such a bril-liant light that it was brighter than at noon-day: never formerly had the grandmother been so beautiful and so tall. She took the little maiden, on her arm, and both flew in brightness and in joy so high, so very high, and then above was neither cold, nor hun-ger, nor anxiety—they were with God.

But in the corner, at the cold hour of dawn, sat the poor girl, with rosy cheeks and with a smiling mouth, leaning against the wall—frozen to death on the last evening of the old year. Stiff and stark sat the child there with her matches, of which one bundle had been burnt. "She wanted to warm herself," people said. No one had the slightest suspicion of what beautiful things she had seen; no one even dreamed of the splendor in which, with her grandmother she had entered on the joys of a new year.

The Shadow

It is in the hot lands that the sun burns, sure enough! there the people become quite a mahogany brown, ay, and in the HOT-TEST lands they are burnt darkest. But now it was only to the HOT lands that a learned man had come from the cold; there he thought that he could run about just as when at home, but he soon found out his mistake.

He, and all sensible folks, were obliged to stay within doors— the window-shutters and doors were closed the whole day; it looked as if the whole house slept, or there was no one at home.

The narrow street with the high houses, was built so that the sunshine must fall there from morning till evening—it was really not to be borne.

The learned man from the cold lands—he was a young man, and seemed to be a clever man—sat in a glowing oven; it took effect on him, he became quite meagre—even his shadow shrunk in, for the sun had also an effect on it. It was first towards evening when the sun was down, that they began to freshen up again.

In the warm lands every window has a balcony, and the people came out on all the balconies in the street—for one must have air, even if one be accustomed to the warm weather. It was lively both up and down the street. Tailors, and shoemakers, and all the folks, moved out into the street—chairs and tables were brought forth—and candles burnt—yes, above a thousand lights were burning—and the one talked and the other sung; and people walked and church-bells rang, and asses went along with a dingle-dingle-dong! for they too had bells on. The street boys were screaming and hooting, and shouting and shooting, with devils and detonating balls—and there came corpse bearers and hood wearers—for there were funerals with psalm and hymn— and then the din of carriages driving and company arriving: yes, it was, in truth, lively enough down in the street. Only in that single house, which stood opposite that in which the learned foreigner lived, it was quite still; and yet some one lived there, for there stood flowers in the balcony—they grew so well in the sun's heat! and that they could not do unless they were watered—and some one must water them—there must be somebody there. The door opposite was also opened late in the evening, but it was dark within, at least in the front room; further in there was heard the sound of music. The learned foreigner thought it quite marvellous, but now—it might be that he only imagined it—for he found everything marvellous out there, in the warm lands, if there had only been no sun. The stranger's landlord said that he didn't know who had taken the house opposite, one saw no person about, and as to the music, it appeared to him to be extremely tiresome. "It is as if some one sat there, and practised a piece that he could not master—always the same piece. 'I shall master it!' says he; but yet he cannot master it, however long he plays."

One night the stranger awoke—he slept with the doors of the balcony open—the curtain before it was raised by the wind, and he thought that a strange lustre came from the opposite neighbor's house; all the flowers shone like flames, in the most beautiful colors, and in the midst of the flowers stood a slender, graceful maiden—it was as if she also shone; the light really hurt his eyes. He now opened them quite wide—yes, he was quite awake; with one spring he was on the floor; he crept gently behind the curtain, but the maiden was gone; the flowers shone no longer, but there they stood, fresh and blooming as ever; the door was ajar, and, far within, the music sounded so soft and delightful, one could really melt away in sweet thoughts from it. Yet it was like a piece of enchantment. And who lived there? Where was the actual entrance? The whole of the ground-floor was a row of shops, and there people could not always be running through.

One evening the stranger sat out on the balcony. The light burnt in the room behind him; and thus it was quite natural that his shadow should fall on his opposite neighbor's wall. Yes! there it sat, directly opposite, between the flowers on the balcony; and when the stranger moved, the shadow also moved: for that it always does.

"I think my shadow is the only living thing one sees over there," said the learned man. "See, how nicely it sits between the flowers. The door stands half-open: now the shadow should be cunning, and go into the room, look about, and then come and tell me what it had seen. Come, now! Be useful, and do me a service," said he, in jest. "Have the kindness to step in. Now! Art thou going?" and then he nodded to the shadow, and the shadow nodded again. "Well then, go! But don't stay away."

The stranger rose, and his shadow on the opposite neighbor's balcony rose also; the stranger turned round and the shadow also turned round. Yes! if anyone had paid particular attention to it, they would have seen, quite distinctly, that the shadow went in through the half-open balcony-door of their opposite neighbor, just as the stranger went into his own room, and let the long curtain fall down after him.

Next morning, the learned man went out to drink coffee and read the newspapers.

"What is that?" said he, as he came out into the sunshine. "I have no shadow! So then, it has actually gone last night, and not come again. It is really tiresome!"

This annoyed him: not so much because the shadow was gone, but because he knew there was a story about a man without a shadow. It was known to everybody at home, in the cold lands; and if the learned man now came there and told his story, they would say that he was imitating it, and that he had no need to do. He would, therefore, not talk about it at all; and that was wisely thought.

In the evening he went out again on the balcony. He had placed the light directly behind him, for he knew that the shadow would always have its master for a screen, but he could not entice it. He made himself little; he made himself great: but no shadow came again. He said, "Hem! hem!" but it was of no use.

It was vexatious; but in the warm lands everything grows so quickly; and after the lapse of eight days he observed, to his great joy, that a new shadow came in the sunshine. In the course of three weeks he had a very fair shadow, which, when he set out for his home in the northern lands, grew more and more in the journey, so that at last it was so long and so large, that it was more than sufficient.

The learned man then came home, and he wrote books about what was true in the world, and about what was good and what was beautiful; and there passed days and years—yes! many years passed away.

One evening, as he was sitting in his room, there was a gentle knocking at the door.

"Come in!" said he; but no one came in; so he opened the door, and there stood before him such an extremely lean man, that he felt quite strange. As to the rest, the man was very finely dressed—he must be a gentleman.

"Whom have I the honor of speaking?" asked the learned man.

"Yes! I thought as much," said the fine man. "I thought you would not know me. I have got so much body. I have even got flesh and clothes. You certainly never thought of seeing me so well off. Do you not know your old shadow? You certainly thought I should never more return. Things have gone on well with me since I was last with you. I have, in all respects, become very well off. Shall I purchase my freedom from service? If so, I can do it"; and then he rattled a whole bunch of valuable seals that hung to his watch, and he stuck his hand in the thick gold chain he wore around his neck—nay! how all his fingers glittered with diamond rings; and then all were pure gems.

"Nay; I cannot recover from my surprise!" said the learned man. "What is the meaning of all this?"

"Something common, is it not," said the shadow. "But you

yourself do not belong to the common order; and I, as you know well, have from a child followed in your footsteps. As soon as you found I was capable to go out alone in the world, I went my own way. I am in the most brilliant circumstances, but there came a sort of desire over me to see you once more before you die; you will die, I suppose? I also wished to see this land again—for you know we always love our native land. I know you have got another shadow again; have I anything to pay to it or you? If so, you will oblige me by saying what it is."

"Nay, is it really thou?" said the learned man. "It is most remarkable: I never imagined that one's old shadow could come again as a man."

"Tell me what I have to pay," said the shadow; "for I don't like to be in any sort of debt."

"How canst thou talk so?" said the learned man. "What debt is there to talk about? Make thyself as free as anyone else. I am extremely glad to hear of thy good fortune: sit down, old friend, and tell me a little how it has gone with thee, and what thou hast seen at our opposite neighbor's there—in the warm lands."

"Yes, I will tell you all about it," said the shadow, and sat down: "but then you must also promise me, that, wherever you may meet me, you will never say to anyone here in the town that I have been your shadow. I intend to get betrothed, for I can provide for more than one family."

"Be quite at thy ease about that," said the learned man; "I shall not say to anyone who thou actually art: here is my hand—I promise it, and a man's bond is his word."

"A word is a shadow," said the shadow, "and as such it must speak."

It was really quite astonishing how much of a man it was. It was dressed entirely in black, and of the very finest cloth; it had patent leather boots, and a hat that could be folded together, so that it was bare crown and brim; not to speak of what we already know it had—seals, gold neck-chain, and diamond rings; yes, the

shadow was well-dressed, and it was just that which made it quite
a man.

"Now I shall tell you my adventures," said the shadow; and
then he sat, with the polished boots, as heavily as he could, on
the arm of the learned man's new shadow, which lay like a poo-
dle-dog at his feet. Now this was perhaps from arrogance; and the
shadow on the ground kept itself so still and quiet, that it might
hear all that passed: it wished to know how it could get free, and
work its way up, so as to become its own master.

"Do you know who lived in our opposite neighbor's house?"
said the shadow. "It was the most charming of all beings, it was
Poesy! I was there for three weeks, and that has as much effect as
if one had lived three thousand years, and read all that was composed and written; that is what I say, and it is right. I have seen
everything and I know everything!"

"Poesy!" cried the learned man. "Yes, yes, she often dwells a
recluse in large cities! Poesy! Yes, I have seen her—a single short
moment, but sleep came into my eyes! She stood on the balcony
and shone as the Aurora Borealis shines. Go on, go on—thou
wert on the balcony, and went through the doorway, and then—"

"Then I was in the antechamber," said the shadow. "You always sat and looked over to the antechamber. There was no light;
there was a sort of twilight, but the one door stood open directly
opposite the other through a long row of rooms and saloons, and
there it was lighted up. I should have been completely killed if I
had gone over to the maiden; but I was circumspect, I took time
to think, and that one must always do."

"And what didst thou then see?" asked the learned man.

"I saw everything, and I shall tell all to you: but—it is no pride
on my part—as a free man, and with the knowledge I have, not
to speak of my position in life, my excellent circumstances—I
certainly wish that you would say YOU to me!"

(It is the custom in Denmark for intimate acquaintances to use
the second person singular, "Du," (thou) when speaking to each

other. When a friendship is formed between men, they generally affirm it, when occasion offers, either in public or private, by drinking to each other and exclaiming, "thy health," at the same time striking their glasses together. This is called drinking "Duus": they are then, "Duus Brodre," (thou brothers) and ever afterwards use the pronoun "thou," to each other, it being regarded as more familiar than "De," (you). Father and mother, sister and brother say thou to one another—without regard to age or rank. Master and mistress say thou to their servants the superior to the inferior. But servants and inferiors do not use the same term to their masters, or superiors—nor is it ever used when speaking to a stranger, or anyone with whom they are but slightly acquainted—they then say as in English—you.)

"I beg your pardon," said the learned man; "it is an old habit with me. YOU are perfectly right, and I shall remember it; but now you must tell me all YOU saw!"

"Everything!" said the shadow. "For I saw everything, and I know everything!"

"How did it look in the furthest saloon?" asked the learned man. "Was it there as in the fresh woods? Was it there as in a holy church? Were the saloons like the starlit firmament when we stand on the high mountains?"

"Everything was there!" said the shadow. "I did not go quite in, I remained in the foremost room, in the twilight, but I stood there quite well; I saw everything, and I know everything! I have been in the antechamber at the court of Poesy."

"But WHAT DID you see? Did all the gods of the olden times pass through the large saloons? Did the old heroes combat there? Did sweet children play there, and relate their dreams?"

"I tell you I was there, and you can conceive that I saw everything there was to be seen. Had you come over there, you would not have been a man; but I became so! And besides, I learned to know my inward nature, my innate qualities, the relationship I had with Poesy. At the time I was with you, I thought not of that, but always—you know it well—when the sun rose, and when the sun went down, I became so strangely great; in the moonlight I was very near being more distinct than yourself; at that time I did not understand my nature; it was revealed to me in the ante-chamber! I became a man! I came out matured; but you were no longer in the warm lands; as a man I was ashamed to go as I did. I was in want of boots, of clothes, of the whole human varnish that makes a man perceptible. I took my way—I tell it to you, but you will not put it in any book—I took my way to the cake woman—I hid myself behind her; the woman didn't think how much she concealed. I went out first in the evening; I ran about the streets in the moonlight; I made myself long up the walls—it tickles the back so delightfully! I ran up, and ran down, peeped into the highest windows, into the saloons, and on the roofs, I peeped in where no one could peep, and I saw what no one else saw, what no one else should see! This is, in fact, a base world! I would not be a man if it were not now once accepted and regarded as something to be so! I saw the most unimaginable things with the women, with the men, with parents, and with the sweet, match-less children; I saw," said the shadow, "what no human being must know, but what they would all so willingly know—what is bad in their neighbor. Had I written a newspaper, it would have been read! But I wrote direct to the persons themselves, and there was consternation in all the towns where I came. They were so afraid of me, and yet they were so excessively fond of me. The profes-sors made a professor of me; the tailors gave me new clothes—I am well furnished; the master of the mint struck new coin for me, and the women said I was so handsome! And so I became the man I am. And I now bid you farewell. Here is my card—I live on the sunny side of the street, and am always at home in rainy weather!" And so away went the shadow. "That was most extraordinary!" said the learned man. Years and days passed away, then the shadow came again. "How goes it?" said the shadow.

"Alas!" said the learned man. "I write about the true, and the good, and the beautiful, but no one cares to hear such things; I am quite desperate, for I take it so much to heart!"

"But I don't!" said the shadow. "I become fat, and it is that one wants to become! You do not understand the world. You will become ill by it. You must travel! I shall make a tour this summer; will you go with me? I should like to have a travelling companion! Will you go with me, as shadow? It will be a great pleasure for me to have you with me; I shall pay the travelling expenses!"

"Nay, this is too much!" said the learned man.

"It is just as one takes it!" said the shadow. "It will do you much good to travel! Will you be my shadow? You shall have everything free on the journey!"

"Nay, that is too bad!" said the learned man.

"But it is just so with the world!" said the shadow, "and so it will be!" and away it went again.

The learned man was not at all in the most enviable state; grief and torment followed him, and what he said about the true, and the good, and the beautiful, was, to most persons, like roses for a cow! He was quite ill at last.

"You really look like a shadow!" said his friends to him; and the learned man trembled, for he thought of it.

"You must go to a watering-place!" said the shadow, who came and visited him. "There is nothing else for it! I will take you with me for old acquaintance' sake; I will pay the travelling expenses, and you write the descriptions—and if they are a little amusing for me on the way! I will go to a watering-place—my beard does not grow out as it ought—that is also a sickness—and one must have a beard! Now you be wise and accept the offer; we shall travel as comrades!"

And so they travelled; the shadow was master, and the master was the shadow; they drove with each other, they rode and walked together, side by side, before and behind, just as the sun was; the shadow always took care to keep itself in the master's place. Now the learned man didn't think much about that; he was a very kind-hearted man, and particularly mild and friendly, and so he said one day to the shadow: "As we have now become companions, and in this way have grown up together from childhood, shall we not drink 'thou' together, it is more familiar?"

"You are right," said the shadow, who was now the proper master. "It is said in a very straight-forward and well-meant manner. You, as a learned man, certainly know how strange nature is. Some persons cannot bear to touch grey paper, or they become ill; others shiver in every limb if one rub a pane of glass with a nail: I have just such a feeling on hearing you say thou to me; I feel myself as if pressed to the earth in my first situation with you. You see that it is a feeling; that it is not pride: I cannot allow you to say THOU to me, but I will willingly say THOU to you, so it is half done!"

So the shadow said THOU to its former master.

"This is rather too bad," thought he, "that I must say YOU and he say THOU," but he was now obliged to put up with it.

So they came to a watering-place where there were many strangers, and amongst them was a princess, who was troubled with seeing too well; and that was so alarming!

She directly observed that the stranger who had just come was quite a different sort of person to all the others; "He has come here in order to get his beard to grow, they say, but I see the real cause, he cannot cast a shadow."

She had become inquisitive; and so she entered into conversation directly with the strange gentleman, on their promenades. As the daughter of a king, she needed not to stand upon trifles, so she said, "Your complaint is, that you cannot cast a shadow?"

"Your Royal Highness must be improving considerably," said the shadow, "I know your complaint is, that you see too clearly, but it has decreased, you are cured. I just happen to have a very unusual shadow! Do you not see that person who always goes with me? Other persons have a common shadow, but I do not like what is common to all. We give our servants finer cloth for their livery than we ourselves use, and so I had my shadow trimmed up into a man: yes, you see I have even given him a shadow. It is somewhat expensive, but I like to have something for myself!"

"What!" thought the princess. "Should I really be cured! These baths are the first in the world! In our time water has wonderful powers. But I shall not leave the place, for it now begins to be amusing here. I am extremely fond of that stranger: would that his beard should not grow, for in that case he will leave us!"

In the evening, the princess and the shadow danced together in the large ball-room. She was light, but he was still lighter; she had never had such a partner in the dance. She told him from what land she came, and he knew that land; he had been there, but then she was not at home; he had peeped in at the window, above and below—he had seen both the one and the other, and so he could answer the princess, and make insinuations, so that she was quite astonished; he must be the wisest man in the whole world! She felt such respect for what he knew! So that when they again danced together she fell in love with him; and that the shadow could remark, for she almost pierced him through with her eyes. So they danced once more together; and she was about to declare herself, but she was discreet; she thought of her country and kingdom, and of the many persons she would have to reign over.

"He is a wise man," said she to herself—"It is well; and he dances delightfully—that is also good; but has he solid knowledge? That is just as important! He must be examined."

So she began, by degrees, to question him about the most difficult things she could think of, and which she herself could not have answered; so that the shadow made a strange face.

"You cannot answer these questions?" said the princess.

"They belong to my childhood's learning," said the shadow. "I really believe my shadow, by the door there, can answer them!"

"Your shadow!" said the princess. "That would indeed be marvellous!"

"I will not say for a certainty that he can," said the shadow, "but I think so; he has now followed me for so many years, and listened to my conversation—I should think it possible. But your royal highness will permit me to observe, that he is so proud of passing himself off for a man, that when he is to be in a proper humor—and he must be so to answer well—he must be treated quite like a man."

"Oh! I like that!" said the princess.

So she went to the learned man by the door, and she spoke to him about the sun and the moon, and about persons out of and in the world, and he answered with wisdom and prudence.

"What a man that must be who has so wise a shadow!" thought she. "It will be a real blessing to my people and kingdom if I choose him for my consort—I will do it!"

They were soon agreed, both the princess and the shadow; but no one was to know about it before she arrived in her own kingdom.

"No one—not even my shadow!" said the shadow, and he had his own thoughts about it!

Now they were in the country where the princess reigned when she was at home.

"Listen, my good friend," said the shadow to the learned man. "I have now become as happy and mighty as anyone can be; I will, therefore, do something particular for thee! Thou shalt always live with me in the palace, drive with me in my royal carriage, and have ten thousand pounds a year; but then thou must submit to be called SHADOW by all and everyone; thou must not say that thou hast ever been a man; and once a year, when I sit on the balcony in the sunshine, thou must lie at my feet, as a shadow shall do! I must tell thee: I am going to marry the king's daughter, and the nuptials are to take place this evening!"

"Nay, this is going too far!" said the learned man. "I will not have it; I will not do it! It is to deceive the whole country and the princess too! I will tell everything! That I am a man, and that thou art a shadow—thou art only dressed up!"

"There is no one who will believe it!" said the shadow. "Be reasonable, or I will call the guard!"

"I will go directly to the princess!" said the learned man.

"But I will go first!" said the shadow. "And thou wilt go to prison!" and that he was obliged to do—for the sentinels obeyed him whom they knew the king's daughter was to marry.

"You tremble!" said the princess, as the shadow came into her chamber. "Has anything happened? You must not be unwell this evening, now that we are to have our nuptials celebrated."

"I have lived to see the most cruel thing that anyone can live to see!" said the shadow. "Only imagine—yes, it is true, such a poor shadow-skull cannot bear much—only think, my shadow has become mad; he thinks that he is a man, and that I—now only think—that I am his shadow!"

"It is terrible!" said the princess; "but he is confined, is he not?"

"That he is. I am afraid that he will never recover."

"Poor shadow!" said the princess. "He is very unfortunate; it would be a real work of charity to deliver him from the little life he has, and, when I think properly over the matter, I am of opinion that it will be necessary to do away with him in all stillness!"

"It is certainly hard," said the shadow, "for he was a faithful servant!" and then he gave a sort of sigh.

"You are a noble character!" said the princess.

The whole city was illuminated in the evening, and the cannons went off with a bum! bum! and the soldiers presented arms. That was a marriage! The princess and the shadow went out on the balcony to show themselves, and get another hurrah!

The learned man heard nothing of all this—for they had deprived him of life.

The Brave Tin Soldier

There were once five-and-twenty tin soldiers, who were all brothers, for they had been made out of the same old tin spoon. They shouldered arms and looked straight before them, and wore a splendid uniform, red and blue. The first thing in the world they ever heard were the words, "Tin soldiers!" uttered by a little boy, who clapped his hands with delight when the lid of the box, in which they lay, was taken off. They were given him for a birthday present, and he stood at the table to set them up. The soldiers were all exactly alike, excepting one, who had only one leg; he had been left to the last, and then there was not enough of the melted tin to finish him, so they made him to stand firmly on one leg, and this caused him to be very remarkable.

The table on which the tin soldiers stood, was covered with other playthings, but the most attractive to the eye was a pretty little paper castle. Through the small windows the rooms could be seen. In front of the castle a number of little trees surrounded a piece of looking-glass, which was intended to represent a transparent lake. Swans, made of wax, swam on the lake, and were reflected in it. All this was very pretty, but the prettiest of all was a tiny little lady, who stood at the open door of the castle; she, also, was made of paper, and she wore a dress of clear muslin, with a narrow blue ribbon over her shoulders just like a scarf. In front of these was fixed a glittering tinsel rose, as large as her whole face. The little lady was a dancer, and she stretched out both her arms, and raised one of her legs so high, that the tin soldier could not see it at all, and he thought that she, like himself, had only one leg. "That is the wife for me," he thought; "but she is too grand, and lives in a castle, while I have only a box to live in, five-and-twenty of us altogether, that is no place for her. Still I must try and make her acquaintance." Then he laid himself at full length on the table behind a snuff-box that stood upon it, so that he could peep at the little delicate lady, who continued to stand on one leg without losing her balance. When evening came, the other tin soldiers were all placed in the box, and the people of the house went to bed. Then the playthings began to have their own games together, to pay visits, to have sham fights, and to give balls. The tin soldiers rattled in their box; they wanted to get out and join the amusements, but they could not open the lid. The nut-crackers played at leap-frog, and the pencil jumped about the table. There was such a noise that the canary woke up and began to talk, and in poetry too. Only the tin soldier and the dancer remained in their places. She stood on tiptoe, with her legs stretched out, as firmly as he did on his one leg. He never took his eyes from her for even a moment. The clock struck twelve, and, with a bounce, up sprang the lid of the snuff-box; but, instead of snuff, there jumped up a little black goblin; for the snuff-box was a toy puzzle.

"Tin soldier," said the goblin, "don't wish for what does not belong to you."

But the tin soldier pretended not to hear.

"Very well; wait till to-morrow, then," said the goblin.

When the children came in the next morning, they placed the tin soldier in the window. Now, whether it was the goblin who did it, or the draught, is not known, but the window flew open, and out fell the tin soldier, heels over head, from the third story, into the street beneath. It was a terrible fall; for he came head downwards, his helmet and his bayonet stuck in between the flag-stones, and his one leg up in the air. The servant maid and the little boy went down stairs directly to look for him; but he was nowhere to be seen, although once they nearly trod upon him. If he had called out, "Here I am," it would have been all right, but he was too proud to cry out for help while he wore a uniform.

Presently it began to rain, and the drops fell faster and faster, till there was a heavy shower. When it was over, two boys happened to pass by, and one of them said, "Look, there is a tin soldier. He ought to have a boat to sail in."

So they made a boat out of a newspaper, and placed the tin soldier in it, and sent him sailing down the gutter, while the two boys ran by the side of it, and clapped their hands. Good gracious, what large waves arose in that gutter! and how fast the stream rolled on! for the rain had been very heavy. The paper boat rocked up and down, and turned itself round sometimes so quickly that the tin soldier trembled; yet he remained firm; his countenance did not change; he looked straight before him, and shouldered his musket. Suddenly the boat shot under a bridge which formed a part of a drain, and then it was as dark as the tin soldier's box.

"Where am I going now?" thought he. "This is the black goblin's fault, I am sure. Ah, well, if the little lady were only here with me in the boat, I should not care for any darkness."

Suddenly there appeared a great water-rat, who lived in the drain.

"Have you a passport?" asked the rat, "give it to me at once." But the tin soldier remained silent and held his musket tighter than ever. The boat sailed on and the rat followed it. How he did gnash his teeth and cry out to the bits of wood and straw, "Stop him, stop him; he has not paid toll, and has not shown his pass." But the stream rushed on stronger and stronger. The tin soldier could already see daylight shining where the arch ended. Then he heard a roaring sound quite terrible enough to frighten the bravest man. At the end of the tunnel the drain fell into a large canal over a steep place, which made it as dangerous for him as a waterfall would be to us. He was too close to it to stop, so the boat rushed on, and the poor tin soldier could only hold himself as stiffly as possible, without moving an eyelid, to show that he was not afraid. The boat whirled round three or four times, and then filled with water to the very edge; nothing could save it from sinking. He now stood up to his neck in water, while deeper and deeper sank the boat, and the paper became soft and loose with the wet, till at last the water closed over the soldier's head. He thought of the elegant little dancer whom he should never see again, and the words of the song sounded in his ears—

"Farewell, warrior! ever brave,
Drifting onward to thy grave."

Then the paper boat fell to pieces, and the soldier sank into the water and immediately afterwards was swallowed up by a great fish. Oh how dark it was inside the fish! A great deal darker than in the tunnel, and narrower too, but the tin soldier continued firm, and lay at full length shouldering his musket. The fish swam to and fro, making the most wonderful movements, but at last he became quite still. After a while, a flash of lightning seemed to pass through him, and then the daylight approached, and a voice cried out, "I declare here is the tin soldier." The fish had been caught, taken to the market and sold to the cook, who took him into the kitchen and cut him open with a large knife. She picked up the soldier and held him by the waist between her finger and thumb, and carried him into the room. They were all anxious to see this wonderful soldier who had travelled about inside a fish; but he was not at all proud. They placed him on the table, and— how many curious things do happen in the world!—there he was in the very same room from the window of which he had fallen, there were the same children, the same playthings, standing on the table, and the pretty castle with the elegant little dancer at the door; she still balanced herself on one leg, and held up the other, so she was as firm as himself. It touched the tin soldier so much to see her that he almost wept tin tears, but he kept them back. He only looked at her and they both remained silent. Presently one of the little boys took up the tin soldier, and threw him into the stove. He had no reason for doing so, therefore it must have been the fault of the goblin who lived in the snuff-box. The flames lighted up the tin soldier, as he stood, the heat was very terrible, but whether it proceeded from the real fire or from the fire of love he could not tell. Then he could see that the bright colors were faded from his uniform, but whether they had been washed off during his journey or from the effects of his sorrow, no one could say. He looked at the little lady, and she looked at him. He felt himself melting away, but he still remained firm with his gun on his shoulder. Suddenly the door of the room flew open and the draught of air caught up the little dancer, she fluttered like a sylph right into the stove by the side of the tin soldier, and was instantly in flames and was gone. The tin soldier melted down into a lump, and the next morning, when the maid servant took the ashes out of the stove, she found him in the shape of a little tin heart. But of the little dancer nothing remained but the tinsel rose, which was burnt black as a cinder.

The Dream of Little Tuk

Ah! yes, that was little Tuk: in reality his name was not Tuk, but that was what he called himself before he could speak plain: he meant it for Charles, and it is all well enough if one does but know it. He had now to take care of his little sister Augusta, who was much younger than himself, and he was, besides, to learn his lesson at the same time; but these two things would not do together at all. There sat the poor little fellow, with his sister on his lap, and he sang to her all the songs he knew; and he glanced the while from time to time into the geography-book that lay open before him. By the next morning he was to have learnt all the towns in Zealand by heart, and to know about them all that is possible to be known.

His mother now came home, for she had been out, and took little Augusta on her arm. Tuk ran quickly to the window, and read so eagerly that he pretty nearly read his eyes out; for it got darker and darker, but his mother had no money to buy a candle.

"There goes the old washerwoman over the way," said his mother, as she looked out of the window. "The poor woman can hardly drag herself along, and she must now drag the pail home from the fountain. Be a good boy, Tukey, and run across and help the old woman, won't you?"

So Tuk ran over quickly and helped her; but when he came back again into the room it was quite dark, and as to a light, there was no thought of such a thing. He was now to go to bed; that was an old turn-up bedstead; in it he lay and thought about his geography lesson, and of Zealand, and of all that his master had told him. He ought, to be sure, to have read over his lesson again, but that, you know, he could not do. He therefore put his geography-book under his pillow, because he had heard that was a very good thing to do when one wants to learn one's lesson; but one cannot, however, rely upon it entirely. Well, there he lay, and thought and thought, and all at once it was just as if someone kissed his eyes and mouth: he slept, and yet he did not sleep; it was as though the old washerwoman gazed on him with her mild eyes and said, "It were a great sin if you were not to know your lesson tomorrow morning. You have aided me, I therefore will now help you; and the loving God will do so at all times." And all of a sudden the book under Tuk's pillow began scraping and scratching.

"Kickery-ki! kluk! kluk! kluk!"—that was an old hen who came creeping along, and she was from Kjoge. "I am a Kjoger hen," said she, and then she related how many inhabitants there were there, and about the battle that had taken place, and which, after all, was hardly worth talking about.

(Kjoge, a town in the bay of Kjoge. "To see the Kjoge hens," is an expression similar to "showing a child London," which is said to be done by taking his head in both bands, and so lifting him off the ground. At the invasion of the English in 1807, an encounter of a no very glorious nature took place between the British troops and the undisciplined Danish militia.)

"Kribledy, krabledy—plump!" down fell somebody: it was a wooden bird, the popinjay used at the shooting-matches at Prastoe. Now he said that there were just as many inhabitants as he had nails in his body; and he was very proud. "Thorwaldsen lived almost next door to me. Plump! Here I lie capitally."

(Prastoe, a still smaller town than Kjoge. Some hundred paces from it lies the manor-house Ny Soe, where Thorwaldsen, the famed sculptor, generally sojourned during his stay in Denmark, and where he called many of his immortal works into existence.)

But little Tuk was no longer lying down: all at once he was on horseback. On he went at full gallop, still galloping on and on. A knight with a gleaming plume, and most magnificently dressed, held him before him on the horse, and thus they rode through the wood to the old town of Bordingborg, and that was a large and very lively town. High towers rose from the castle of the king, and the brightness of many candles streamed from all the windows; within was dance and song, and King Waldemar and the young, richly-attired maids of honor danced together. The morn now came; and as soon as the sun appeared, the whole town and the king's palace crumbled together, and one tower after the other; and at last only a single one remained standing where the castle had been before,* and the town was so small and poor, and the school boys came along with their books under their arms, and said, "2000 inhabitants!" but that was not true, for there were not so many.

(Bordingborg, in the reign of King Waldemar, a considerable place, now an unimportant little town. One solitary tower only, and some remains of a wall, show where the castle once stood.)

And little Tukey lay in his bed: it seemed to him as if he dreamed, and yet as if he were not dreaming; however, somebody was close beside him.

"Little Tukey! Little Tukey!" cried someone near. It was a seaman, quite a little personage, so little as if he were a midshipman; but a midshipman it was not.

"Many remembrances from Corsor. That is a town that is just rising into importance; a lively town that has steam-boats and stagecoaches: formerly people called it ugly, but that is no longer true. I lie on the sea," said Corsor; "I have high roads and gardens, and I have given birth to a poet who was witty and amusing, which all poets are not. I once intended to equip a ship that was to sail all round the earth; but I did not do it, although I could have done so: and then, too, I smell so deliciously, for close before the gate bloom the most beautiful roses."

(Corsor, on the Great Belt, called, formerly, before the introduction of steam-vessels, when travellers were often obliged to wait a long time for a favorable wind, "the most tiresome of towns." The poet Baggesen was born here.)

Little Tuk looked, and all was red and green before his eyes; but as soon as the confusion of colors was somewhat over, all of a sudden there appeared a wooded slope close to the bay, and high up above stood a magnificent old church, with two high pointed towers. From out the hill-side spouted fountains in thick streams of water, so that there was a continual splashing; and close beside them sat an old king with a golden crown upon his white head: that was King Hroar, near the fountains, close to the town of Roeskilde, as it is now called. And up the slope into the old church went all the kings and queens of Denmark, hand in hand, all with their golden crowns; and the organ played and the fountains rustled. Little Tuk saw all, heard all. "Do not forget the diet," said King Hroar.

(Roeskilde, once the capital of Denmark. The town takes its name from King Hroar, and the many fountains in the neighborhood. In the beautiful cathedral the greater number of the kings and queens of Denmark are interred. In Roeskilde, too, the members of the Danish Diet assemble.)

Again all suddenly disappeared. Yes, and whither? It seemed to him just as if one turned over a leaf in a book. And now stood there an old peasant-woman, who came from Soroe, where grass grows in the market-place. She had an old grey linen apron hanging over her head and back: it was so wet, it certainly must have been raining. "Yes, that it has," said she; and she now related many pretty things out of Holberg's comedies, and about Waldemar and Absalon; but all at once she cowered together, and her head began shaking backwards and forwards, and she looked as she were going to make a spring. "Croak! croak!" said she. "It is wet, it is wet; there is such a pleasant deathlike stillness in Sorbe!" She was now suddenly a frog, "Croak"; and now she was an old woman. "One must dress according to the weather," said she. "It is wet; it is wet. My town is just like a bottle; and one gets in by the neck, and by the neck one must get out again! In former times I had the finest fish, and now I have fresh rosy-cheeked boys at the bottom of the bottle, who learn wisdom, Hebrew, Greek—Croak!"

(Sorbe, a very quiet little town, beautifully situated, surrounded by woods and lakes. Holberg, Denmark's Moliere, founded here an academy for the sons of the nobles. The poets Hauch and Ingemann were appointed professors here. The latter lives there still.)

When she spoke it sounded just like the noise of frogs, or as if one walked with great boots over a moor; always the same tone, so uniform and so tiring that little Tuk fell into a good sound sleep, which, by the bye, could not do him any harm.

But even in this sleep there came a dream, or whatever else it was: his little sister Augusta, she with the blue eyes and the fair curling hair, was suddenly a tall, beautiful girl, and without having wings was yet able to fly; and she now flew over Zealand— over the green woods and the blue lakes.

"Do you hear the cock crow, Tukey? Cock-a-doodle-doo! The cocks are flying up from Kjoge! You will have a farm-yard, so large, oh! so very large! You will suffer neither hunger nor thirst! You will get on in the world! You will be a rich and happy man! Your house will exalt itself like King Waldemar's tower, and will be richly decorated with marble statues, like that at Prastoe. You understand what I mean. Your name shall circulate with renown all round the earth, like unto the ship that was to have sailed from Corsor; and in Roeskilde—"

"Do not forget the diet!" said King Hroar.

"Then you will speak well and wisely, little Tukey; and when at last you sink into your grave, you shall sleep as quietly—"

"As if I lay in Soroe," said Tuk, awaking. It was bright day, and he was now quite unable to call to mind his dream; that, however, was not at all necessary, for one may not know what the future will bring.

And out of bed he jumped, and read in his book, and now all

at once he knew his whole lesson. And the old washerwoman popped her head in at the door, nodded to him friendly, and said, "Thanks, many thanks, my good child, for your help! May the good ever-loving God fulfil your loveliest dream!"

Little Tukey did not at all know what he had dreamed, but the loving God knew it.

The Emperor's New Clothes

Many years ago, there was an Emperor, who was so excessively fond of new clothes, that he spent all his money in dress. He did not trouble himself in the least about his soldiers; nor did he care to go either to the theatre or the chase, except for the opportunities then afforded him for displaying his new clothes. He had a different suit for each hour of the day; and as of any other king or emperor, one is accustomed to say, "he is sitting in council," it was always said of him, "The Emperor is sitting in his wardrobe."

Time passed merrily in the large town which was his capital; strangers arrived every day at the court. One day, two rogues, calling themselves weavers, made their appearance. They gave out that they knew how to weave stuffs of the most beautiful colors and elaborate patterns, the clothes manufactured from which should have the wonderful property of remaining invisible to everyone who was unfit for the office he held, or who was extraordinarily simple in character.

"These must, indeed, be splendid clothes!" thought the Emperor. "Had I such a suit, I might at once find out what men in my realms are unfit for their office, and also be able to distinguish the wise from the foolish! This stuff must be woven for me immediately." And he caused large sums of money to be given to both the weavers in order that they might begin their work directly.

So the two pretended weavers set up two looms, and affected to work very busily, though in reality they did nothing at all. They asked for the most delicate silk and the purest gold thread; put both into their own knapsacks; and then continued their pretended work at the empty looms until late at night.

"I should like to know how the weavers are getting on with my cloth," said the Emperor to himself, after some little time had elapsed; he was, however, rather embarrassed, when he remembered that a simpleton, or one unfit for his office, would be unable to see the manufacture. To be sure, he thought he had nothing to risk in his own person; but yet, he would prefer sending somebody else, to bring him intelligence about the weavers, and their work, before he troubled himself in the affair. All the people throughout the city had heard of the wonderful property the cloth was to possess; and all were anxious to learn how wise, or how ignorant, their neighbors might prove to be.

"I will send my faithful old minister to the weavers," said the Emperor at last, after some deliberation, "he will be best able to see how the cloth looks; for he is a man of sense, and no one can be more suitable for his office than he is."

So the faithful old minister went into the hall, where the knaves were working with all their might, at their empty looms. "What can be the meaning of this?" thought the old man, opening his eyes very wide. "I cannot discover the least bit of thread on the looms." However, he did not express his thoughts aloud.

The impostors requested him very courteously to be so good as to come nearer their looms; and then asked him whether the design pleased him, and whether the colors were not very beautiful; at the same time pointing to the empty frames. The poor old minister looked and looked, he could not discover anything on the looms, for a very good reason, viz: there was nothing there. "What!" thought he again. "Is it possible that I am a simpleton? I have never thought so myself; and no one must know it now if I am so. Can it be, that I am unfit for my office? No, that must not be said either. I will never confess that I could not see the stuff."

"Well, Sir Minister!" said one of the knaves, still pretending to work. "You do not say whether the stuff pleases you."

"Oh, it is excellent!" replied the old minister, looking at the loom through his spectacles. "This pattern, and the colors, yes, I will tell the Emperor without delay, how very beautiful I think them."

"We shall be much obliged to you," said the impostors, and then they named the different colors and described the pattern of the pretended stuff. The old minister listened attentively to their words, in order that he might repeat them to the Emperor; and then the knaves asked for more silk and gold, saying that it was necessary to complete what they had begun. However, they put all that was given them into their knapsacks; and continued to work with as much apparent diligence as before at their empty looms.

The Emperor now sent another officer of his court to see how the men were getting on, and to ascertain whether the cloth would soon be ready. It was just the same with this gentleman as with the minister; he surveyed the looms on all sides, but could see nothing at all but the empty frames.

"Does not the stuff appear as beautiful to you, as it did to my lord the minister?" asked the impostors of the Emperor's second ambassador; at the same time making the same gestures as before, and talking of the design and colors which were not there.

"I certainly am not stupid!" thought the messenger. "It must be, that I am not fit for my good, profitable office! That is very odd; however, no one shall know anything about it." And accordingly he praised the stuff he could not see, and declared that he was delighted with both colors and patterns. "Indeed, please your Imperial Majesty," said he to his sovereign when he returned, "the cloth which the weavers are preparing is extraordinarily magnificent."

The whole city was talking of the splendid cloth which the Emperor had ordered to be woven at his own expense.

And now the Emperor himself wished to see the costly manufacture, while it was still in the loom. Accompanied by a select number of officers of the court, among whom were the two honest men who had already admired the cloth, he went to the crafty impostors, who, as soon as they were aware of the Emperor's approach, went on working more diligently than ever; although they still did not pass a single thread through the looms.

"Is not the work absolutely magnificent?" said the two officers of the crown, already mentioned. "If your Majesty will only be pleased to look at it! What a splendid design! What glorious colors!" and at the same time they pointed to the empty frames; for they imagined that everyone else could see this exquisite piece of workmanship.

"How is this?" said the Emperor to himself. "I can see nothing! This is indeed a terrible affair! Am I a simpleton, or am I unfit to be an Emperor? That would be the worst thing that could happen—Oh! the cloth is charming," said he, aloud. "It has my complete approbation." And he smiled most graciously, and looked closely at the empty looms; for on no account would he say that he could not see what two of the officers of his court had praised so much. All his retinue now strained their eyes, hoping to discover something on the looms, but they could see no more than the others; nevertheless, they all exclaimed, "Oh, how beautiful!" and advised his majesty to have some new clothes made from this splendid material, for the approaching procession. "Magnificent! Charming! Excellent!" resounded on all sides; and everyone was uncommonly gay. The Emperor shared in the general satisfaction; and presented the impostors with the riband of an order of knighthood, to be worn in their button-holes, and the title of "Gentlemen Weavers."

The rogues sat up the whole of the night before the day on which the procession was to take place, and had sixteen lights burning, so that everyone might see how anxious they were to finish the Emperor's new suit. They pretended to roll the cloth off the looms; cut the air with their scissors; and sewed with needles without any thread in them. "See!" cried they, at last. "The Emperor's new clothes are ready!"

And now the Emperor, with all the grandees of his court, came to the weavers; and the rogues raised their arms, as if in the act of holding something up, saying, "Here are your Majesty's trousers! Here is the scarf! Here is the mantle! The whole suit is as light as a cobweb; one might fancy one has nothing at all on, when dressed in it; that, however, is the great virtue of this delicate cloth."

"Yes indeed!" said all the courtiers, although not one of them could see anything of this exquisite manufacture.

"If your Imperial Majesty will be graciously pleased to take off your clothes, we will fit on the new suit, in front of the looking glass."

The Emperor was accordingly undressed, and the rogues pretended to array him in his new suit; the Emperor turning round, from side to side, before the looking glass.

"How splendid his Majesty looks in his new clothes, and how well they fit!" everyone cried out. "What a design! What colors! These are indeed royal robes!"

"The canopy which is to be borne over your Majesty, in the procession, is waiting," announced the chief master of the ceremonies.

"I am quite ready," answered the Emperor. "Do my new clothes fit well?" asked he, turning himself round again before the looking glass, in order that he might appear to be examining his handsome suit.

The lords of the bedchamber, who were to carry his Majesty's train felt about on the ground, as if they were lifting up the ends of the mantle; and pretended to be carrying something; for they would by no means betray anything like simplicity, or unfitness for their office.

So now the Emperor walked under his high canopy in the midst of the procession, through the streets of his capital; and all the people standing by, and those at the windows, cried out, "Oh! How beautiful are our Emperor's new clothes! What a magnificent train there is to the mantle; and how gracefully the scarf hangs!" in short, no one would allow that he could not see these much-admired clothes; because, in doing so, he would have declared himself either a simpleton or unfit for his office. Certainly, none of the Emperor's various suits, had ever made so great an impression, as these invisible ones.

"But the Emperor has nothing at all on!" said a little child.

"Listen to the voice of innocence!" exclaimed his father; and what the child had said was whispered from one to another.

"But he has nothing at all on!" at last cried out all the people. The Emperor was vexed, for he knew that the people were right; but he thought the procession must go on now! And the lords of the bedchamber took greater pains than ever, to appear holding up a train, although, in reality, there was no train to hold.

The Happy Family

Really, the largest green leaf in this country is a dock-leaf; if one holds it before one, it is like a whole apron, and if one holds it over one's head in rainy weather, it is almost as good as an umbrella, for it is so immensely large. The burdock never grows alone, but where there grows one there always grow several: it is a great delight, and all this delightfulness is snails' food. The great white snails which persons of quality in former times made fricassees of, ate, and said, "Hem, hem! how delicious!" for they thought it tasted so delicate—lived on dock-leaves, and therefore burdock seeds were sown.

Now, there was an old manor-house, where they no longer ate snails, they were quite extinct; but the burdocks were not extinct, they grew and grew all over the walks and all the beds; they could not get the mastery over them—it was a whole forest of burdocks. Here and there stood an apple and a plum-tree, or else one never would have thought that it was a garden; all was burdocks, and there lived the two last venerable old snails.

They themselves knew not how old they were, but they could remember very well that there had been many more; that they were of a family from foreign lands, and that for them and theirs the whole forest was planted. They had never been outside it, but they knew that there was still something more in the world, which was called the manor-house, and that there they were boiled, and then they became black, and were then placed on a silver dish; but what happened further they knew not; or, in fact, what it was to be boiled, and to lie on a silver dish, they could not possibly imagine; but it was said to be delightful, and particularly genteel. Neither the chafers, the toads, nor the earth-worms, whom they asked about it could give them any information—none of them had been boiled or laid on a silver dish.

The old white snails were the first persons of distinction in the world, that they knew; the forest was planted for their sake, and the manor-house was there that they might be boiled and laid on a silver dish.

Now they lived a very lonely and happy life; and as they had no children themselves, they had adopted a little common snail, which they brought up as their own; but the little one would not grow, for he was of a common family; but the old ones, especially Dame Mother Snail, thought they could observe how he increased in size, and she begged father, if he could not see it, that he would at least feel the little snail's shell; and then he felt it, and found the good dame was right.

One day there was a heavy storm of rain.

"Hear how it beats like a drum on the dock-leaves!" said Father Snail.

"There are also rain-drops!" said Mother Snail. "And now the rain pours right down the stalk! You will see that it will be wet here! I am very happy to think that we have our good house, and the little one has his also! There is more done for us than for all other creatures, sure enough; but can you not see that we are folks of quality in the world? We are provided with a house from our birth, and the burdock forest is planted for our sakes! I should like to know how far it extends, and what there is outside!"

"There is nothing at all," said Father Snail. "No place can be better than ours, and I have nothing to wish for!"

"Yes," said the dame. "I would willingly go to the manorhouse, be boiled, and laid on a silver dish; all our forefathers have been treated so; there is something extraordinary in it, you may be sure!"

"The manor-house has most likely fallen to ruin!" said Father Snail. "Or the burdocks have grown up over it, so that they cannot come out. There need not, however, be any haste about that; but you are always in such a tremendous hurry, and the little one is beginning to be the same. Has he not been creeping up that stalk these three days? It gives me a headache when I look up to him!"

"You must not scold him," said Mother Snail. "He creeps so carefully; he will afford us much pleasure—and we have nothing but him to live for! But have you not thought of it? Where shall we get a wife for him? Do you not think that there are some of our species at a great distance in the interior of the burdock forest?"

"Black snails, I dare say, there are enough of," said the old one. "Black snails without a house—but they are so common, and so conceited. But we might give the ants a commission to look out for us; they run to and fro as if they had something to do, and they certainly know of a wife for our little snail!"

"I know one, sure enough—the most charming one!" said one of the ants. "But I am afraid we shall hardly succeed, for she is a queen!"

"That is nothing!" said the old folks. "Has she a house?"

"She has a palace!" said the ant. "The finest ant's palace, with seven hundred passages!"

"I thank you!" said Mother Snail. "Our son shall not go into an ant-hill; if you know nothing better than that, we shall give the commission to the white gnats. They fly far and wide, in rain and sunshine; they know the whole forest here, both within and without."

"We have a wife for him," said the gnats. "At a hundred human paces from here there sits a little snail in her house, on a goose-berry bush; she is quite lonely, and old enough to be married. It is only a hundred human paces!"

"Well, then, let her come to him!" said the old ones. "He has a whole forest of burdocks, she has only a bush!"

And so they went and fetched little Miss Snail. It was a whole week before she arrived; but therein was just the very best of it, for one could thus see that she was of the same species.

And then the marriage was celebrated. Six earth-worms shone

as well as they could. In other respects the whole went off very quietly, for the old folks could not bear noise and merriment; but old Dame Snail made a brilliant speech. Father Snail could not speak, he was too much affected; and so they gave them as a dowry and inheritance, the whole forest of burdocks, and said—what they had always said—that it was the best in the world; and if they lived honestly and decently, and increased and multiplied, they and their children would once in the course of time come to the manor-house, be boiled black, and laid on silver dishes. After this speech was made, the old ones crept into their shells, and never more came out. They slept; the young couple governed in the forest, and had a numerous progeny, but they were never boiled, and never came on the silver dishes; so from this they concluded that the manor-house had fallen to ruins, and that all the men in the world were extinct; and as no one contradicted them, so, of course it was so. And the rain beat on the dock-leaves to make drum-music for their sake, and the sun shone in order to give the burdock forest a color for their sakes; and they were very happy, and the whole family was happy; for they, indeed were so.

The Princess and the Pea

There was once a Prince who wished to marry a Princess; but then she must be a real Princess. He travelled all over the world in hopes of finding such a lady; but there was always something wrong. Princesses he found in plenty; but whether they were real Princesses it was impossible for him to decide, for now one thing, now another, seemed to him not quite right about the ladies. At last he returned to his palace quite cast down, because he wished so much to have a real Princess for his wife.

One evening a fearful tempest arose, it thundered and lightened, and the rain poured down from the sky in torrents: besides, it was as dark as pitch. All at once there was heard a violent knocking at the door, and the old King, the Prince's father, went out himself to open it.

It was a Princess who was standing outside the door. What with the rain and the wind, she was in a sad condition; the water trickled down from her hair, and her clothes clung to her body. She said she was a real Princess.

"Ah! we shall soon see that!" thought the old Queen-mother; however, she said not a word of what she was going to do; but went quietly into the bedroom, took all the bed-clothes off the bed, and put three little peas on the bedstead. She then laid twenty mattresses one upon another over the three peas, and put twenty feather beds over the mattresses.

Upon this bed the Princess was to pass the night.

The next morning she was asked how she had slept. "Oh, very badly indeed!" she replied. "I have scarcely closed my eyes the whole night through. I do not know what was in my bed, but I had something hard under me, and am all over black and blue. It has hurt me so much!"

Now it was plain that the lady must be a real Princess, since she had been able to feel the three little peas through the twenty

173

mattresses and twenty feather beds. None but a real Princess could have had such a delicate sense of feeling.

The Prince accordingly made her his wife; being now convinced that he had found a real Princess. The three peas were however put into the cabinet of curiosities, where they are still to be seen, provided they are not lost.

Wasn't this a lady of real delicacy?

The Roses and the Sparrows

It really appeared as if something very important were going on by the duck pond, but this was not the case.

A few minutes before, all the ducks had been resting on the water or standing on their heads—for that they can do—and then they all swam in a bustle to the shore. The traces of their feet could be seen on the wet earth, and far and wide could be heard their quacking. The water, so lately clear and bright as a mirror, was in quite a commotion.

But a moment before, every tree and bush near the old farmhouse—and even the house itself with the holes in the roof and the swallows' nests and, above all, the beautiful rosebush covered with roses—had been clearly reflected in the water. The rosebush on the wall hung over the water, which resembled a picture only that everything appeared upside down, but when the water was set in motion all vanished, and the picture disappeared.

Two feathers, dropped by the fluttering ducks, floated to and fro on the water. All at once they took a start as if the wind were coming, but it did not come, so they were obliged to lie still, as the water became again quiet and at rest. The roses could once more behold their own reflections. They were very beautiful, but they knew it not, for no one had told them. The sun shone between the delicate leaves, and the sweet fragrance spread itself, carrying happiness everywhere.

"How beautiful is our existence!" said one of the roses. "I feel as if I should like to kiss the sun, it is so bright and warm. I should like to kiss the roses too, our images in the water, and the pretty birds there in their nests. There are some birds too in the nest above us; they stretch out their heads and cry 'Tweet, tweet,' very faintly. They have no feathers yet, such as their father and mother have. Both above us and below us we have good neighbors. How beautiful is our life!"

The young birds above and the young ones below were the same; they were sparrows, and their nest was reflected in the water. Their parents were sparrows also, and they had taken possession of an empty swallow's nest of the year before, occupying it now as if it were their own.

"Are those ducks' children that are swimming about? asked the young sparrows, as they spied the feathers on the water.

"If you must ask questions, pray ask sensible ones," said the mother. "Can you not see that these are feathers, the living stuff for clothes, which I wear and which you will wear soon, only ours are much finer? I should like, however, to have them up here in the nest, they would make it so warm. I am rather curious to know why the ducks were so alarmed just now. It could not be from fear of us, certainly, though I did say 'tweet' rather loudly. The thick-headed roses really ought to know, but they are very ignorant; they only look at one another and smell. I am heartily tired of such neighbors."

"Listen to the sweet little birds above us," said the roses; "they are trying to sing. They cannot manage it yet, but it will be done in time. What a pleasure it will be, and how nice to have such lively neighbors!"

Suddenly two horses came prancing along to drink at the water. A peasant boy rode on one of them; he had a broad-brimmed black hat on, but had taken off the most of his clothes, that he might ride into the deepest part of the pond; he whistled like a bird, and while passing the rosebush he plucked a rose and placed it in his hat and then rode on thinking himself very fine. The other roses looked at their sister and asked each other where she could be going, but they did not know.

"I should like for once to go out into the world," said one, "although it is very lovely here in our home of green leaves. The sun shines warmly by day, and in the night we can see that heaven is more beautiful still, as it sparkles through the holes in the sky."

She meant the stars, for she knew no better.

"We make the house very lively," said the mother sparrow, "and people say that a swallow's nest brings luck, therefore they are pleased to see us; but as to our neighbors, a rosebush on the wall produces damp. It will most likely be removed, and perhaps corn will grow here instead of it. Roses are good for nothing but to be looked at and smelt, or perhaps one may chance to be stuck in a hat. I have heard from my mother that they fall off every year. The farmer's wife preserves them by laying them in salt, and then they receive a French name which I neither can nor will pronounce; then they are sprinkled on the fire to produce a pleasant smell. Such you see is their life. They are only formed to please the eye and the nose. Now you know all about them."

As the evening approached, the gnats played about in the warm air beneath the rosy clouds, and the nightingale came and sang to the roses that the beautiful was like sunshine to the world, and that the beautiful lives forever. The roses thought that the nightingale was singing of herself, which any one indeed could easily suppose; they never imagined that her song could refer to them. But it was a joy to them, and they wondered to themselves whether all the little sparrows in the nest would become nightingales.

"We understood that bird's song very well," said the young sparrows, "but one word was not clear. What is the beautiful?"

"Oh, nothing of any consequence," replied the mother sparrow. "It is something relating to appearances over yonder at the nobleman's house. The pigeons have a house of their own, and every day they have corn and peas spread for them. I have dined there with them sometimes, and so shall you by and by, for I believe the old maxim—'Tell me what company you keep, and I will tell you what you are.' Well, over at the noble house there are two birds with green throats and crests on their heads. They can spread out their tails like large wheels, and they reflect so many beautiful colors that it dazzles the eyes to look at them. These birds are called peacocks, and they belong to the beautiful; but if only a few of their feathers were plucked off, they would not appear better than we do. I would myself have plucked some out had they not been so large."

"I will pluck them," squeaked the youngest sparrow, who had as yet no feathers of his own.

In the cottage dwelt two young married people, who loved each other very much and were industrious and active so that everything looked neat and pretty around them. Early on Sunday mornings the young wife came out, gathered a handful of the most beautiful roses, and put them in a glass of water, which she placed on a side table.

"I see now that it is Sunday," said the husband, as he kissed his little wife. Then they sat down and read in their hymn books, holding each other's hands, while the sun shone down upon the young couple and upon the fresh roses in the glass.

"This sight is really too wearisome," said the mother sparrow, who from her nest could look into the room; and she flew away.

The same thing occurred the next Sunday; and indeed every Sunday fresh roses were gathered and placed in a glass, but the rose tree continued to bloom in all its beauty. After a while the young sparrows were fledged and wanted to fly, but the mother would not allow it, and so they were obliged to remain in the nest for the present, while she flew away alone. It so happened that some boys had fastened a snare made of horsehair to the branch of a tree, and before she was aware, her leg became entangled in the horsehair so tightly as almost to cut it through. What pain and terror she felt! The boys ran up quickly and seized her, not in a very gentle manner.

"It is only a sparrow," they said. However they did not let her fly, but took her home with them, and every time she cried they tapped her on the beak.

In the farmyard they met an old man who knew how to make

soap for shaving and washing, in cakes or in balls. When he saw the sparrow which the boys had brought home and which they said they did not know what to do with, he said, "Shall we make it beautiful?"

A cold shudder passed over the sparrow when she heard this. The old man then took a shell containing a quantity of glittering gold leaf from a box full of beautiful colors and told the youngsters to fetch the white of an egg, with which he besmeared the sparrow all over and then laid the gold leaf upon it, so that the mother sparrow was now gilded from head to tail. She thought not of her appearance, but trembled in every limb. Then the soap maker tore a little piece out of the red lining of his jacket, cut notches in it, so that it looked like a cock'scomb, and stuck it on the bird's head.

"Now you shall see gold-jacket fly," said the old man, and he released the sparrow, which flew away in deadly terror with the sunlight shining upon her. How she did glitter! All the sparrows, and even a crow, who is a knowing old boy, were startled at the sight, yet they all followed it to discover what foreign bird it could be. Driven by anguish and terror, she flew homeward almost ready to sink to the earth for want of strength. The flock of birds that were following increased and some even tried to peck her.

"Look at him! look at him!" they all cried. "Look at him! look at him!" cried the young ones as their mother approached the nest, for they did not know her. "That must be a young peacock, for he glitters in all colors. It quite hurts one's eyes to look at him, as mother told us; 'tweet,' this is the beautiful." And then they pecked the bird with their little beaks so that she was quite unable to get into the nest and was too much exhausted even to say "tweet," much less "I am your mother." So the other birds fell upon the sparrow and pulled out feather after feather till she sank bleeding into the rosebush.

"You poor creature," said the roses, "be at rest. We will hide you; lean your little head against us."

The sparrow spread out her wings once more, then drew them in close about her and lay dead among the roses, her fresh and lovely neighbors.

"Tweet," sounded from the nest; "where can our mother be staying? It is quite unaccountable. Can this be a trick of hers to show us that we are now to take care of ourselves? She has left us the house as an inheritance, but as it cannot belong to us all when we have families, who is to have it?"

"It won't do for you all to stay with me when I increase my household with a wife and children," remarked the youngest.

"I shall have more wives and children than you," said the second.

"But I am the eldest," cried a third.

Then they all became angry, beat each other with their wings, pecked with their beaks, till one after another bounced out of the nest. There they lay in a rage, holding their heads on one side and twinkling the eye that looked upward. This was their way of looking sulky.

They could all fly a little, and by practice they soon learned to do so much better. At length they agreed upon a sign by which they might be able to recognize each other in case they should meet in the world after they had separated. This sign was to be the cry of "tweet, tweet," and a scratching on the ground three times with the left foot.

The youngster who was left behind in the nest spread himself out as broad as ever he could; he was the householder now. But his glory did not last long, for during that night red flames of fire burst through the windows of the cottage, seized the thatched roof, and blazed up frightfully. The whole house was burned, and the sparrow perished with it, while the young couple fortunately escaped with their lives.

When the sun rose again, and all nature looked refreshed as

after a quiet sleep, nothing remained of the cottage but a few blackened, charred beams leaning against the chimney, that now was the only master of the place. Thick smoke still rose from the ruins, but outside on the wall the rosebush remained unhurt, blooming and fresh as ever, while each flower and each spray was mirrored in the clear water beneath.

"How beautifully the roses are blooming on the walls of that ruined cottage," said a passer-by. "A more lovely picture could scarcely be imagined. I must have it."

And the speaker took out of his pocket a little book full of white leaves of paper (for he was an artist), and with a pencil he made a sketch of the smoking ruins, the blackened rafters, and the chimney that overhung them and which seemed more and more to totter; and quite in the foreground stood the large, blooming rosebush, which added beauty to the picture; indeed, it was for the sake of the roses that the sketch had been made. Later in the day two of the sparrows who had been born there came by.

"Where is the house?" they asked. "Where is the nest? Tweet, tweet; all is burned down, and our strong brother with it. That is all he got by keeping the nest. The roses have escaped famously; they look as well as ever, with their rosy cheeks; they do not trouble themselves about their neighbors' misfortunes. I won't speak to them. And really, in my opinion, the place looks very ugly"; so they flew away.

On a fine, bright, sunny day in autumn, so bright that any one might have supposed it was still the middle of summer, a number of pigeons were hopping about in the nicely kept courtyard of the nobleman's house, in front of the great steps. Some were black, others white, and some of various colors, and their plumage glittered in the sunshine. An old mother pigeon said to her young ones, "Place yourselves in groups! place yourselves in groups! it has a much better appearance."

"What are those little gray creatures which are running about behind us?" asked an old pigeon with red and green round her eyes. "Little gray ones, little gray ones," she cried.

"They are sparrows—good little creatures enough. We have always had the character of being very good-natured, so we allow them to pick up some corn with us; they do not interrupt our conversation, and they draw back their left foot so prettily."

Sure enough, so they did, three times each, and with the left foot too, and said "tweet," by which we recognize them as the sparrows that were brought up in the nest on the house that was burned down.

"The food here is very good," said the sparrows; while the pigeons strutted round each other, puffed out their throats, and formed their own opinions on what they observed.

"Do you see the pouter pigeon?" asked one pigeon of another. "Do you see how he swallows the peas? He takes too much and always chooses the best of everything. Coo-oo, coo-oo. How the ugly, spiteful creature erects his crest." And all their eyes sparkled with malice. "Place yourselves in groups, place yourselves in groups. Little gray coats, little gray coats. Coo-oo, coo-oo."

So they went on, and it will be the same a thousand years hence.

The sparrows feasted bravely and listened attentively; they even stood in ranks like the pigeons, but it did not suit them. So having satisfied their hunger, they left the pigeons passing their own opinions upon them to each other and slipped through the garden railings. The door of a room in the house, leading into the garden, stood open, and one of them, feeling brave after his good dinner, hopped upon the threshold crying, "Tweet, I can venture so far."

"Tweet," said another, "I can venture that, and a great deal more," and into the room he hopped.

The first followed, and, seeing no one there, the third became courageous and flew right across the room, saying: "Venture everything, or do not venture at all. This is a wonderful place—a man's nest, I suppose; and look! what can this be?"

Just in front of the sparrows stood the ruins of the burned cottage; roses were blooming over it, and their reflection appeared in the water beneath, and the black, charred beams rested against the tottering chimney. How could it be? How came the cottage and the roses in a room in the nobleman's house? And then the sparrows tried to fly over the roses and the chimney, but they only struck themselves against a flat wall. It was a picture—a large, beautiful picture which the artist had painted from the little sketch he had made.

"Tweet," said the sparrows, "it is really nothing, after all; it only looks like reality. Tweet, I suppose that is the beautiful. Can you understand it? I cannot."

Then some persons entered the room and the sparrows flew away. Days and years passed. The pigeons had often "coo-oo-d"— we must not say quarreled, though perhaps they did, the naughty things! The sparrows had suffered from cold in the winter and lived gloriously in summer. They were all betrothed, or married, or whatever you like to call it. They had little ones, and each considered its own brood the wisest and the prettiest.

One flew in this direction and another in that, and when they met they recognized each other by saying "tweet" and three times drawing back the left foot. The eldest remained single; she had no nest nor young ones. Her great wish was to see a large town, so she flew to Copenhagen.

Close by the castle, and by the canal, in which swam many ships laden with apples and pottery, there was to be seen a great house. The windows were broader below than at the top, and when the sparrows peeped through they saw a room that looked to them like a tulip with beautiful colors of every shade. Within the tulip were white figures of human beings, made of marble— some few of plaster, but this is the same thing to a sparrow. Upon the roof stood a metal chariot and horses, and the goddess of victory, also of metal, was seated in the chariot driving the horses.

It was Thorwaldsen's museum. "How it shines and glitters," said the maiden sparrow. "This must be the beautiful,—tweet,—only this is larger than a peacock." She remembered what her mother had told them in her childhood, that the peacock was one of the greatest examples of the beautiful. She flew down into the courtyard, where everything also was very grand. The walls were painted to represent palm branches, and in the midst of the court stood a large, blooming rose tree, spreading its young, sweet, rose-covered branches over a grave. Thither the maiden sparrow flew, for she saw many others of her own kind.

"Tweet," said she, drawing back her foot three times. She had, during the years that had passed, often made the usual greeting to the sparrows she met, but without receiving any acknowledgment; for friends who are once separated do not meet every day. This manner of greeting was become a habit to her, and to-day two old sparrows and a young one returned the greeting.

"Tweet," they replied and drew back the left foot three times. They were two old sparrows out of the nest, and a young one belonging to the family. "Ah, good day; how do you do? To think of our meeting here! This is a very grand place, but there is not much to eat; this is the beautiful. Tweet!"

A great many people now came out of the side rooms, in which the marble statues stood, and approached the grave where rested the remains of the great master who carved them. As they stood round Thorwaldsen's grave, each face had a reflected glory, and some few gathered up the fallen rose leaves to preserve them. They had all come from afar; one from mighty England, others from Germany and France. One very handsome lady plucked a rose and concealed it in her bosom. Then the sparrows thought that the roses ruled in this place, and that the whole house had been built for them—which seemed really too much honor; but as all the people showed their love for the roses, the sparrows thought they would not remain behindhand in paying their respects.

"Tweet," they said, and swept the ground with their tails, and glanced with one eye at the roses. They had not looked at them very long, however, before they felt convinced that they were old acquaintances, and so they actually were. The artist who had sketched the rosebush and the ruins of the cottage had since then received permission to transplant the bush and had given it to the architect, for more beautiful roses had never been seen. The architect had planted it on the grave of Thorwaldsen, where it continued to bloom, the image of the beautiful, scattering its fragrant, rosy leaves to be gathered and carried away into distant lands in memory of the spot on which they fell.

"Have you obtained a situation in town?" then asked the sparrows of the roses.

The roses nodded. They recognized their little brown neighbors and were rejoiced to see them again.

"It is very delightful," said the roses, "to live here and to blossom, to meet old friends, and to see cheerful faces every day. It is as if each day were a holiday."

"Tweet," said the sparrows to each other. "Yes, these really are our old neighbors. We remember their origin near the pond. Tweet! how they have risen, to be sure. Some people seem to get on while they are asleep. Ah! there's a withered leaf. I can see it quite plainly."

And they pecked at the leaf till it fell, but the rosebush continued fresher and greener than ever. The roses bloomed in the sunshine on Thorwaldsen's grave and thus became linked with his immortal name.

The Bell

People said "The Evening Bell is sounding, the sun is setting." For a strange wondrous tone was heard in the narrow streets of a large town. It was like the sound of a church-bell: but it was only heard for a moment, for the rolling of the carriages and the voices of the multitude made too great a noise.

Those persons who were walking outside the town, where the houses were farther apart, with gardens or little fields between them, could see the evening sky still better, and heard the sound of the bell much more distinctly. It was as if the tones came from a church in the still forest; people looked thitherward, and felt their minds attuned most solemnly.

A long time passed, and people said to each other—"I wonder if there is a church out in the wood? The bell has a tone that is wondrous sweet; let us stroll thither, and examine the matter nearer." And the rich people drove out, and the poor walked, but the way seemed strangely long to them; and when they came to a clump of willows which grew on the skirts of the forest, they sat down, and looked up at the long branches, and fancied they were now in the depth of the green wood. The confectioner of the town came out, and set up his booth there; and soon after came another confectioner, who hung a bell over his stand, as a sign or ornament, but it had no clapper, and it was tarred over to preserve it from the rain. When all the people returned home, they said it had been very romantic, and that it was quite a different sort of thing to a pic-nic or tea-party. There were three persons who asserted they had penetrated to the end of the forest, and that they had always heard the wonderful sounds of the bell, but it had seemed to them as if it had come from the town. One wrote a whole poem about it, and said the bell sounded like the voice of a mother to a good dear child, and that no melody was sweeter than the tones of the bell. The king of the country was also observant of it, and vowed that he who could discover whence the sounds proceeded, should have the title of "Universal Bell-ringer," even if it were not really a bell.

Many persons now went to the wood, for the sake of getting the place, but one only returned with a sort of explanation; for nobody went far enough, that one not further than the others. However, he said that the sound proceeded from a very large owl, in a hollow tree; a sort of learned owl, that continually knocked its head against the branches. But whether the sound came from his head or from the hollow tree, that no one could say with certainty. So now he got the place of "Universal Bell-ringer," and wrote yearly a short treatise "On the Owl"; but everybody was just as wise as before.

It was the day of confirmation. The clergyman had spoken so touchingly, the children who were confirmed had been greatly moved; it was an eventful day for them; from children they become all at once grown-up-persons; it was as if their infant souls were now to fly all at once into persons with more understanding. The sun was shining gloriously; the children that had been confirmed went out of the town; and from the wood was borne towards them the sounds of the unknown bell with wonderful distinctness. They all immediately felt a wish to go thither; all except three. One of them had to go home to try on a ball-dress; for it was just the dress and the ball which had caused her to be confirmed this time, for otherwise she would not have come; the other was a poor boy, who had borrowed his coat and boots to be confirmed in from the innkeeper's son, and he was to give them back by a certain hour; the third said that he never went to a strange place if his parents were not with him—that he had always been a good boy hitherto, and would still be so now that he was confirmed, and that one ought not to laugh at him for it: the others, however, did make fun of him, after all.

There were three, therefore, that did not go; the others hastened on. The sun shone, the birds sang, and the children sang too, and each held the other by the hand; for as yet they had none of them any high office, and were all of equal rank in the eye of God.

But two of the youngest soon grew tired, and both returned to town; two little girls sat down, and twined garlands, so they did not go either; and when the others reached the willow-tree, where the confectioner was, they said, "Now we are there! In reality the bell does not exist; it is only a fancy that people have taken into their heads!"

At the same moment the bell sounded deep in the wood, so clear and solemnly that five or six determined to penetrate somewhat further. It was so thick, and the foliage so dense, that it was quite fatiguing to proceed. Woodroof and anemonies grew almost too high; blooming convolvuluses and blackberry-bushes hung in long garlands from tree to tree, where the nightingale sang and the sunbeams were playing: it was very beautiful, but it was no place for girls to go; their clothes would get so torn. Large blocks of stone lay there, overgrown with moss of every color; the fresh spring bubbled forth, and made a strange gurgling sound.

"That surely cannot be the bell," said one of the children, lying down and listening. "This must be looked to." So he remained, and let the others go on without him.

They afterwards came to a little house, made of branches and the bark of trees; a large wild apple-tree bent over it, as if it would shower down all its blessings on the roof, where roses were blooming. The long stems twined round the gable, on which there hung a small bell.

Was it that which people had heard? Yes, everybody was unanimous on the subject, except one, who said that the bell was too small and too fine to be heard at so great a distance, and besides it was very different tones to those that could move a human heart in such a manner. It was a king's son who spoke; whereon the others said, "Such people always want to be wiser than everybody else."

They now let him go on alone; and as he went, his breast was filled more and more with the forest solitude; but he still heard the little bell with which the others were so satisfied, and now and then, when the wind blew, he could also hear the people singing who were sitting at tea where the confectioner had his tent; but the deep sound of the bell rose louder; it was almost as if an organ were accompanying it, and the tones came from the left hand, the side where the heart is placed. A rustling was heard in the bushes, and a little boy stood before the King's Son, a boy in wooden shoes, and with so short a jacket that one could see what long wrists he had. Both knew each other: the boy was that one among the children who could not come because he had to go home and return his jacket and boots to the innkeeper's son. This he had done, and was now going on in wooden shoes and in his humble dress, for the bell sounded with so deep a tone, and with such strange power, that proceed he must.

"Why, then, we can go together," said the King's Son. But the poor child that had been confirmed was quite ashamed; he looked at his wooden shoes, pulled at the short sleeves of his jacket, and said that he was afraid he could not walk so fast; besides, he thought that the bell must be looked for to the right; for that was the place where all sorts of beautiful things were to be found.

"But there we shall not meet," said the King's Son, nodding at the same time to the poor boy, who went into the darkest, thickest part of the wood, where thorns tore his humble dress, and scratched his face and hands and feet till they bled. The King's Son got some scratches too; but the sun shone on his path, and it is him that we will follow, for he was an excellent and resolute youth.

"I must and will find the bell," said he, "even if I am obliged to go to the end of the world."

The ugly apes sat upon the trees, and grinned. "Shall we thrash him?" said they. "Shall we thrash him? He is the son of a king!"

But on he went, without being disheartened, deeper and deeper into the wood, where the most wonderful flowers were growing. There stood white lilies with blood-red stamina, skyblue tulips, which shone as they waved in the winds, and apple-trees, the apples of which looked exactly like large soapbubbles: so only think how the trees must have sparkled in the sunshine! Around the nicest green meads, where the deer were playing in the grass, grew magnificent oaks and beeches; and if the bark of one of the trees was cracked, there grass and long creeping plants grew in the crevices. And there were large calm lakes there too, in which white swans were swimming, and beat the air with their wings. The King's Son often stood still and listened. He thought the bell sounded from the depths of these still lakes; but then he remarked again that the tone proceeded not from there, but farther off, from out the depths of the forest.

The sun now set: the atmosphere glowed like fire. It was still in the woods, so very still; and he fell on his knees, sung his evening hymn, and said: "I cannot find what I seek; the sun is going down, and night is coming—the dark, dark night. Yet perhaps I may be able once more to see the round red sun before he entirely disappears. I will climb up yonder rock."

And he seized hold of the creeping-plants, and the roots of trees—climbed up the moist stones where the water-snakes were writhing and the toads were croaking—and he gained the summit before the sun had quite gone down. How magnificent was the sight from this height! The sea—the great, the glorious sea, that dashed its long waves against the coast—was stretched out before him. And yonder, where sea and sky meet, stood the sun, like a large shining altar, all melted together in the most glowing colors. And the wood and the sea sang a song of rejoicing, and his heart sang with the rest: all nature was a vast holy church, in which the trees and the buoyant clouds were the pillars, flowers and grass the velvet carpeting, and heaven itself the large cupola. The red colors above faded away as the sun vanished, but a million stars were lighted, a million lamps shone; and the King's Son spread out his arms towards heaven, and wood, and sea; when at the same moment, coming by a path to the right, appeared, in his wooden shoes and jacket, the poor boy who had been confirmed with him. He had followed his own path, and had reached the spot just as soon as the son of the king had done. They ran towards each other, and stood together hand in hand in the vast church of nature and of poetry, while over them sounded the invisible holy bell: blessed spirits floated around them, and lifted up their voices in a rejoicing hallelujah!

The Elderbush

Once upon a time there was a little boy who had taken cold. He had gone out and got his feet wet; though nobody could imagine how it had happened, for it was quite dry weather. So his mother undressed him, put him to bed, and had the tea-pot brought in, to make him a good cup of Elderflower tea. Just at that moment the merry old man came in who lived up a-top of the house all alone; for he had neither wife nor children—but he liked children very much, and knew so many fairy tales, that it was quite delightful.

"Now drink your tea," said the boy's mother; "then, perhaps, you may hear a fairy tale."

"If I had but something new to tell," said the old man. "But how did the child get his feet wet?"

"That is the very thing that nobody can make out," said his mother.

"Am I to hear a fairy tale?" asked the little boy.

"Yes, if you can tell me exactly—for I must know that first— how deep the gutter is in the little street opposite, that you pass through in going to school."

"Just up to the middle of my boot," said the child; "but then I must go into the deep hole."

"Ah, ah! That's where the wet feet came from," said the old man. "I ought now to tell you a story; but I don't know any more."

"You can make one in a moment," said the little boy. "My mother says that all you look at can be turned into a fairy tale: and that you can find a story in everything."

"Yes, but such tales and stories are good for nothing. The right sort come of themselves; they tap at my forehead and say, 'Here we are.'"

"Won't there be a tap soon?" asked the little boy. And his mother laughed, put some Elder-flowers in the tea-pot, and poured boiling water upon them.

"Do tell me something! Pray do!"

"Yes, if a fairy tale would come of its own accord; but they are proud and haughty, and come only when they choose. Stop!" said he, all on a sudden. "I have it! Pay attention! There is one in the tea-pot!"

And the little boy looked at the tea-pot. The cover rose more and more; and the Elder-flowers came forth so fresh and white, and shot up long branches. Out of the spout even did they spread themselves on all sides, and grew larger and larger; it was a splendid Elderbush, a whole tree; and it reached into the very bed, and pushed the curtains aside. How it bloomed! And what an odour! In the middle of the bush sat a friendly-looking old woman in a most strange dress. It was quite green, like the leaves of the elder, and was trimmed with large white Elder-flowers; so that at first one could not tell whether it was a stuff, or a natural green and real flowers.

"What's that woman's name?" asked the little boy.

"The Greeks and Romans," said the old man, "called her a Dryad; but that we do not understand. The people who live in the New Booths [a row of buildings for seamen in Copenhagen] have a much better name for her; they call her 'old Granny'—and she it is to whom you are to pay attention. Now listen, and look at the beautiful Elderbush.

"Just such another large blooming Elder Tree stands near the New Booths. It grew there in the corner of a little miserable court-yard; and under it sat, of an afternoon, in the most splendid sunshine, two old people; an old, old seaman, and his old, old wife. They had great-grand-children, and were soon to celebrate the fiftieth anniversary of their marriage; but they could not exactly recollect the date: and old Granny sat in the tree, and looked as pleased as now. 'I know the date,' said she; but those below did not hear her, for they were talking about old times.

"'Yes, can't you remember when we were very little,' said the old seaman, 'and ran and played about? It was the very same court-yard where we now are, and we stuck slips in the ground, and made a garden.'

"'I remember it well,' said the old woman; 'I remember it quite well. We watered the slips, and one of them was an Elderbush. It took root, put forth green shoots, and grew up to be the large tree under which we old folks are now sitting.'

"'To be sure,' said he. 'And there in the corner stood a water-pail, where I used to swim my boats.'

"'True; but first we went to school to learn somewhat,' said she; 'and then we were confirmed. We both cried; but in the afternoon we went up the Round Tower, and looked down on Copenhagen, and far, far away over the water; then we went to Friedericksberg, where the King and the Queen were sailing about in their splen-did barges.'

"'But I had a different sort of sailing to that, later; and that, too, for many a year; a long way off, on great voyages.'

"'Yes, many a time have I wept for your sake,' said she. 'I thought you were dead and gone, and lying down in the deep waters. Many a night have I got up to see if the wind had not changed: and changed it had, sure enough; but you never came. I remember so well one day, when the rain was pouring down in torrents, the scavengers were before the house where I was in ser-vice, and I had come up with the dust, and remained standing at the door—it was dreadful weather—when just as I was there, the postman came and gave me a letter. It was from you! What a tour that letter had made! I opened it instantly and read: I laughed and wept. I was so happy. In it I read that you were in warm lands where the coffee-tree grows. What a blessed land that must be! You related so much, and I saw it all the while the rain was pour-ing down, and I standing there with the dust-box. At the same moment came someone who embraced me.'

"'Yes; but you gave him a good box on his ear that made it tingle!'

"'But I did not know it was you. You arrived as soon as your letter, and you were so handsome—that you still are—and had a long yellow silk handkerchief round your neck, and a bran new hat on; oh, you were so dashing! Good heavens! What weather it was, and what a state the street was in!'

"'And then we married,' said he. 'Don't you remember? And then we had our first little boy, and then Mary, and Nicholas, and Peter, and Christian.'

"'Yes, and how they all grew up to be honest people, and were beloved by everybody.'

"'And their children also have children,' said the old sailor; 'yes, those are our grand-children, full of strength and vigor. It was, methinks about this season that we had our wedding.'

"'Yes, this very day is the fiftieth anniversary of the marriage,' said old Granny, sticking her head between the two old people; who thought it was their neighbor who nodded to them. They looked at each other and held one another by the hand. Soon after came their children, and their grand-children; for they knew well enough that it was the day of the fiftieth anniversary, and had come with their gratulations that very morning; but the old people had forgotten it, although they were able to remember all that had happened many years ago. And the Elderbush sent forth a strong odour in the sun, that was just about to set, and shone right in the old people's faces. They both looked so rosy-cheeked; and the youngest of the grandchildren danced around them, and called out quite delighted, that there was to be something very splendid that evening—they were all to have hot potatoes. And old Nanny nodded in the bush, and shouted 'hurrah!' with the rest."

"But that is no fairy tale," said the little boy, who was listening to the story.

"The thing is, you must understand it," said the narrator; "let us ask old Nanny."

"That was no fairy tale, 'tis true," said old Nanny; "but now it's coming. The most wonderful fairy tales grow out of that which is reality; were that not the case, you know, my magnificent Elder-bush could not have grown out of the tea-pot." And then she took the little boy out of bed, laid him on her bosom, and the branches of the Elder Tree, full of flowers, closed around her. They sat in an aerial dwelling, and it flew with them through the air. Oh, it was wondrous beautiful! Old Nanny had grown all of a sudden a young and pretty maiden; but her robe was still the same green stuff with white flowers, which she had worn before. On her bo-som she had a real Elderflower, and in her yellow waving hair a wreath of the flowers; her eyes were so large and blue that it was a pleasure to look at them; she kissed the boy, and now they were of the same age and felt alike.

Hand in hand they went out of the bower, and they were stand-ing in the beautiful garden of their home. Near the green lawn papa's walking-stick was tied, and for the little ones it seemed to be endowed with life; for as soon as they got astride it, the round polished knob was turned into a magnificent neighing head, a long black mane fluttered in the breeze, and four slender yet strong legs shot out. The animal was strong and handsome, and away they went at full gallop round the lawn.

"Huzza! Now we are riding miles off," said the boy. "We are rid-ing away to the castle where we were last year!"

And on they rode round the grass-plot; and the little maiden, who, we know, was no one else but old Nanny, kept on crying out, "Now we are in the country! Don't you see the farm-house yonder? And there is an Elder Tree standing beside it; and the cock is scraping away the earth for the hens, look, how he struts! And now we are close to the church. It lies high upon the hill, between the large oak-trees, one of which is half decayed. And now we are by the smithy, where the fire is blazing, and where the half-naked men are banging with their hammers till the sparks fly about. Away! away! To the beautiful country-seat!"

And all that the little maiden, who sat behind on the stick, spoke of, flew by in reality. The boy saw it all, and yet they were only going round the grass-plot. Then they played in a side avenue, and marked out a little garden on the earth; and they took Elder-blossoms from their hair, planted them, and they grew just like those the old people planted when they were children, as related before. They went hand in hand, as the old people had done when they were children; but not to the Round Tower, or to Friedericksberg; no, the little damsel wound her arms round the boy, and then they flew far away through all Denmark. And spring came, and summer; and then it was autumn, and then winter; and a thousand pictures were reflected in the eye and in the heart of the boy; and the little girl always sang to him, "This you will never forget." And during their whole flight the Elder Tree smelt so sweet and odorous; he remarked the roses and the fresh beeches, but the Elder Tree had a more wondrous fragrance, for its flowers hung on the breast of the little maiden; and there, too, did he often lay his head during the flight.

"It is lovely here in spring!" said the young maiden. And they stood in a beech-wood that had just put on its first green, where the woodroof at their feet sent forth its fragrance, and the pale-red anemony looked so pretty among the verdure. "Oh, would it were always spring in the sweetly-smelling Danish beech-forests!"

"It is lovely here in summer!" said she. And she flew past old castles of by-gone days of chivalry, where the red walls and the embattled gables were mirrored in the canal, where the swans were swimming, and peered up into the old cool avenues. In the fields the corn was waving like the sea; in the ditches red and yellow flowers were growing; while wild-drone flowers, and blooming convolvuluses were creeping in the hedges; and towards evening the moon rose round and large, and the haycocks in the meadows smelt so sweetly. "This one never forgets!"

"It is lovely here in autumn!" said the little maiden. And suddenly the atmosphere grew as blue again as before; the forest grew red, and green, and yellow-colored. The dogs came leaping along, and whole flocks of wild-fowl flew over the cairn, where blackberry-bushes were hanging round the old stones. The sea was dark blue, covered with ships full of white sails; and in the barn old women, maidens, and children were sitting picking hops into a large cask; the young sang songs, but the old told fairy tales of mountain-sprites and soothsayers. Nothing could be more charming.

"It is delightful here in winter!" said the little maiden. And all the trees were covered with hoar-frost; they looked like white corals; the snow crackled under foot, as if one had new boots on; and one falling star after the other was seen in the sky. The Christmas-tree was lighted in the room; presents were there, and good-humor reigned. In the country the violin sounded in the room of the peasant; the newly-baked cakes were attacked; even the poorest child said, "It is really delightful here in winter!"

Yes, it was delightful; and the little maiden showed the boy everything; and the Elder Tree still was fragrant, and the red flag, with the white cross, was still waving: the flag under which the old seaman in the New Booths had sailed. And the boy grew up to be a lad, and was to go forth in the wide world-far, far away to warm lands, where the coffee-tree grows; but at his departure the little maiden took an Elder-blossom from her bosom, and gave it him to keep; and it was placed between the leaves of his Prayer-Book; and when in foreign lands he opened the book, it was always at the place where the keepsake-flower lay; and the more he looked at it, the fresher it became; he felt as it were, the fragrance of the Danish groves; and from among the leaves of the flowers he could distinctly see the little maiden, peeping forth with her bright blue eyes—and then she whispered, "It is delightful here in Spring, Summer, Autumn, and Winter"; and a hundred visions glided before his mind.

Thus passed many years, and he was now an old man, and sat with his old wife under the blooming tree. They held each other by the hand, as the old grand-father and grand-mother yonder in the New Booths did, and they talked exactly like them of old times, and of the fiftieth anniversary of their wedding. The little maiden, with the blue eyes, and with Elder-blossoms in her hair, sat in the tree, nodded to both of them, and said, "To-day is the fiftieth anniversary!" And then she took two flowers out of her hair, and kissed them. First, they shone like silver, then like gold; and when they laid them on the heads of the old people, each flower became a golden crown. So there they both sat, like a king and a queen, under the fragrant tree, that looked exactly like an elder: the old man told his wife the story of "Old Nanny," as it had been told him when a boy. And it seemed to both of them it contained much that resembled their own history; and those parts that were like it pleased them best.

"Thus it is," said the little maiden in the tree, "some call me 'Old Nanny,' others a 'Dryad,' but, in reality, my name is 'Remembrance'; 'tis I who sit in the tree that grows and grows! I can remember; I can tell things! Let me see if you have my flower still?"

And the old man opened his Prayer-Book. There lay the Elder-blossom, as fresh as if it had been placed there but a short time before; and Remembrance nodded, and the old people, decked with crowns of gold, sat in the flush of the evening sun. They closed their eyes, and—and—! Yes, that's the end of the story!

The little boy lay in his bed; he did not know if he had dreamed or not, or if he had been listening while someone told him the story. The tea-pot was standing on the table, but no Elder Tree was growing out of it! And the old man, who had been talking, was just on the point of going out at the door, and he did go.

"How splendid that was!" said the little boy. "Mother, I have been to warm countries."

"So I should think," said his mother. "When one has drunk two good cupfuls of Elder-flower tea, 'tis likely enough one goes into warm climates"; and she tucked him up nicely, least he should take cold. "You have had a good sleep while I have been sitting here, and arguing with him whether it was a story or a fairy tale."

"And where is old Nanny?" asked the little boy.

"In the tea-pot," said his mother; "and there she may remain."

The Leap-Frog

A Flea, a Grasshopper, and a Leap-frog once wanted to see which could jump highest; and they invited the whole world, and everybody else besides who chose to come to see the festival. Three famous jumpers were they, as everyone would say, when they all met together in the room.

"I will give my daughter to him who jumps highest," exclaimed the King; "for it is not so amusing where there is no prize to jump for."

The Flea was the first to step forward. He had exquisite manners, and bowed to the company on all sides; for he had noble blood, and was, moreover, accustomed to the society of man alone; and that makes a great difference.

Then came the Grasshopper. He was considerably heavier, but he was well-mannered, and wore a green uniform, which he had by right of birth; he said, moreover, that he belonged to a very ancient Egyptian family, and that in the house where he then was, he was thought much of. The fact was, he had been just brought out of the fields, and put in a pasteboard house, three stories high, all made of court-cards, with the colored side inwards; and doors and windows cut out of the body of the Queen of Hearts. "I sing so well," said he, "that sixteen native grasshoppers who have chirped from infancy, and yet got no house built of cards to live in, grew thinner than they were before for sheer vexation when they heard me."

It was thus that the Flea and the Grasshopper gave an account of themselves, and thought they were quite good enough to marry a Princess.

The Leap-frog said nothing; but people gave it as their opinion, that he therefore thought the more; and when the housedog snuffed at him with his nose, he confessed the Leap-frog was of good family. The old councillor, who had had three orders given him to make him hold his tongue, asserted that the Leap-frog was a prophet; for that one could see on his back, if there would be a severe or mild winter, and that was what one could not see even on the back of the man who writes the almanac.

"I say nothing, it is true," exclaimed the King; "but I have my own opinion, notwithstanding."

Now the trial was to take place. The Flea jumped so high that nobody could see where he went to; so they all asserted he had not jumped at all; and that was dishonorable.

The Grasshopper jumped only half as high; but he leaped into the King's face, who said that was ill-mannered.

The Leap-frog stood still for a long time lost in thought; it was believed at last he would not jump at all.

"I only hope he is not unwell," said the house-dog; when, pop! he made a jump all on one side into the lap of the Princess, who was sitting on a little golden stool close by.

Hereupon the King said, "There is nothing above my daughter; therefore to bound up to her is the highest jump that can be made; but for this, one must possess understanding, and the Leap-frog has shown that he has understanding. He is brave and intellectual."

And so he won the Princess.

"It's all the same to me," said the Flea. "She may have the old Leap-frog, for all I care. I jumped the highest; but in this world merit seldom meets its reward. A fine exterior is what people look at now-a-days."

The Flea then went into foreign service, where, it is said, he was killed.

The Grasshopper sat without on a green bank, and reflected on worldly things; and he said too, "Yes, a fine exterior is everything—a fine exterior is what people care about." And then he began chirping his peculiar melancholy song, from which we have taken this history; and which may, very possibly, be all untrue, although it does stand here printed in black and white.

The Naughty Boy

Along time ago, there lived an old poet, a thoroughly kind old poet. As he was sitting one evening in his room, a dreadful storm arose without, and the rain streamed down from heaven; but the old poet sat warm and comfortable in his chimney-corner, where the fire blazed and the roasting apple hissed.

"Those who have not a roof over their heads will be wetted to the skin," said the good old poet.

"Oh let me in! Let me in! I am cold, and I'm so wet!" exclaimed suddenly a child that stood crying at the door and knocking for admittance, while the rain poured down, and the wind made all the windows rattle.

"Poor thing!" said the old poet, as he went to open the door. There stood a little boy, quite naked, and the water ran down from his long golden hair; he trembled with cold, and had he not come into a warm room he would most certainly have perished in the frightful tempest.

"Poor child!" said the old poet, as he took the boy by the hand. "Come in, come in, and I will soon restore thee! Thou shalt have wine and roasted apples, for thou art verily a charming child!" And the boy was so really. His eyes were like two bright stars; and although the water trickled down his hair, it waved in beautiful curls. He looked exactly like a little angel, but he was so pale, and his whole body trembled with cold. He had a nice little bow in his hand, but it was quite spoiled by the rain, and the tints of his many-colored arrows ran one into the other.

The old poet seated himself beside his hearth, and took the little fellow on his lap; he squeezed the water out of his dripping hair, warmed his hands between his own, and boiled for him some sweet wine. Then the boy recovered, his cheeks again grew rosy, he jumped down from the lap where he was sitting, and danced round the kind old poet.

"You are a merry fellow," said the old man. "What's your name?"

"My name is Cupid," answered the boy. "Don't you know me? There lies my bow; it shoots well, I can assure you! Look, the weather is now clearing up, and the moon is shining clear again through the window."

"Why, your bow is quite spoiled," said the old poet.

"That were sad indeed," said the boy, and he took the bow in his hand and examined it on every side. "Oh, it is dry again, and is not hurt at all; the string is quite tight. I will try it directly." And he bent his bow, took aim, and shot an arrow at the old poet, right into his heart. "You see now that my bow was not spoiled," said he laughing; and away he ran.

The naughty boy, to shoot the old poet in that way; he who had taken him into his warm room, who had treated him so kindly, and who had given him warm wine and the very best apples!

The poor poet lay on the earth and wept, for the arrow had really flown into his heart.

"Fie!" said he. "How naughty a boy Cupid is! I will tell all children about him, that they may take care and not play with him, for he will only cause them sorrow and many a heartache."

And all good children to whom he related this story, took great heed of this naughty Cupid; but he made fools of them still, for he is astonishingly cunning. When the university students come from the lectures, he runs beside them in a black coat, and with a book under his arm. It is quite impossible for them to know him, and they walk along with him arm in arm, as if he, too, were a student like themselves; and then, unperceived, he thrusts an arrow to their bosom. When the young maidens come from being examined by the clergyman, or go to church to be confirmed, there he is again close behind them. Yes, he is forever following people. At the play, he sits in the great chandelier and burns in bright flames, so that people think it is really a flame, but they soon discover it is something else. He roves about in the garden of the palace and upon the ramparts: yes, once he even shot your father and mother right in the heart. Ask them only and you will hear what they'll tell you. Oh, he is a naughty boy, that Cupid; you must never have anything to do with him. He is forever running after everybody. Only think, he shot an arrow once at your old grandmother! But that is a long time ago, and it is all past now; however, a thing of that sort she never forgets. Fie, naughty Cupid! But now you know him, and you know, too, how ill-behaved he is!

The Storks

On the last house in a little village stood a stork's nest. The Mother Stork sat in it with her four young ones, who stretched out their heads with the pointed black beaks, for their beaks had not yet turned red. A little way off stood the Father Stork, all alone on the ridge of the roof, quite upright and stiff; he had drawn up one of his legs, so as not to be quite idle while he stood sentry. One would have thought he had been carved out of wood, so still did he stand. He thought, "It must look very grand, that my wife has a sentry standing by her nest. They can't tell that it is her husband. They certainly think I have been commanded to stand here. That looks so aristocratic!" And he went on standing on one leg.

Below in the street a whole crowd of children were playing; and when they caught sight of the Storks, one of the boldest of the boys, and afterwards all of them, sang the old verse about the Storks. But they only sang it just as he could remember it:— "The first he will be hanged,

"The first he will be hanged,
"Stork, stork, long-legged stork;
Off to thy home I prithee walk.
Thy dear wife is in the nest,
Where she rocks her young to rest.
The second will be hit,
The third he will be shot,
And the fourth put on the spit."

"Just hear what those boys are saying!" said the little Stork children. "They say we're to be hanged and killed."

"You're not to care for that!" said the Mother Stork. "Don't listen to it, and then it won't matter."

But the boys went on singing, and pointed at the Storks

206

mockingly with their fingers; only one boy, whose name was Peter, declared that it was a sin to make a jest of animals, and he would not join in it at all.

The Mother Stork comforted her children. "Don't you mind it at all," she said; "see how quiet your father stands, though it's only on one leg."

"We are very much afraid," said the young Storks; and they drew their heads far back into the nest.

Now to-day, when the children came out again to play, and saw the Storks, they sang their song,—

"The first he will be hanged,
The second will be hit."

"Shall we be hanged and beaten?" asked the young Storks.

"No, certainly not," replied the mother. "You shall learn to fly; I'll exercise you; then we shall fly into the meadows and pay a visit to the frogs; they will bow before us in the water, and sing 'Co-ax! co-ax!' and then we shall eat them up. That will be a real pleasure."

"And what then?" asked the young Storks.

"Then all the Storks will assemble, all that are here in the whole country, and the autumn exercises begin: then one must fly well, for that is highly important, for whoever cannot fly properly will be thrust dead by the general's beak; so take care and learn well when the exercising begins."

"But then we shall be killed, as the boys say—and only listen, now they're singing again."

"Listen to me, and not to them," said the Mother Stork. "After the great review we shall fly away to the warm countries, far away from here, over mountains and forests. We shall fly to Egypt, where there are three covered houses of stone, which curl in a point and tower above the clouds; they are called pyramids, and are older than a stork can imagine. There is a river in that country which runs out of its bed, and then all the land is turned to mud. One walks about in the mud, and eats frogs."

"O!" cried all the young ones.

"Yes! It is glorious there! One does nothing all day long but eat; and while we are so comfortable over there, here there is not a green leaf on the trees; here it is so cold that the clouds freeze to pieces, and fall down in little white rags!"

It was the snow that she meant, but she could not explain it in any other way.

"And do the naughty boys freeze to pieces?" asked the young Storks.

"No, they don't freeze to pieces; but they are not far from it, and must sit in the dark room and cower. You, on the other hand, can fly about in foreign lands, where there are flowers, and the sun shines warm."

Now some time had elapsed, and the nestlings had grown so large that they could stand upright in the nest and look far around; and the Father Stork came every day with delicious frogs, little snakes, and all kinds of stork-dainties as he found them. O! it looked funny when he performed feats before them. He laid his head quite back upon his tail, and clapped with his beak as if he had been a little clapper; and then he told them stories, all about the marshes.

"Listen! now you must learn to fly," said the Mother Stork one day; and all the four young ones had to go out on the ridge of the roof. O, how they tottered! how they balanced themselves with their wings, and yet they were nearly falling down.

"Only look at me," said the mother. "Thus you must hold your heads! Thus you must pitch your feet! One, two! one, two! That's what will help you on in the world."

Then she flew a little way, and the young ones made a little clumsy leap. Bump!—there they lay, for their bodies were too heavy.

"I will not fly!" said one of the young Storks, and crept back into the nest. "I don't care about getting to the warm countries."

"Do you want to freeze to death here, when the winter comes? Are the boys to come and hang you, and singe you, and roast you? Now I'll call them."

"O no!" cried the young Stork, and hopped out on to the roof again like the rest.

On the third day they could actually fly a little, and then they thought they could also soar and hover in the air. They tried it, but—bump!—down they tumbled, and they had to shoot their wings again quickly enough. Now the boys came into the street again and sang their song,—

"Stork, stork, long-legged stork!"

"Shall we fly down and pick their eyes out?" asked the young Storks.

"No," replied the mother, "let them alone. Only listen to me; that's far more important. One, two, three!—now we fly round to the right. One, two, three!—now to the left round the chimney! See, that was very good! the last kick with the feet was so neat and correct that you shall have permission to-morrow to fly with me to the marsh! Several nice Stork families go there with their young: show them that mine are the nicest, and that you can start proudly; that looks well, and will get you consideration."

"But are we not to take revenge on the rude boys?" asked the young Storks.

"Let them scream as much as they like. You will fly up to the clouds, and get to the land of the pyramids, when they will have to shiver, and not have a green leaf or a sweet apple."

"Yes, we will revenge ourselves!" they whispered to one another; and then the exercising went on.

Among all the boys down in the street, the one most bent upon singing the teasing song was he who had begun it, and he was quite a little boy. He could hardly be more than six years old. The young Storks certainly thought he was a hundred, for he was much bigger than their mother and father; and how should they know how old children and grown-up people can be! Their revenge was to come upon this boy, for it was he who had begun, and he always kept on. The young Storks were very angry; and as they grew bigger they were less inclined to bear it: at last their mother had to promise them that they should be revenged, but not till the last day of their stay.

"We must first see how you behave at the grand review. If you get through badly, so that the general stabs you through the chest with his beak, the boys will be right, at least in one way. Let us see."

"Yes, you shall see!" cried the young Storks; and then they took all imaginable pains. They practiced every day, and flew so neatly and so lightly that it was a pleasure to see them.

Now the autumn came on; all the Storks began to assemble, to fly away to the warm countries while it is winter here. That was a review. They had to fly over forests and villages, to show how well they could soar, for it was a long journey they had before them. The young Storks did their parts so well that they got as a mark, "Remarkably well, with frogs and snakes." That was the highest mark; and they might eat the frogs and snakes; and that is what they did.

"Now we will be revenged!" they said.

"Yes, certainly!" said the Mother Stork. "What I have thought of will be the best. I know the pond in which all the little mortals lie till the stork comes and brings them to their parents. The pretty little babies lie there and dream so sweetly as they never dream afterwards. All parents are glad to have such a child, and all children want to have a sister or a brother. Now we will fly to the pond, and bring one for each of the children who have not sung the naughty song and laughed at the Storks."

"But he who began to sing,—that naughty, ugly boy!" screamed the young Storks; "what shall we do with him?"

"There is a little dead child in the pond, one that has dreamed itself to death; we will bring that for him. Then he will cry because we have brought him a little dead brother. But that good boy—you have not forgotten him, the one who said, "It is wrong to laugh at animals!'—for him we will bring a brother and a sister too. And as his name is Peter, all of you shall be called Peter too."

And it was done as she said; all the storks were named Peter, and so they are all called even now.

The Old House

In the street, up there, was an old, a very old house—it was almost three hundred years old, for that might be known by reading the great beam on which the date of the year was carved: together with tulips and hop-binds there were whole verses spelled as in former times, and over every window was a distorted face cut out in the beam. The one story stood forward a great way over the other; and directly under the eaves was a leaden spout with a dragon's head; the rain-water should have run out of the mouth, but it ran out of the belly, for there was a hole in the spout.

All the other houses in the street were so new and so neat, with large window panes and smooth walls, one could easily see that they would have nothing to do with the old house: they certainly thought, "How long is that old decayed thing to stand here as a spectacle in the street? And then the projecting windows stand so far out, that no one can see from our windows what happens in that direction! The steps are as broad as those of a palace, and as high as to a church tower. The iron railings look just like the door to an old family vault, and then they have brass tops—that's so stupid!"

On the other side of the street were also new and neat houses, and they thought just as the others did; but at the window opposite the old house there sat a little boy with fresh rosy cheeks and bright beaming eyes: he certainly liked the old house best, and that both in sunshine and moonshine. And when he looked across at the wall where the mortar had fallen out, he could sit and find out there the strangest figures imaginable; exactly as the street had appeared before, with steps, projecting windows, and pointed gables; he could see soldiers with halberds, and spouts where the water ran, like dragons and serpents. That was a house to look at; and there lived an old man, who wore plush breeches; and he had a coat with large brass buttons, and a wig that one could see was a real wig. Every morning there came an old fellow to him who put his rooms in order, and went on errands; otherwise, the old man in the plush breeches was quite alone in the old house. Now and then he came to the window and looked out, and the little boy nodded to him, and the old man nodded again, and so they became acquaintances, and then they were friends, although they had never spoken to each other—but that made no difference. The little boy heard his parents say, "The old man opposite is very well off, but he is so very, very lonely!"

The Sunday following, the little boy took something, and wrapped it up in a piece of paper, went downstairs, and stood in the doorway; and when the man who went on errands came past, he said to him—

"I say, master! will you give this to the old man over the way from me? I have two pewter soldiers—this is one of them, and he shall have it, for I know he is so very, very lonely."

And the old errand man looked quite pleased, nodded, and took the pewter soldier over to the old house. Afterwards there came a message; it was to ask if the little boy himself had not a wish to come over and pay a visit; and so he got permission of his parents, and then went over to the old house.

And the brass balls on the iron railings shone much brighter than ever; one would have thought they were polished on account of the visit; and it was as if the carved-out trumpeters—for there were trumpeters, who stood in tulips, carved out on the door—blew with all their might, their cheeks appeared so much rounder than before. Yes, they blew—"Trateratra! The little boy comes! Trateratra!"—and then the door opened.

The whole passage was hung with portraits of knights in armor, and ladies in silken gowns; and the armor rattled, and the silken gowns rustled! And then there was a flight of stairs which went a good way upwards, and a little way downwards, and then one came on a balcony which was in a very dilapidated state, sure enough, with large holes and long crevices, but grass grew there and leaves out of them altogether, for the whole balcony outside, the yard, and the walls, were overgrown with so much green stuff, that it looked like a garden; only a balcony. Here stood old flower-pots with faces and asses' ears, and the flowers grew just as they liked. One of the pots was quite overrun on all sides with pinks, that is to say, with the green part; shoot stood by shoot, and it said quite distinctly, "The air has cherished me, the sun has kissed me, and promised me a little flower on Sunday! a little flower on Sunday!"

And then they entered a chamber where the walls were covered with hog's leather, and printed with gold flowers.

"The gilding decays,　But hog's leather stays!" said the walls.

And there stood easy-chairs, with such high backs, and so carved out, and with arms on both sides. "Sit down! sit down!" said they. "Ugh! how I creak; now I shall certainly get the gout, like the old clothespress, ugh!"

And then the little boy came into the room where the projecting windows were, and where the old man sat.

"I thank you for the pewter soldier, my little friend!" said the old man. "And I thank you because you come over to me."

"Thankee! thankee!" or "cranky! cranky!" sounded from all the furniture; there was so much of it, that each article stood in the other's way, to get a look at the little boy.

In the middle of the wall hung a picture representing a beautiful lady, so young, so glad, but dressed quite as in former times, with clothes that stood quite stiff, and with powder in her hair; she neither said "thankee, thankee!" nor "cranky, cranky!" but looked with her mild eyes at the little boy, who directly asked the old man, "Where did you get her?"

"Yonder, at the broker's," said the old man, "where there are so many pictures hanging. No one knows or cares about them, for they are all of them buried; but I knew her in by-gone days, and now she has been dead and gone these fifty years!"

Under the picture, in a glazed frame, there hung a bouquet of withered flowers; they were almost fifty years old; they looked so very old!

The pendulum of the great clock went to and fro, and the hands turned, and everything in the room became still older; but they did not observe it.

"They say at home," said the little boy, "that you are so very, very lonely!"

"Oh!" said he. "The old thoughts, with what they may bring with them, come and visit me, and now you also come! I am very well off!"

Then he took a book with pictures in it down from the shelf; there were whole long processions and pageants, with the strangest characters, which one never sees now-a-days; soldiers like the knave of clubs, and citizens with waving flags: the tailors had theirs, with a pair of shears held by two lions—and the shoemakers theirs, without boots, but with an eagle that had two heads, for the shoemakers must have everything so that they can say, it is a pair! Yes, that was a picture book!

The old man now went into the other room to fetch preserves, apples, and nuts—yes, it was delightful over there in the old house.

"I cannot bear it any longer!" said the pewter soldier, who sat on the drawers. "It is so lonely and melancholy here! But when one has been in a family circle one cannot accustom oneself to this life! I cannot bear it any longer! The whole day is so long, and the evenings are still longer! Here it is not at all as it is over the way at your home, where your father and mother spoke so pleasantly, and where you and all your sweet children made such a delightful noise. Nay, how lonely the old man is—do you think that he gets kisses? Do you think he gets mild eyes, or a Christmas tree? He will get nothing but a grave! I can bear it no longer!"

"You must not let it grieve you so much," said the little boy. "I find it so very delightful here, and then all the old thoughts, with what they may bring with them, they come and visit here."

"Yes, it's all very well, but I see nothing of them, and I don't know them!" said the pewter soldier. "I cannot bear it!"

"But you must!" said the little boy.

Then in came the old man with the most pleased and happy face, the most delicious preserves, apples, and nuts, and so the little boy thought no more about the pewter soldier.

The little boy returned home happy and pleased, and weeks and days passed away, and nods were made to the old house, and from the old house, and then the little boy went over there again.

The carved trumpeters blew, "Trateratra! There is the little boy! Trateratra!" and the swords and armor on the knights' portraits rattled, and the silk gowns rustled; the hog's leather spoke, and the old chairs had the gout in their legs and rheumatism in their backs: Ugh! it was exactly like the first time, for over there one day and hour was just like another.

"I cannot bear it!" said the pewter soldier. "I have shed pewter tears! It is too melancholy! Rather let me go to the wars and lose arms and legs! It would at least be a change. I cannot bear it longer! Now, I know what it is to have a visit from one's old thoughts, with what they may bring with them! I have had a visit from mine, and you may be sure it is no pleasant thing in the end; I was at last about to jump down from the drawers.

"I saw you all over there at home so distinctly, as if you really were here; it was again that Sunday morning; all you children stood before the table and sung your Psalms, as you do every morning. You stood devoutly with folded hands; and father and mother were just as pious; and then the door was opened, and little sister Mary, who is not two years old yet, and who always dances when she hears music or singing, of whatever kind it may be, was put into the room—though she ought not to have been there—and then she began to dance, but could not keep time, because the tones were so long; and then she stood, first on the one leg, and bent her head forwards, and then on the other leg, and bent her head forwards—but all would not do. You stood very seriously all together, although it was difficult enough; but I laughed to myself, and then I fell off the table, and got a bump, which I have still—for it was not right of me to laugh. But the whole now passes before me again in thought, and everything that I have lived to see; and these are the old thoughts, with what they may bring with them.

"Tell me if you still sing on Sundays? Tell me something about little Mary! And how my comrade, the other pewter soldier, lives! Yes, he is happy enough, that's sure! I cannot bear it any longer!"

"You are given away as a present!" said the little boy. "You must remain. Can you not understand that?"

The old man now came with a drawer, in which there was much to be seen, both "tin boxes" and "balsam boxes," old cards, so large and so gilded, such as one never sees them now. And several drawers were opened, and the piano was opened; it had landscapes on the inside of the lid, and it was so hoarse when the old man played on it! and then he hummed a song.

"Yes, she could sing that!" said he, and nodded to the portrait, which he had bought at the broker's, and the old man's eyes shone so bright!

"I will go to the wars! I will go to the wars!" shouted the pewter soldier as loud as he could, and threw himself off the drawers right down on the floor. What became of him? The old man sought, and the little boy sought; he was away, and he stayed away.

"I shall find him!" said the old man; but he never found him. The floor was too open—the pewter soldier had fallen through a crevice, and there he lay as in an open tomb.

That day passed, and the little boy went home, and that week passed, and several weeks too. The windows were quite frozen, the little boy was obliged to sit and breathe on them to get a peep-hole over to the old house, and there the snow had been blown into all the carved work and inscriptions; it lay quite up over the steps, just as if there was no one at home—nor was there any one at home—the old man was dead!

In the evening there was a hearse seen before the door, and he was borne into it in his coffin: he was now to go out into the country, to lie in his grave. He was driven out there, but no one followed; all his friends were dead, and the little boy kissed his hand to the coffin as it was driven away.

Some days afterwards there was an auction at the old house, and the little boy saw from his window how they carried the old knights and the old ladies away, the flower-pots with the long ears, the old chairs, and the old clothes-presses. Something came here, and something came there; the portrait of her who had been found at the broker's came to the broker's again; and there it hung, for no one knew her more—no one cared about the old picture.

In the spring they pulled the house down, for, as people said, it was a ruin. One could see from the street right into the room with the hog's-leather hanging, which was slashed and torn; and the green grass and leaves about the balcony hung quite wild about the falling beams. And then it was put to rights.

"That was a relief," said the neighboring houses.

A fine house was built there, with large windows, and smooth white walls; but before it, where the old house had in fact stood, was a little garden laid out, and a wild grapevine ran up the wall of the neighboring house. Before the garden there was a large iron railing with an iron door, it looked quite splendid, and people stood still and peeped in, and the sparrows hung by scores in the vine, and chattered away at each other as well as they could, but it was not about the old house, for they could not remember it, so many years had passed—so many that the little boy had grown up to a whole man, yes, a clever man, and a pleasure to his parents; and he had just been married, and, together with his little wife, had come to live in the house here, where the garden was; and he stood by her there whilst she planted a field-flower that she found so pretty; she planted it with her little hand, and pressed the earth around it with her fingers. Oh! what was that? She had stuck herself. There sat something pointed, straight out of the soft mould.

It was—yes, guess! It was the pewter soldier, he that was lost up at the old man's, and had tumbled and turned about amongst the timber and the rubbish, and had at last laid for many years in the ground.

The young wife wiped the dirt off the soldier, first with a green leaf, and then with her fine handkerchief—it had such a delightful smell, that it was to the pewter soldier just as if he had awaked from a trance.

"Let me see him," said the young man. He laughed, and then shook his head. "Nay, it cannot be he; but he reminds me of a story about a pewter soldier which I had when I was a little boy!" And then he told his wife about the old house, and the old man, and about the pewter soldier that he sent over to him because he was so very, very lonely; and he told it as correctly as it had really been, so that the tears came into the eyes of his young wife, on account of the old house and the old man.

"It may possibly be, however, that it is the same pewter soldier!" said she. "I will take care of it, and remember all that you have told me; but you must show me the old man's grave!"

"But I do not know it," said he, "and no one knows it! All his friends were dead, no one took care of it, and I was then a little boy!"

"How very, very lonely he must have been!" said she.

"Very, very lonely!" said the pewter soldier. "But it is delightful not to be forgotten!"

"Delightful!" shouted something close by; but no one, except the pewter soldier, saw that it was a piece of the hog's-leather hangings; it had lost all its gilding, it looked like a piece of wet clay, but it had an opinion, and it gave it:

"The gilding decays,   But hog's leather stays!"

This the pewter soldier did not believe.

The Shoes of Fortune

I. A Beginning~

Every author has some peculiarity in his descriptions or in his style of writing. Those who do not like him, magnify it, shrug up their shoulders, and exclaim—there he is again! I, for my part, know very well how I can bring about this movement and this exclamation. It would happen immediately if I were to begin here, as I intended to do, with: "Rome has its Corso, Naples its Toledo"—"Ah! that Andersen; there he is again!" they would cry; yet I must, to please my fancy, continue quite quietly, and add: "But Copenhagen has its East Street."

Here, then, we will stay for the present. In one of the houses not far from the new market a party was invited—a very large party, in order, as is often the case, to get a return invitation from the others. One half of the company was already seated at the card-table, the other half awaited the result of the stereotype preliminary observation of the lady of the house:

"Now let us see what we can do to amuse ourselves."

They had got just so far, and the conversation began to crystallise, as it could but do with the scanty stream which the commonplace world supplied. Amongst other things they spoke of the middle ages: some praised that period as far more interesting, far more poetical than our own too sober present; indeed Councillor Knap defended this opinion so warmly, that the hostess declared immediately on his side, and both exerted themselves with unwearied eloquence. The Councillor boldly declared the time of King Hans to be the noblest and the most happy period.

(A.D. 1482-1513)

While the conversation turned on this subject, and was only for a moment interrupted by the arrival of a journal that con-

220

tained nothing worth reading, we will just step out into the antechamber, where cloaks, mackintoshes, sticks, umbrellas, and shoes, were deposited. Here sat two female figures, a young and an old one. One might have thought at first they were servants come to accompany their mistresses home; but on looking nearer, one soon saw they could scarcely be mere servants; their forms were too noble for that, their skin too fine, the cut of their dress too striking. Two fairies were they; the younger, it is true, was not Dame Fortune herself, but one of the waiting-maids of her handmaidens who carry about the lesser good things that she distributes; the other looked extremely gloomy—it was Care. She always attends to her own serious business herself, as then she is sure of having it done properly.

They were telling each other, with a confidential interchange of ideas, where they had been during the day. The messenger of Fortune had only executed a few unimportant commissions, such as saving a new bonnet from a shower of rain, etc.; but what she had yet to perform was something quite unusual.

"I must tell you," said she, "that to-day is my birthday; and in honor of it, a pair of walking-shoes or galoshes has been entrusted to me, which I am to carry to mankind. These shoes possess the property of instantly transporting him who has them on to the place or the period in which he most wishes to be; every wish, as regards time or place, or state of being, will be immediately fulfilled, and so at last man will be happy, here below."

"Do you seriously believe it?" replied Care, in a severe tone of reproach. "No; he will be very unhappy, and will assuredly bless the moment when he feels that he has freed himself from the fatal shoes."

"Stupid nonsense!" said the other angrily. "I will put them here by the door. Some one will make a mistake for certain and take the wrong ones—he will be a happy man."

Such was their conversation.

II. What Happened to the Councillor~

It was late; Councillor Knap, deeply occupied with the times of King Hans, intended to go home, and malicious Fate managed matters so that his feet, instead of finding their way to his own galoshes, slipped into those of Fortune. Thus caparisoned the good man walked out of the well-lighted rooms into East Street. By the magic power of the shoes he was carried back to the times of King Hans; on which account his foot very naturally sank in the mud and puddles of the street, there having been in those days no pavement in Copenhagen.

"Well! This is too bad! How dirty it is here!" sighed the Councillor. "As to a pavement, I can find no traces of one, and all the lamps, it seems, have gone to sleep."

The moon was not yet very high; it was besides rather foggy, so that in the darkness all objects seemed mingled in chaotic confusion. At the next corner hung a votive lamp before a Madonna, but the light it gave was little better than none at all; indeed, he did not observe it before he was exactly under it, and his eyes fell upon the bright colors of the pictures which represented the well-known group of the Virgin and the infant Jesus.

"That is probably a wax-work show," thought he; "and the people delay taking down their sign in hopes of a late visitor or two."

A few persons in the costume of the time of King Hans passed quickly by him.

"How strange they look! The good folks come probably from a masquerade!"

Suddenly was heard the sound of drums and fifes; the bright blaze of a fire shot up from time to time, and its ruddy gleams seemed to contend with the bluish light of the torches. The Councillor stood still, and watched a most strange procession pass by. First came a dozen drummers, who understood pretty well how to handle their instruments; then came halberdiers, and some armed with cross-bows. The principal person in the pro-

222

cession was a priest. Astonished at what he saw, the Councillor asked what was the meaning of all this mummery, and who that man was.

"That's the Bishop of Zealand," was the answer.

"Good Heavens! What has taken possession of the Bishop?" sighed the Councillor, shaking his head. It certainly could not be the Bishop; even though he was considered the most absent man in the whole kingdom, and people told the drollest anecdotes about him. Reflecting on the matter, and without looking right or left, the Councillor went through East Street and across the Habro-Platz. The bridge leading to Palace Square was not to be found; scarcely trusting his senses, the nocturnal wanderer discovered a shallow piece of water, and here fell in with two men who very comfortably were rocking to and fro in a boat.

"Does your honor want to cross the ferry to the Holme?" asked they.

"Across to the Holme!" said the Councillor, who knew nothing of the age in which he at that moment was. "No, I am going to Christianshafen, to Little Market Street."

Both men stared at him in astonishment.

"Only just tell me where the bridge is," said he. "It is really unpardonable that there are no lamps here; and it is as dirty as if one had to wade through a morass."

The longer he spoke with the boatmen, the more unintelligible did their language become to him.

"I don't understand your Bornholmish dialect," said he at last, angrily, and turning his back upon them. He was unable to find the bridge: there was no railway either. "It is really disgraceful what a state this place is in," muttered he to himself. Never had his age, with which, however, he was always grumbling, seemed so miserable as on this evening. "I'll take a hackney-coach!" thought he. But where were the hackney-coaches? Not one was to be seen.

"I must go back to the New Market; there, it is to be hoped,

I shall find some coaches; for if I don't, I shall never get safe to Christianshafen."

So off he went in the direction of East Street, and had nearly got to the end of it when the moon shone forth.

"God bless me! What wooden scaffolding is that which they have set up there?" cried he involuntarily, as he looked at East Gate, which, in those days, was at the end of East Street.

He found, however, a little side-door open, and through this he went, and stepped into our New Market of the present time. It was a huge desolate plain; some wild bushes stood up here and there, while across the field flowed a broad canal or river. Some wretched hovels for the Dutch sailors, resembling great boxes, and after which the place was named, lay about in confused disorder on the opposite bank.

"I either behold a fata morgana, or I am regularly tipsy," whimpered out the Councillor. "But what's this?"

He turned round anew, firmly convinced that he was seriously ill. He gazed at the street formerly so well known to him, and now so strange in appearance, and looked at the houses more attentively: most of them were of wood, slightly put together; and many had a thatched roof.

"No—I am far from well," sighed he; "and yet I drank only one glass of punch; but I cannot suppose it—it was, too, really very wrong to give us punch and hot salmon for supper. I shall speak about it at the first opportunity. I have half a mind to go back again, and say what I suffer. But no, that would be too silly; and Heaven only knows if they are up still."

He looked for the house, but it had vanished.

"It is really dreadful," groaned he with increasing anxiety; "I cannot recognise East Street again; there is not a single decent shop from one end to the other! Nothing but wretched huts can I see anywhere; just as if I were at Ringstead. Oh! I am ill! I can scarcely bear myself any longer. Where the deuce can the house be? It must be here on this very spot; yet there is not the slightest idea of resemblance, to such a degree has everything changed this night! At all events here are some people up and stirring. Oh! oh! I am certainly very ill."

He now hit upon a half-open door, through a chink of which a faint light shone. It was a sort of hostelry of those times; a kind of public-house. The room had some resemblance to the clay-floored halls in Holstein; a pretty numerous company, consisting of seamen, Copenhagen burghers, and a few scholars, sat here in deep converse over their pewter cans, and gave little heed to the person who entered.

"By your leave!" said the Councillor to the Hostess, who came bustling towards him. "I've felt so queer all of a sudden; would you have the goodness to send for a hackney-coach to take me to Christianshafen?"

The woman examined him with eyes of astonishment, and shook her head; she then addressed him in German. The Councillor thought she did not understand Danish, and therefore repeated his wish in German. This, in connection with his costume, strengthened the good woman in the belief that he was a foreigner. That he was ill, she comprehended directly; so she brought him a pitcher of water, which tasted certainly pretty strong of the sea, although it had been fetched from the well.

The Councillor supported his head on his hand, drew a long breath, and thought over all the wondrous things he saw around him.

"Is this the Daily News of this evening?" he asked mechanically, as he saw the Hostess push aside a large sheet of paper.

The meaning of this councillorship query remained, of course, a riddle to her, yet she handed him the paper without replying. It was a coarse wood-cut, representing a splendid meteor "as seen in the town of Cologne," which was to be read below in bright letters.

"That is very old!" said the Councillor, whom this piece of antiquity began to make considerably more cheerful. "Pray how did you come into possession of this rare print? It is extremely interesting, although the whole is a mere fable. Such meteorous appearances are to be explained in this way—that they are the reflections of the Aurora Borealis, and it is highly probable they are caused principally by electricity."

Those persons who were sitting nearest him and heard his speech, stared at him in wonderment; and one of them rose, took off his hat respectfully, and said with a serious countenance, "You are no doubt a very learned man, Monsieur."

"Oh no," answered the Councillor, "I can only join in conversation on this topic and on that, as indeed one must do according to the demands of the world at present."

"Modestia is a fine virtue," continued the gentleman; "however, as to your speech, I must say mihi secus videtur: yet I am willing to suspend my judicium."

"May I ask with whom I have the pleasure of speaking?" asked the Councillor.

"I am a Bachelor in Theologia," answered the gentleman with a stiff reverence.

This reply fully satisfied the Councillor; the title suited the dress. "He is certainly," thought he, "some village schoolmaster—some queer old fellow, such as one still often meets with in Jutland."

"This is no locus docendi, it is true," began the clerical gentleman; "yet I beg you earnestly to let us profit by your learning. Your reading in the ancients is, sine dubio, of vast extent?"

"Oh yes, I've read something, to be sure," replied the Councillor. "I like reading all useful works; but I do not on that account despise the modern ones; 'tis only the unfortunate 'Tales of Every-day Life' that I cannot bear—we have enough and more than enough such in reality."

"'Tales of Every-day Life?'" said our Bachelor inquiringly.

"I mean those new fangled novels, twisting and writhing themselves in the dust of commonplace, which also expect to find a
reading public."

"Oh," exclaimed the clerical gentleman smiling, "there is much
wit in them; besides they are read at court. The King likes the history of Sir Iffven and Sir Gaudian particularly, which treats of
King Arthur, and his Knights of the Round Table; he has more
than once joked about it with his high vassals."

"I have not read that novel," said the Councillor; "it must be
quite a new one, that Heiberg has published lately."

"No," answered the theologian of the time of King Hans: "that
book is not written by a Heiberg, but was imprinted by Godfrey
von Gehmen."

"Oh, is that the author's name?" said the Councillor. "It is a
very old name, and, as well as I recollect, he was the first printer
that appeared in Denmark."

"Yes, he is our first printer," replied the clerical gentleman
hastily.

So far all went on well. Some one of the worthy burghers now
spoke of the dreadful pestilence that had raged in the country a
few years back, meaning that of 1484. The Councillor imagined
it was the cholera that was meant, which people made so much
fuss about; and the discourse passed off satisfactorily enough. The
war of the buccaneers of 1490 was so recent that it could not fail
being alluded to; the English pirates had, they said, most shame-
fully taken their ships while in the roadstead; and the Councillor,
before whose eyes the Herostratic event of 1801 still floated vividly, agreed entirely with the others in abusing the rascally English. With other topics he was not so fortunate; every moment
brought about some new confusion, and threatened to become
a perfect Babel; for the worthy Bachelor was really too ignorant,
and the simplest observations of the Councillor sounded to him
too daring and phantastical. They looked at one another from the
crown of the head to the soles of the feet; and when matters grew

to too high a pitch, then the Bachelor talked Latin, in the hope of being better understood—but it was of no use after all.

"What's the matter?" asked the Hostess, plucking the Councillor by the sleeve; and now his recollection returned, for in the course of the conversation he had entirely forgotten all that had preceded it.

"Merciful God, where am I!" exclaimed he in agony; and while he so thought, all his ideas and feelings of overpowering dizziness, against which he struggled with the utmost power of desperation, encompassed him with renewed force. "Let us drink claret and mead, and Bremen beer," shouted one of the guests—"and you shall drink with us!"

Two maidens approached. One wore a cap of two staring colors, denoting the class of persons to which she belonged. They poured out the liquor, and made the most friendly gesticulations; while a cold perspiration trickled down the back of the poor Councillor.

"What's to be the end of this! What's to become of me!" groaned he; but he was forced, in spite of his opposition, to drink with the rest. They took hold of the worthy man; who, hearing on every side that he was intoxicated, did not in the least doubt the truth of this certainly not very polite assertion; but on the contrary, implored the ladies and gentlemen present to procure him a hackney-coach: they, however, imagined he was talking Russian.

Never before, he thought, had he been in such a coarse and ignorant company; one might almost fancy the people had turned heathens again. "It is the most dreadful moment of my life: the whole world is leagued against me!" But suddenly it occurred to him that he might stoop down under the table, and then creep unobserved out of the door. He did so; but just as he was going, the others remarked what he was about; they laid hold of him by the legs; and now, happily for him, off fell his fatal shoes—and with them the charm was at an end.

The Councillor saw quite distinctly before him a lantern burning, and behind this a large handsome house. All seemed to him in proper order as usual; it was East Street, splendid and elegant as we now see it. He lay with his feet towards a doorway, and exactly opposite sat the watchman asleep.

"Gracious Heaven!" said he. "Have I lain here in the street and dreamed? Yes; 'tis East Street! How splendid and light it is! But really it is terrible what an effect that one glass of punch must have had on me!"

Two minutes later, he was sitting in a hackney-coach and driving to Frederickshafen. He thought of the distress and agony he had endured, and praised from the very bottom of his heart the happy reality—our own time—which, with all its deficiencies, is yet much better than that in which, so much against his inclination, he had lately been.

III. The Watchman's Adventure~

"Why, there is a pair of galoshes, as sure as I'm alive!" said the watchman, awaking from a gentle slumber. "They belong no doubt to the lieutenant who lives over the way. They lie close to the door."

The worthy man was inclined to ring and deliver them at the house, for there was still a light in the window; but he did not like disturbing the other people in their beds, and so very considerately he left the matter alone.

"Such a pair of shoes must be very warm and comfortable," said he; "the leather is so soft and supple." They fitted his feet as though they had been made for him. "'Tis a curious world we live in," continued he, soliloquizing. "There is the lieutenant, now, who might go quietly to bed if he chose, where no doubt he could stretch himself at his ease; but does he do it? No; he saunters up and down his room, because, probably, he has enjoyed too many of the good things of this world at his dinner. That's a happy fellow! He has neither an infirm mother, nor a whole troop of everlastingly hungry children to torment him. Every evening he goes to a party, where his nice supper costs him nothing: would to Heaven I could but change with him! How happy should I be!"

While expressing his wish, the charm of the shoes, which he had put on, began to work; the watchman entered into the being and nature of the lieutenant. He stood in the handsomely furnished apartment, and held between his fingers a small sheet of rose-colored paper, on which some verses were written—written indeed by the officer himself; for who has not, at least once in his life, had a lyrical moment? And if one then marks down one's thoughts, poetry is produced. But here was written:

OH, WERE I RICH!
"Oh, were I rich! Such was my wish, yea such
When hardly three feet high, I longed for much.
Oh, were I rich! an officer were I,
With sword, and uniform, and plume so high.
And the time came, and officer was I!
But yet I grew not rich. Alas, poor me!
Have pity, Thou, who all man's wants dost see.
"I sat one evening sunk in dreams of bliss,
A maid of seven years old gave me a kiss,
I at that time was rich in poesy
And tales of old, though poor as poor could be;
But all she asked for was this poesy.
Then was I rich, but not in gold, poor me!
As Thou dost know, who all men's hearts canst see.
"Oh, were I rich! Oft asked I for this boon.
The child grew up to womanhood full soon.
She is so pretty, clever, and so kind
Oh, did she know what's hidden in my mind—

A tale of old. Would she to me were kind!
But I'm condemned to silence! oh, poor me!
As Thou dost know, who all men's hearts canst see.
"Oh, were I rich in calm and peace of mind,
My grief you then would not here written find!
O thou, to whom I do my heart devote,
Oh read this page of glad days now remote,
A dark, dark tale, which I tonight devote!
Dark is the future now. Alas, poor me!
Have pity Thou, who all men's pains dost see."

Such verses as these people write when they are in love! But no man in his senses ever thinks of printing them. Here one of the sorrows of life, in which there is real poetry, gave itself vent; not that barren grief which the poet may only hint at, but never depict in its detail—misery and want: that animal necessity, in short, to snatch at least at a fallen leaf of the bread-fruit tree, if not at the fruit itself. The higher the position in which one finds oneself transplanted, the greater is the suffering. Everyday necessity is the stagnant pool of life—no lovely picture reflects itself therein. Lieutenant, love, and lack of money—that is a symbolic triangle, or much the same as the half of the shattered die of Fortune. This the lieutenant felt most poignantly, and this was the reason he leant his head against the window, and sighed so deeply.

"The poor watchman out there in the street is far happier than I. He knows not what I term privation. He has a home, a wife, and children, who weep with him over his sorrows, who rejoice with him when he is glad. Oh, far happier were I, could I exchange with him my being—with his desires and with his hopes perform the weary pilgrimage of life! Oh, he is a hundred times happier than I!"

In the same moment the watchman was again watchman. It

was the shoes that caused the metamorphosis by means of which, unknown to himself, he took upon him the thoughts and feelings of the officer; but, as we have just seen, he felt himself in his new situation much less contented, and now preferred the very thing which but some minutes before he had rejected. So then the watchman was again watchman.

"That was an unpleasant dream," said he; "but 'twas droll enough altogether. I fancied that I was the lieutenant over there: and yet the thing was not very much to my taste after all. I missed my good old mother and the dear little ones; who almost tear me to pieces for sheer love."

He seated himself once more and nodded: the dream continued to haunt him, for he still had the shoes on his feet. A falling star shone in the dark firmament.

"There falls another star," said he: "but what does it matter; there are always enough left. I should not much mind examining the little glimmering things somewhat nearer, especially the moon; for that would not slip so easily through a man's fingers. When we die—so at least says the student, for whom my wife does the washing—we shall fly about as light as a feather from one such a star to the other. That's, of course, not true: but 'twould be pretty enough if it were so. If I could but once take a leap up there, my body might stay here on the steps for what I care."

Behold—there are certain things in the world to which one ought never to give utterance except with the greatest caution; but doubly careful must one be when we have the Shoes of Fortune on our feet. Now just listen to what happened to the watchman.

As to ourselves, we all know the speed produced by the employment of steam; we have experienced it either on railroads, or in boats when crossing the sea; but such a flight is like the travelling of a sloth in comparison with the velocity with which light moves. It flies nineteen million times faster than the best race-horse; and yet electricity is quicker still. Death is an electric shock which our heart receives; the freed soul soars upwards on the wings of electricity. The sun's light wants eight minutes and some seconds to perform a journey of more than twenty million of our Danish miles; borne by electricity, the soul wants even some minutes less to accomplish the same flight. To it the space between the heavenly bodies is not greater than the distance between the homes of our friends in town is for us, even if they live a short way from each other; such an electric shock in the heart, however, costs us the use of the body here below; unless, like the watchman of East Street, we happen to have on the Shoes of Fortune.

In a few seconds the watchman had done the fifty-two thousand of our miles up to the moon, which, as everyone knows, was formed out of matter much lighter than our earth; and is, so we should say, as soft as newly-fallen snow. He found himself on one of the many circumjacent mountain-ridges with which we are acquainted by means of Dr. Madler's "Map of the Moon." Within, down it sunk perpendicularly into a caldron, about a Danish mile in depth; while below lay a town, whose appearance we can, in some measure, realize to ourselves by beating the white of an egg in a glass of water. The matter of which it was built was just as soft, and formed similar towers, and domes, and pillars, transparent and rocking in the thin air; while above his head our earth was rolling like a large fiery ball.

He perceived immediately a quantity of beings who were certainly what we call "men"; yet they looked different to us. A far more correct imagination than that of the pseudo-Herschel* had created them; and if they had been placed in rank and file, and copied by some skilful painter's hand, one would, without doubt, have exclaimed involuntarily, "What a beautiful arabesque!"

They had a language too; but surely nobody can expect that the soul of the watchman should understand it. Be that as it may, it did comprehend it; for in our souls there germinate far greater powers than we poor mortals, despite all our cleverness, have any notion of. Does she not show us—she the queen in the land of enchantment—her astounding dramatic talent in all our dreams? There every acquaintance appears and speaks upon the stage, so entirely in character, and with the same tone of voice, that none of us, when awake, were able to imitate it. How well can she re-call persons to our mind, of whom we have not thought for years; when suddenly they step forth "every inch a man," resembling the real personages, even to the finest features, and become the heroes or heroines of our world of dreams. In reality, such remem-brances are rather unpleasant: every sin, every evil thought, may, like a clock with alarm or chimes, be repeated at pleasure; then the question is if we can trust ourselves to give an account of ev-ery unbecoming word in our heart and on our lips.

The watchman's spirit understood the language of the inhabit-ants of the moon pretty well. The Selenites disputed variously about our earth, and expressed their doubts if it could be inhab-ited: the air, they said, must certainly be too dense to allow any rational dweller in the moon the necessary free respiration. They considered the moon alone to be inhabited: they imagined it was the real heart of the universe or planetary system, on which the genuine Cosmopolites, or citizens of the world, dwelt. What strange things men—no, what strange things Selenites some-times take into their heads!

About politics they had a good deal to say. But little Denmark must take care what it is about, and not run counter to the moon; that great realm, that might in an ill-humor bestir itself, and dash down a hail-storm in our faces, or force the Baltic to overflow the sides of its gigantic basin.

We will, therefore, not listen to what was spoken, and on no condition run in the possibility of telling tales out of school; but we will rather proceed, like good quiet citizens, to East Street, and observe what happened meanwhile to the body of the watchman.

He sat lifeless on the steps: the morning-star, the name for his, the heavy wooden club, headed with iron spikes, and which had nothing else in common with its sparkling brother in the sky, had glided from his hand; while his eyes were fixed with glassy stare on the moon, looking for the good old fellow of a spirit which still haunted it.

"What's the hour, watchman?" asked a passer-by. But when the watchman gave no reply, the merry roysterer, who was now returning home from a noisy drinking bout, took it into his head to try what a tweak of the nose would do, on which the supposed sleeper lost his balance, the body lay motionless, stretched out on the pavement: the man was dead. When the patrol came up, all his comrades, who comprehended nothing of the whole affair, were seized with a dreadful fright, for dead he was, and he remained so. The proper authorities were informed of the circumstance, people talked a good deal about it, and in the morning the body was carried to the hospital.

Now that would be a very pretty joke, if the spirit when it came back and looked for the body in East Street, were not to find one. No doubt it would, in its anxiety, run off to the police, and then to the "Hue and Cry" office, to announce that "the finder will be handsomely rewarded," and at last away to the hospital; yet we may boldly assert that the soul is shrewdest when it shakes off every fetter, and every sort of leading-string—the body only makes it stupid.

The seemingly dead body of the watchman wandered, as we have said, to the hospital, where it was brought into the general viewing-room: and the first thing that was done here was naturally to pull off the galoshes—when the spirit, that was merely gone out on adventures, must have returned with the quickness of lightning to its earthly tenement. It took its direction towards the body in a straight line; and a few seconds after, life began to show itself in the man. He asserted that the preceding night had been the worst that ever the malice of fate had allotted him; he would not for two silver marks again go through what he had endured while moon-stricken; but now, however, it was over.

The same day he was discharged from the hospital as perfectly cured; but the Shoes meanwhile remained behind.

IV. A Moment of Head Importance—An Evening's "Dramatic Readings"—A Most Strange Journey~

Every inhabitant of Copenhagen knows, from personal inspection, how the entrance to Frederick's Hospital looks; but as it is possible that others, who are not Copenhagen people, may also read this little work, we will beforehand give a short description of it.

The extensive building is separated from the street by a pretty high railing, the thick iron bars of which are so far apart, that in all seriousness, it is said, some very thin fellow had of a night occasionally squeezed himself through to go and pay his little visits in the town. The part of the body most difficult to manage on such occasions was, no doubt, the head; here, as is so often the case in the world, long-headed people get through best. So much, then, for the introduction.

One of the young men, whose head, in a physical sense only, might be said to be of the thickest, had the watch that evening. The rain poured down in torrents; yet despite these two obstacles, the young man was obliged to go out, if it were but for a quarter of an hour; and as to telling the door-keeper about it, that, he thought, was quite unnecessary, if, with a whole skin, he were able to slip through the railings. There, on the floor lay the galoshes, which the watchman had forgotten; he never dreamed for a moment that they were those of Fortune; and they promised to do him good service in the wet; so he put them on. The question now was, if he could squeeze himself through the grating, for he had never tried before. Well, there he stood.

"Would to Heaven I had got my head through!" said he, involuntarily; and instantly through it slipped, easily and without pain, notwithstanding it was pretty large and thick. But now the rest of the body was to be got through!

"Ah! I am much too stout," groaned he aloud, while fixed as in a vice. "I had thought the head was the most difficult part of the matter—oh! oh! I really cannot squeeze myself through!"

He now wanted to pull his over-hasty head back again, but he could not. For his neck there was room enough, but for nothing more. His first feeling was of anger; his next that his temper fell to zero. The Shoes of Fortune had placed him in the most dreadful situation; and, unfortunately, it never occurred to him to wish himself free. The pitch-black clouds poured down their contents in still heavier torrents; not a creature was to be seen in the streets. To reach up to the bell was what he did not like; to cry aloud for help would have availed him little; besides, how ashamed would he have been to be found caught in a trap, like an outwitted fox! How was he to twist himself through! He saw clearly that it was his irrevocable destiny to remain a prisoner till dawn, or, perhaps, even late in the morning; then the smith must be fetched to file away the bars; but all that would not be done so quickly as he could think about it. The whole Charity School, just opposite, would be in motion; all the new booths, with their not very courtier-like swarm of seamen, would join them out of curiosity, and would greet him with a wild "hurrah!" while he was standing in his pillory: there would be a mob, a hissing, and rejoicing, and jeering, ten times worse than in the rows about the Jews some years ago—"Oh, my blood is mounting to my brain; 'tis enough to drive one mad! I shall go wild! I know not what to do. Oh! were I but loose; my dizziness would then cease; oh, were my head but loose!"

You see he ought to have said that sooner; for the moment he expressed the wish his head was free; and cured of all his paroxysms of love, he hastened off to his room, where the pains consequent on the fright the Shoes had prepared for him, did not so soon take their leave.

But you must not think that the affair is over now; it grows much worse.

The night passed, the next day also; but nobody came to fetch the Shoes.

In the evening "Dramatic Readings" were to be given at the little theatre in King Street. The house was filled to suffocation; and among other pieces to be recited was a new poem by H. C. Andersen, called, My Aunt's Spectacles; the contents of which were pretty nearly as follows:

"A certain person had an aunt, who boasted of particular skill in fortune-telling with cards, and who was constantly being stormed by persons that wanted to have a peep into futurity. But she was full of mystery about her art, in which a certain pair of magic spectacles did her essential service. Her nephew, a merry boy, who was his aunt's darling, begged so long for these spectacles, that, at last, she lent him the treasure, after having informed him, with many exhortations, that in order to execute the interesting trick, he need only repair to some place where a great many persons were assembled; and then, from a higher position, whence he could overlook the crowd, pass the company in review before him through his spectacles. Immediately 'the inner man' of each individual would be displayed before him, like a game of cards, in which he unerringly might read what the future of every person presented was to be. Well pleased the little magician hastened away to prove the powers of the spectacles in the theatre; no place seeming to him more fitted for such a trial. He begged permission of the worthy audience, and set his spectacles on his nose. A motley phantasmagoria presents itself before him, which he describes in a few satirical touches, yet without expressing his opinion openly: he tells the people enough to set them all thinking and guessing; but in order to hurt nobody, he wraps his witty oracular judgments in a transparent veil, or rather in a lurid thundercloud, shooting forth bright sparks of wit, that they may fall in the powder-magazine of the expectant audience."

The humorous poem was admirably recited, and the speaker much applauded. Among the audience was the young man of the hospital, who seemed to have forgotten his adventure of the preceding night. He had on the Shoes; for as yet no lawful owner had appeared to claim them; and besides it was so very dirty out-of-doors, they were just the thing for him, he thought.

The beginning of the poem he praised with great generosity: he even found the idea original and effective. But that the end of it, like the Rhine, was very insignificant, proved, in his opinion, the author's want of invention; he was without genius, etc. This was an excellent opportunity to have said something clever.

Meanwhile he was haunted by the idea—he should like to possess such a pair of spectacles himself; then, perhaps, by using them circumspectly, one would be able to look into people's hearts, which, he thought, would be far more interesting than merely to see what was to happen next year; for that we should all know in proper time, but the other never.

"I can now," said he to himself, "fancy the whole row of ladies and gentlemen sitting there in the front row; if one could but see into their hearts—yes, that would be a revelation—a sort of bazar. In that lady yonder, so strangely dressed, I should find for certain a large milliner's shop; in that one the shop is empty, but it wants cleaning plain enough. But there would also be some good stately shops among them. Alas!" sighed he, "I know one in which all is stately; but there sits already a spruce young shopman, which is the only thing that's amiss in the whole shop. All would be splendidly decked out, and we should hear, 'Walk in, gentlemen, pray walk in; here you will find all you please to want.' Ah! I wish to Heaven I could walk in and take a trip right through the hearts of those present!"

And behold! to the Shoes of Fortune this was the cue; the whole man shrunk together and a most uncommon journey through the hearts of the front row of spectators, now began. The first heart through which he came, was that of a middle-aged lady, but he instantly fancied himself in the room of the "Institution for the cure of the crooked and deformed," where casts of mis-shapen limbs are displayed in naked reality on the wall. Yet there was this difference, in the institution the casts were taken at the entry of the patient; but here they were retained and guarded in the heart while the sound persons went away. They were, namely, casts of female friends, whose bodily or mental deformities were here most faithfully preserved.

With the snake-like writhings of an idea he glided into another female heart; but this seemed to him like a large holy temple. The white dove of innocence fluttered over the altar. How gladly would he have sunk upon his knees; but he must away to the next heart; yet he still heard the pealing tones of the organ, and he himself seemed to have become a newer and a better man; he felt unworthy to tread the neighboring sanctuary which a poor garret, with a sick bed-rid mother, revealed. But God's warm sun streamed through the open window; lovely roses nodded from the wooden flower-boxes on the roof, and two sky-blue birds sang re-joicingly, while the sick mother implored God's richest blessings on her pious daughter.

He now crept on hands and feet through a butcher's shop; at least on every side, and above and below, there was nought but flesh. It was the heart of a most respectable rich man, whose name is certain to be found in the Directory.

He was now in the heart of the wife of this worthy gentleman. It was an old, dilapidated, mouldering dovecot. The husband's portrait was used as a weather-cock, which was connected in some way or other with the doors, and so they opened and shut of their own accord, whenever the stern old husband turned round.

Hereupon he wandered into a boudoir formed entirely of mir-rors, like the one in Castle Rosenburg; but here the glasses mag-nified to an astonishing degree. On the floor, in the middle of the room, sat, like a Dalai-Lama, the insignificant "Self" of the person, quite confounded at his own greatness. He then imagined he had got into a needle-case full of pointed needles of every size.

"This is certainly the heart of an old maid," thought he. But he was mistaken. It was the heart of a young military man; a man, as people said, of talent and feeling.

In the greatest perplexity, he now came out of the last heart in the row; he was unable to put his thoughts in order, and fancied that his too lively imagination had run away with him.

"Good Heavens!" sighed he. "I have surely a disposition to madness—'tis dreadfully hot here; my blood boils in my veins and my head is burning like a coal." And he now remembered the important event of the evening before, how his head had got jammed in between the iron railings of the hospital. "That's what it is, no doubt," said he. "I must do something in time: under such circumstances a Russian bath might do me good. I only wish I were already on the upper level.

And so there he lay on the uppermost level in the vapor-bath; but with all his clothes on, in his boots and galoshes, while the hot drops fell scalding from the ceiling on his face.

"Holloa!" cried he, leaping down. The bathing attendant, on his side, uttered a loud cry of astonishment when he beheld in the bath, a man completely dressed.

The other, however, retained sufficient presence of mind to whisper to him, "'Tis a bet, and I have won it!" But the first thing he did as soon as he got home, was to have a large blister put on his chest and back to draw out his madness.

The next morning he had a sore chest and a bleeding back; and, excepting the fright, that was all that he had gained by the Shoes of Fortune.

V. *Metamorphosis of the Copying-Clerk*~

The watchman, whom we have certainly not forgotten,

thought meanwhile of the galoshes he had found and taken with him to the hospital; he now went to fetch them; and as neither the lieutenant, nor anybody else in the street, claimed them as his property, they were delivered over to the police-office.

As on the continent, in all law and police practices nothing is verbal, but any circumstance, however trifling, is reduced to writing, the labor, as well as the number of papers that thus accumulate, is enormous. In a police-office, consequently, we find copying-clerks among many other scribes of various denominations, of which, it seems, our hero was one.

"Why, I declare the Shoes look just like my own," said one of the clerks, eying the newly-found treasure, whose hidden powers, even he, sharp as he was, was not able to discover. "One must have more than the eye of a shoemaker to know one pair from the other," said he, soliloquizing; and putting, at the same time, the galoshes in search of an owner, beside his own in the corner.

"Here, sir!" said one of the men, who panting brought him a tremendous pile of papers.

The copying-clerk turned round and spoke awhile with the man about the reports and legal documents in question; but when he had finished, and his eye fell again on the Shoes, he was unable to say whether those to the left or those to the right belonged to him. "At all events it must be those which are wet," thought he; but this time, in spite of his cleverness, he guessed quite wrong, for it was just those of Fortune which played as it were into his hands, or rather on his feet. And why, I should like to know, are the police never to be wrong? So he put them on quickly, stuck his papers in his pocket, and took besides a few under his arm, intending to look them through at home to make the necessary notes. It was noon; and the weather, that had threatened rain, began to clear up, while gaily dressed holiday folks filled the streets. "A little trip to Fredericksburg would do me no great harm," thought he; "for I, poor beast of burden that I am, have so much to annoy me, that I don't know what a good appetite is. 'Tis a bitter crust, alas! at which I am condemned to gnaw!"

Nobody could be more steady or quiet than this young man; we therefore wish him joy of the excursion with all our heart; and it will certainly be beneficial for a person who leads so sedentary a life. In the park he met a friend, one of our young poets, who told him that the following day he should set out on his long-intended tour.

"So you are going away again!" said the clerk. "You are a very free and happy being; we others are chained by the leg and held fast to our desk."

"Yes; but it is a chain, friend, which ensures you the blessed bread of existence," answered the poet. "You need feel no care for the coming morrow: when you are old, you receive a pension."

"True," said the clerk, shrugging his shoulders; "and yet you are the better off. To sit at one's ease and poetise—that is a pleasure; everybody has something agreeable to say to you, and you are always your own master. No, friend, you should but try what it is to sit from one year's end to the other occupied with and judging the most trivial matters."

The poet shook his head, the copying-clerk did the same. Each one kept to his own opinion, and so they separated.

"It's a strange race, those poets!" said the clerk, who was very fond of soliloquizing. "I should like some day, just for a trial, to take such nature upon me, and be a poet myself; I am very sure I should make no such miserable verses as the others. Today, me-thinks, is a most delicious day for a poet. Nature seems anew to celebrate her awakening into life. The air is so unusually clear, the clouds sail on so buoyantly, and from the green herbage a fra-grance is exhaled that fills me with delight. For many a year have I not felt as at this moment."

We see already, by the foregoing effusion, that he is become a poet; to give further proof of it, however, would in most cases be insipid, for it is a most foolish notion to fancy a poet different from other men. Among the latter there may be far more poetical natures than many an acknowledged poet, when examined more closely, could boast of; the difference only is, that the poet possesses a better mental memory, on which account he is able to retain the feeling and the thought till they can be embodied by means of words; a faculty which the others do not possess. But the transition from a commonplace nature to one that is richly endowed, demands always a more or less breakneck leap over a certain abyss which yawns threateningly below; and thus must the sudden change with the clerk strike the reader.

"The sweet air!" continued he of the police-office, in his dreamy imaginings; "how it reminds me of the violets in the garden of my aunt Magdalena! Yes, then I was a little wild boy, who did not go to school very regularly. O heavens! 'tis a long time since I have thought on those times. The good old soul! She lived behind the Exchange. She always had a few twigs or green shoots in water—let the winter rage without as it might. The violets exhaled their sweet breath, whilst I pressed against the windowpanes covered with fantastic frost-work the copper coin I had heated on the stove, and so made peep-holes. What splendid vistas were then opened to my view! What change—what magnificence! Yonder in the canal lay the ships frozen up, and deserted by their whole crews, with a screaming crow for the sole occupant. But when the spring, with a gentle stirring motion, announced her arrival, a new and busy life arose; with songs and hurrahs the ice was sawn asunder, the ships were fresh tarred and rigged, that they might sail away to distant lands. But I have remained here—must always remain here, sitting at my desk in the office, and patiently see other people fetch their passports to go abroad. Such is my fate! Alas!"—sighed he, and was again silent. "Great Heaven! What is come to me! Never have I thought or felt like this before! It must be the summer air that affects me with feelings almost as disquieting as they are refreshing."

He felt in his pocket for the papers. "These police-reports will soon stem the torrent of my ideas, and effectually hinder any rebellious overflowing of the time-worn banks of official duties"; he said to himself consolingly, while his eye ran over the first page. "DAME TIGBRITH, tragedy in five acts." "What is that? And yet it is undeniably my own handwriting. Have I written the tragedy? Wonderful, very wonderful!—And this—what have I here? 'INTRIGUE ON THE RAMPARTS; or THE DAY OF REPENTANCE: vaudeville with new songs to the most favorite airs.' The deuce! Where did I get all this rubbish? Some one must have slipped it slyly into my pocket for a joke. There is too a letter to me; a crumpled letter and the seal broken."

Yes; it was not a very polite epistle from the manager of a theatre, in which both pieces were flatly refused.

"Hem! hem!" said the clerk breathlessly, and quite exhausted he seated himself on a bank. His thoughts were so elastic, his heart so tender; and involuntarily he picked one of the nearest flowers. It is a simple daisy, just bursting out of the bud. What the botanist tells us after a number of imperfect lectures, the flower proclaimed in a minute. It related the mythus of its birth, told of the power of the sun-light that spread out its delicate leaves, and forced them to impregnate the air with their incense—and then he thought of the manifold struggles of life, which in like manner awaken the budding flowers of feeling in our bosom. Light and air contend with chivalric emulation for the love of the fair flower that bestowed her chief favors on the latter; full of longing she turned towards the light, and as soon as it vanished, rolled her tender leaves together and slept in the embraces of the air. "It is the light which adorns me," said the flower.

"But 'tis the air which enables thee to breathe," said the poet's voice.

Close by stood a boy who dashed his stick into a wet ditch. The drops of water splashed up to the green leafy roof, and the clerk thought of the million of ephemera which in a single drop were thrown up to a height, that was as great doubtless for their size, as for us if we were to be hurled above the clouds. While he thought of this and of the whole metamorphosis he had undergone, he smiled and said, "I sleep and dream; but it is wonderful how one can dream so naturally, and know besides so exactly that it is but a dream. If only to-morrow on awaking, I could again call all to mind so vividly! I seem in unusually good spirits; my perception of things is clear, I feel as light and cheerful as though I were in heaven; but I know for a certainty, that if to-morrow a dim remembrance of it should swim before my mind, it will then seem nothing but stupid nonsense, as I have often experienced already—especially before I enlisted under the banner of the police, for that dispels like a whirlwind all the visions of an unfettered imagination. All we hear or say in a dream that is fair and beautiful is like the gold of the subterranean spirits; it is rich and splendid when it is given us, but viewed by daylight we find only withered leaves. Alas!" he sighed quite sorrowful, and gazed at the chirping birds that hopped contentedly from branch to branch, "they are much better off than I! To fly must be a heavenly art; and happy do I prize that creature in which it is innate. Yes! Could I exchange my nature with any other creature, I fain would be such a happy little lark!"

He had hardly uttered these hasty words when the skirts and sleeves of his coat folded themselves together into wings; the clothes became feathers, and the galoshes claws. He observed it perfectly, and laughed in his heart. "Now then, there is no doubt that I am dreaming; but I never before was aware of such mad freaks as these." And up he flew into the green roof and sang; but in the song there was no poetry, for the spirit of the poet was gone. The Shoes, as is the case with anybody who does what he has to do properly, could only attend to one thing at a time. He wanted to be a poet, and he was one; he now wished to be a merry chirping bird: but when he was metamorphosed into one, the former peculiarities ceased immediately. "It is really pleasant enough," said he: "the whole day long I sit in the office amid the driest law-papers, and at night I fly in my dream as a lark in the gardens of Fredericksburg; one might really write a very pretty comedy upon it." He now fluttered down into the grass, turned his head gracefully on every side, and with his bill pecked the pliant blades of grass, which, in comparison to his present size, seemed as majestic as the palm-branches of northern Africa.

Unfortunately the pleasure lasted but a moment. Presently black night overshadowed our enthusiast, who had so entirely missed his part of copying-clerk at a police-office; some vast object seemed to be thrown over him. It was a large oil-skin cap, which a sailor-boy of the quay had thrown over the struggling bird; a coarse hand sought its way carefully in under the broad rim, and seized the clerk over the back and wings. In the first moment of fear, he called, indeed, as loud as he could—"You impudent little blackguard! I am a copying-clerk at the police-office; and you know you cannot insult any belonging to the constabulary force without a chastisement. Besides, you good-for-nothing rascal, it is strictly forbidden to catch birds in the royal gardens of Fredericksburg; but your blue uniform betrays where you come from." This fine tirade sounded, however, to the ungodly sailor-boy like a mere "Pippi-pi." He gave the noisy bird a knock on his beak, and walked on.

He was soon met by two schoolboys of the upper class—that is to say as individuals, for with regard to learning they were in the lowest class in the school; and they bought the stupid bird. So the copying-clerk came to Copenhagen as guest, or rather as prisoner in a family living in Gother Street.

"'Tis well that I'm dreaming," said the clerk, "or I really should get angry. First I was a poet; now sold for a few pence as a lark; no doubt it was that accursed poetical nature which has metamorphosed me into such a poor harmless little creature. It is really pitiable, particularly when one gets into the hands of a little blackguard, perfect in all sorts of cruelty to animals: all I should like to know is, how the story will end."

The two schoolboys, the proprietors now of the transformed clerk, carried him into an elegant room. A stout stately dame received them with a smile; but she expressed much dissatisfaction that a common field-bird, as she called the lark, should appear in such high society. For to-day, however, she would allow it; and they must shut him in the empty cage that was standing in the window. "Perhaps he will amuse my good Polly," added the lady, looking with a benignant smile at a large green parrot that swung himself backwards and forwards most comfortably in his ring, inside a magnificent brass-wired cage. "To-day is Polly's birthday," said she with stupid simplicity: "and the little brown field-bird must wish him joy."

Mr. Polly uttered not a syllable in reply, but swung to and fro with dignified condescension; while a pretty canary, as yellow as gold, that had lately been brought from his sunny fragrant home, began to sing aloud.

"Noisy creature! Will you be quiet!" screamed the lady of the house, covering the cage with an embroidered white pocket handkerchief.

"Chirp, chirp!" sighed he. "That was a dreadful snowstorm"; and he sighed again, and was silent.

The copying-clerk, or, as the lady said, the brown field-bird, was put into a small cage, close to the Canary, and not far from "my good Polly." The only human sounds that the Parrot could bawl out were, "Come, let us be men!" Everything else that he said was as unintelligible to everybody as the chirping of the Canary, except to the clerk, who was now a bird too: he understood his companion perfectly.

"I flew about beneath the green palms and the blossoming almond-trees," sang the Canary; "I flew around, with my brothers and sisters, over the beautiful flowers, and over the glassy lakes, where the bright water-plants nodded to me from below. There, too, I saw many splendidly-dressed paroquets, that told the drollest stories, and the wildest fairy tales without end."

"Oh! those were uncouth birds," answered the Parrot. "They had no education, and talked of whatever came into their head.

"If my mistress and all her friends can laugh at what I say, so may you too, I should think. It is a great fault to have no taste for what is witty or amusing—come, let us be men."

"Ah, you have no remembrance of love for the charming maidens that danced beneath the outspread tents beside the bright fragrant flowers? Do you no longer remember the sweet fruits, and the cooling juice in the wild plants of our never-to-be-forgotten home?" said the former inhabitant of the Canary Isles, continuing his dithyrambic.

"Oh, yes," said the Parrot; "but I am far better off here. I am well fed, and get friendly treatment. I know I am a clever fellow; and that is all I care about. Come, let us be men. You are of a poetical nature, as it is called—I, on the contrary, possess profound knowledge and inexhaustible wit. You have genius; but clear-sighted, calm discretion does not take such lofty flights, and utter such high natural tones. For this they have covered you over—they never do the like to me; for I cost more. Besides, they are afraid of my beak; and I have always a witty answer at hand. Come, let us be men!"

"O warm spicy land of my birth," sang the Canary bird; "I will sing of thy dark-green bowers, of the calm bays where the pendent boughs kiss the surface of the water; I will sing of the rejoicing of all my brothers and sisters where the cactus grows in wanton luxuriance."

"Spare us your elegiac tones," said the Parrot giggling. "Rather speak of something at which one may laugh heartily. Laughing is an infallible sign of the highest degree of mental development. Can a dog, or a horse laugh? No, but they can cry. The gift of laughing was given to man alone. Ha! ha! ha!" screamed Polly, and added his stereotype witticism. "Come, let us be men!"

"Poor little Danish grey-bird," said the Canary; "you have been caught too. It is, no doubt, cold enough in your woods, but there at least is the breath of liberty; therefore fly away. In the hurry they have forgotten to shut your cage, and the upper window is open. Fly, my friend; fly away. Farewell!"

Instinctively the Clerk obeyed; with a few strokes of his wings he was out of the cage; but at the same moment the door, which was only ajar, and which led to the next room, began to creak, and supple and creeping came the large tomcat into the room, and began to pursue him. The frightened Canary fluttered about in his cage; the Parrot flapped his wings, and cried, "Come, let us be men!" The Clerk felt a mortal fright, and flew through the window, far away over the houses and streets. At last he was forced to rest a little.

The neighboring house had a something familiar about it; a window stood open; he flew in; it was his own room. He perched upon the table.

"Come, let us be men!" said he, involuntarily imitating the chatter of the Parrot, and at the same moment he was again a copying-clerk; but he was sitting in the middle of the table.

"Heaven help me!" cried he. "How did I get up here—and so buried in sleep, too? After all, that was a very unpleasant, disagreeable dream that haunted me! The whole story is nothing but silly, stupid nonsense!"

VI. The Best That the Galoshes Gave~

The following day, early in the morning, while the Clerk was still in bed, someone knocked at his door. It was his neighbor, a young Divine, who lived on the same floor. He walked in.

"Lend me your Galoshes," said he; "it is so wet in the garden, though the sun is shining most invitingly. I should like to go out a little."

He got the Galoshes, and he was soon below in a little duodec-imo garden, where between two immense walls a plumtree and an apple-tree were standing. Even such a little garden as this was considered in the metropolis of Copenhagen as a great luxury.

The young man wandered up and down the narrow paths, as well as the prescribed limits would allow; the clock struck six; without was heard the horn of a post-boy.

"To travel! to travel!" exclaimed he, overcome by most pain-ful and passionate remembrances. "That is the happiest thing in the world! That is the highest aim of all my wishes! Then at last would the agonizing restlessness be allayed, which destroys my existence! But it must be far, far away! I would behold magnifi-cent Switzerland; I would travel to Italy, and—"

It was a good thing that the power of the Galoshes worked as instantaneously as lightning in a powder-magazine would do, otherwise the poor man with his overstrained wishes would have travelled about the world too much for himself as well as for us. In short, he was travelling. He was in the middle of Switzerland, but packed up with eight other passengers in the inside of an eternal-ly-creaking diligence; his head ached till it almost split, his weary neck could hardly bear the heavy load, and his feet, pinched by his torturing boots, were terribly swollen. He was in an intermedi-ate state between sleeping and waking; at variance with himself, with his company, with the country, and with the government. In his right pocket he had his letter of credit, in the left, his passport, and in a small leathern purse some double louis d'or, carefully sewn up in the bosom of his waistcoat. Every dream proclaimed that one or the other of these valuables was lost; wherefore he started up as in a fever; and the first movement which his hand made, described a magic triangle from the right pocket to the left, and then up towards the bosom, to feel if he had them all safe or not. From the roof inside the carriage, umbrellas, walking-sticks, hats, and sundry other articles were depending, and hindered the view, which was particularly imposing. He now endeavored as well as he was able to dispel his gloom, which was caused by out-ward chance circumstances merely, and on the bosom of nature imbibe the milk of purest human enjoyment.

Grand, solemn, and dark was the whole landscape around. The gigantic pine-forests, on the pointed crags, seemed almost like little tufts of heather, colored by the surrounding clouds. It began to snow, a cold wind blew and roared as though it were seeking a bride.

"Augh!" sighed he, "were we only on the other side the Alps, then we should have summer, and I could get my letters of cred-it cashed. The anxiety I feel about them prevents me enjoying Switzerland. Were I but on the other side!"

And so saying he was on the other side in Italy, between Flor-ence and Rome. Lake Thracymene, illumined by the evening sun, lay like flaming gold between the dark-blue mountain-ridges; here, where Hannibal defeated Flaminius, the rivers now held each other in their green embraces; lovely, half-naked children tended a herd of black swine, beneath a group of fragrant laurel-trees, hard by the road-side. Could we render this inimitable pic-ture properly, then would everybody exclaim, "Beautiful, unparal-leled Italy!" But neither the young Divine said so, nor anyone of his grumbling companions in the coach of the vetturino.

The poisonous flies and gnats swarmed around by thousands; in vain one waved myrtle-branches about like mad; the audacious insect population did not cease to sting; nor was there a single person in the well-crammed carriage whose face was not swol-len and sore from their ravenous bites. The poor horses, tortured almost to death, suffered most from this truly Egyptian plague; the flies alighted upon them in large disgusting swarms; and if the coachman got down and scraped them off, hardly a minute elapsed before they were there again. The sun now set: a freezing cold, though of short duration pervaded the whole creation; it was like a horrid gust coming from a burial-vault on a warm summer's day—but all around the mountains retained that wonderful green tone which we see in some old pictures, and which, should we not have seen a similar play of color in the South, we declare at once to be unnatural. It was a glorious prospect; but the stomach was empty, the body tired; all that the heart cared and longed for was good night-quarters; yet how would they be? For these one looked much more anxiously than for the charms of nature, which every where were so profusely displayed.

The road led through an olive-grove, and here the solitary inn was situated. Ten or twelve crippled-beggars had encamped outside. The healthiest of them resembled, to use an expression of Marryat's, "Hunger's eldest son when he had come of age"; the others were either blind, had withered legs and crept about on their hands, or withered arms and fingerless hands. It was the most wretched misery, dragged from among the filthiest rags. "Excellenza, miserabili!" sighed they, thrusting forth their deformed limbs to view. Even the hostess, with bare feet, uncombed hair, and dressed in a garment of doubtful color, received the guests grumblingly. The doors were fastened with a loop of string; the floor of the rooms presented a stone paving half torn up; bats fluttered wildly about the ceiling; and as to the smell therein—no—that was beyond description.

"You had better lay the cloth below in the stable," said one of the travellers; "there, at all events, one knows what one is breathing."

The windows were quickly opened, to let in a little fresh air. Quicker, however, than the breeze, the withered, sallow arms of the beggars were thrust in, accompanied by the eternal whine of "Miserabili, miserabili, excellenza!" On the walls were displayed innumerable inscriptions, written in nearly every language of Europe, some in verse, some in prose, most of them not very laudatory of "bella Italia."

The meal was served. It consisted of a soup of salted water, seasoned with pepper and rancid oil. The last ingredient played a very prominent part in the salad; stale eggs and roasted cocks'-combs furnished the grand dish of the repast; the wine even was not without a disgusting taste—it was like a medicinal draught.

At night the boxes and other effects of the passengers were placed against the rickety doors. One of the travellers kept watch while the others slept. The sentry was our young Divine. How close it was in the chamber! The heat oppressive to suffocation—the gnats hummed and stung unceasingly—the "miserabili" without whined and moaned in their sleep.

"Travelling would be agreeable enough," said he groaning, "if one only had no body, or could send it to rest while the spirit went on its pilgrimage unhindered, whither the voice within might call it. Wherever I go, I am pursued by a longing that is insatiable—that I cannot explain to myself, and that tears my very heart. I want something better than what is but what is fled in an instant. But what is it, and where is it to be found? Yet, I know in reality what it is I wish for. Oh! most happy were I, could I but reach one aim—could but reach the happiest of all!"

And as he spoke the word he was again in his home; the long white curtains hung down from the windows, and in the middle of the floor stood the black coffin; in it he lay in the sleep of death. His wish was fulfilled—the body rested, while the spirit went unhindered on its pilgrimage. "Let no one deem himself happy before his end," were the words of Solon; and here was a new and brilliant proof of the wisdom of the old apothegm.

Every corpse is a sphynx of immortality; here too on the black coffin the sphynx gave us no answer to what he who lay within had written two days before:

"O mighty Death! thy silence teaches nought,
Thou leadest only to the near grave's brink;
Is broken now the ladder of my thoughts?
Do I instead of mounting only sink?

Our heaviest grief the world oft seeth not,
Our sorest pain we hide from stranger eyes:
And for the sufferer there is nothing left
But the green mound that o'er the coffin lies."

Two figures were moving in the chamber. We knew them both; it was the fairy of Care, and the emissary of Fortune. They both bent over the corpse.

"Do you now see," said Care, "what happiness your Galoshes have brought to mankind?"

"To him, at least, who slumbers here, they have brought an imperishable blessing," answered the other.

"Ah no!" replied Care. "He took his departure himself; he was not called away. His mental powers here below were not strong enough to reach the treasures lying beyond this life, and which his destiny ordained he should obtain. I will now confer a benefit on him."

And she took the Galoshes from his feet; his sleep of death was ended; and he who had been thus called back again to life arose from his dread couch in all the vigor of youth. Care vanished, and with her the Galoshes. She has no doubt taken them for herself, to keep them to all eternity.

The Butterfly

The butterfly wished to procure a bride for himself—of course, one of the flowers—a pretty little one. He looked about him. Each one sat quietly and thoughtfully on her stalk, as a young maiden should sit, when she is not affianced; but there were many of them, and it was a difficult matter to choose amongst them. The butterfly could not make up his mind; so he flew to the daisy. The French call her Marguerite; they know that she can tell fortunes, and she does this when lovers pluck off leaf after leaf and ask her at each one a question about the beloved one: "How does he love me?—With all his heart?—With sorrow?—Above all?—Can not refrain from it?—Quite secretly?—A little bit?—Not at all?"—or questions to the same import. Each one asks in his own language. The butterfly flew towards her and questioned her; he did not pluck off the leaves, but kissed each separate one, thinking that by so doing, he would make himself more agreeable to the good creature.

"Sweet Margaret Daisy," said he, "of all the flowers you are the wisest woman! You can prophesy! Tell me, shall I obtain this one or that one? Which one? If I but know this, I can fly to the charming one at once, and pay my court!"

Margaret did not answer. She could not bear to be called a woman, for she was a young girl, and when one is a young girl, one is not a woman.

He asked again, he asked a third time, but as she did not answer a single word, he questioned her no more and flew away without further parley, intent on his courtship.

It was early spring time, and there was an abundance of snowdrops and crocuses. "They are very neat," said the butterfly, "pretty little confirmed ones, but a little green!" He, like all young men looked at older girls.

From thence he flew to the anemones; but he found them a little too sentimental; the tulips, too showy; the broom, not of a good family; the linden blossoms, too small—then they had so many relations; as to the apple blossoms, why to look at them you would think them as healthy as roses, but to-day they blossom and to-morrow, if the wind blows, they drop off; a marriage with them would be too short. The pea blossom pleased him most, she was pink and white, she was pure and refined and belonged to the housewifely girls that look well, and still can make themselves useful in the kitchen. He had almost concluded to make love to her, when he saw hanging near to her, a pea-pod with its white blossom. "Who is that?" asked he. "That is my sister," said the pea blossom.

"How now, is that the way you look when older?" This terrified the butterfly and he flew away.

The honeysuckles were hanging over the fence—young ladies with long faces and yellow skins—but he did not fancy their style of beauty. Yes, but which did he like? Ask him!

The spring passed, the summer passed, and then came the autumn. The flowers appeared in their most beautiful dresses, but of what avail was this? The butterfly's fresh youthful feelings had vanished. In old age, the heart longs for fragrance, and dahlias and gillyflowers are scentless. So the butterfly flew to the mint. "She has no flower at all, but she is herself a flower, for she is fragrant from head to foot and each leaf is filled with perfume. I shall take her!"

But the mint stood stiff and still, and at last said: "Friendship— but nothing more! I am old and you are old! We can live very well for one another, but to marry? No! Do not let us make fools of ourselves in our old age."

So the butterfly obtained no one.

The butterfly remained a bachelor.

Many violent and transient showers came late in the autumn; the wind blew so coldly down the back of the old willow trees, that it cracked within them. It did not do to fly about in summer garments, for even love itself would then grow cold. The butterfly however preferred not to fly out at all; he had by chance entered a door-way, and there was fire in the stove—yes, it was just as warm there, as in summer-time;—there he could live. "Life is not enough," said he, "one must have sunshine, liberty and a little flower!"

He flew against the window-panes, was seen, was run through by a pin and placed in a curiosity-box; one could not do more for him.

"Now I also am seated on a stalk like a flower," said the butter-fly, "it is not so comfortable after all! But it is as well as being married, for then one is tied down!" He consoled himself with this.

"What a wretched consolation!" said the flower, that grew in the pot in the room.

"One can not entirely trust to flowers that grow in pots," thought the butterfly, "they have too much intercourse with men."

The Snail and the Rose Tree

A hedge of hazel-nut bushes encircled the garden; without was field and meadow, with cows and sheep; but in the centre of the garden stood a rose-tree, and under it sat a snail—she had much within her, she had herself.

"Wait, until my time comes," said she, "I shall accomplish something more than putting forth roses, bearing nuts, or giving milk, like the cows and sheep!"

"I expect something fearfully grand," said the rose-tree, "may I ask when it will take place?"

"I shall take my time," said the snail, "you are in too great a hurry, and when this is the case, how can one's expectations be fulfilled?"

The next year the snail lay in about the same spot under the rose-tree, which put forth buds and developed roses, ever fresh, ever new. The snail half crept forth, stretched out its feelers and drew itself in again.

"Everything looks as it did a year ago! No progress has been made; the rose-tree still bears roses; it does not get along any farther!"

The summer faded away, the autumn passed, the rose-tree constantly bore flowers and buds, until the snow fell, and the weather was raw and damp. The rose-tree bent itself towards the earth, the snail crept in the earth.

A new year commenced; the roses came out, and the snail came out.

"Now you are an old rose bush," said the snail, "you will soon die away. You have given the world everything that you had in you; whether that be much or little is a question, upon which I have not time to reflect. But it is quite evident, that you have not done the slightest thing towards your inward developement; otherwise I suppose that something different would have sprung from you. Can you answer this? You will soon be nothing but a stick! Can you understand what I say?"

"You startle me," said the rose-tree, "I have never thought upon that!"

"No, I suppose that you have never meddled much with thinking! Can you tell me why you blossom? And how it comes to pass? How? Why?"

"No," said the rose-tree, "I blossom with pleasure because I could not do otherwise. The sun was so warm, the air so refreshing, I drank the clear dew and the fortifying rain; I breathed, I lived! A strength came to me from the earth, a strength came from above, I felt a happiness, ever new, ever great and therefore I must blossom ever, that was my life, I could not do otherwise!"

"You have led a very easy life!" said the snail.

"Certainly, everything has been given to me," said the rose-tree, "but still more has been given to you. You are one of those meditative, pensive, profound natures, one of the highly gifted, that astound the whole world!"

"I have assuredly no such thought in my mind," said the snail, "the world is nothing to me! What have I to do with the world? I have enough with myself, and enough in myself!"

"But should we not all, here on earth, give the best part of us to others? Offer what we can!—It is true, that I have only given roses—but you? You who have received so much, what have you given to the world? What do you give her?"

"What I have given? What I give? I spit upon her! She is good for nothing! I have nought to do with her. Put forth roses, you can do no more! Let the hazel bushes bear nuts! Let the cows and sheep give milk; they have each their public, I have mine within myself! I retire within myself, and there I remain. The world is nothing to me!"

And thereupon the snail withdrew into her house and closed it.

"That is so sad," said the rose-tree, "with the best will, I cannot creep in, I must ever spring out, spring forth in roses. The leaves drop off and are blown away by the wind. Yet, I saw one of the roses laid in the hymn-book of the mother of the family; one of my roses was placed upon the breast of a charming young girl, and one was kissed with joy by a child's mouth. This did me so much good, it was a real blessing! That is my recollection, my life!"

And the rose-tree flowered in innocence, and the snail sat indifferently in her house. The world was nothing to her.

And years passed away. The snail became earth to earth and the rose-tree became earth to earth; the remembrances in the hymn-book were also blown away—but new rose-trees bloomed in the garden, new snails grew in the garden; they crept in their houses and spat.—The world is nothing to them.

Shall we read the story of the past again? It will not be different.

The Conceited Apple Branch

It was the month of May. The wind still blew cold, but from bush and tree, field and flower, came the welcome sound, "Spring is come."

Wild flowers in profusion covered the hedges. Under the little apple tree Spring seemed busy, and he told his tale from one of the branches, which hung fresh and blooming and covered with delicate pink blossoms that were just ready to open.

The branch well knew how beautiful it was; this knowledge exists as much in the leaf as in the blood. I was therefore not surprised when a nobleman's carriage, in which sat the young countess, stopped in the road just by. The apple branch, she said, was a most lovely object, an emblem of spring in its most charming aspect. The branch was broken off for her, and she held it in her delicate hand and sheltered it with her silk parasol.

Then they drove to the castle, in which were lofty halls and splendid drawing-rooms. Pure white curtains fluttered before the open windows, and beautiful flowers stood in transparent vases. In one of them, which looked as if it had been cut out of newly fallen snow, the apple branch was placed among some fresh light twigs of beech. It was a charming sight. And the branch became proud, which was very much like human nature.

People of every description entered the room, and according to their position in society so dared they to express their admiration. Some few said nothing, others expressed too much, and the apple branch very soon got to understand that there was as much difference in the characters of human beings as in those of plants and flowers. Some are all for pomp and parade, others have a great deal to do to maintain their own importance, while the rest might be spared without much loss to society. So thought the apple branch as he stood before the open window, from which he could see out over gardens and fields, where there were flowers and plants enough for him to think and reflect upon—some rich and beautiful, some poor and humble indeed.

"Poor despised herbs," said the apple branch; "there is really a difference between them and such as I am. How unhappy they must be if they can feel as those in my position do! There is a difference indeed, and so there ought to be, or we should all be equals."

And the apple branch looked with a sort of pity upon them, especially on a certain little flower that is found in fields and in ditches. No one bound these flowers together in a nosegay, they were too common,—they were even known to grow between the paving stones, shooting up everywhere like bad weeds,—and they bore the very ugly name of "dog flowers," or "dandelions."

"Poor despised plants," said the apple bough, "it is not your fault that you are so ugly and that you have such an ugly name, but it is with plants as with men—there must be a difference."

"A difference!" cried the sunbeam as he kissed the blooming apple branch and then kissed the yellow dandelion out in the fields. All were brothers, and the sunbeam kissed them—the poor flowers as well as the rich.

The apple bough had never thought of the boundless love of God which extends over all the works of creation, over everything which lives and moves and has its being in Him. He had never thought of the good and beautiful which are so often hidden, but can never remain forgotten by Him, not only among the lower creation, but also among men. The sunbeam, the ray of light, knew better.

"You do not see very far nor very clearly," he said to the apple branch. "Which is the despised plant you so specially pity?"

"The dandelion," he replied. "No one ever places it in a nosegay; it is trodden under foot, there are so many of them; and when they run to seed they have flowers like wool, which fly away in little pieces over the roads and cling to the dresses of the people;

they are only weeds—but of course there must be weeds. Oh, I am really very thankful that I was not made like one of these flowers."

There came presently across the fields a whole group of children, the youngest of whom was so small that he had to be carried by the others; and when he was seated on the grass, among the yellow flowers, he laughed aloud with joy, kicked out his little legs, rolled about, plucked the yellow flowers and kissed them in childlike innocence.

The elder children broke off the flowers with long stems, bent the stalks one round the other to form links, and made first a chain for the neck, then one to go across the shoulders and hang down to the waist, and at last a wreath to wear about the head; so that they looked quite splendid in their garlands of green stems and golden flowers. But the eldest among them gathered carefully the faded flowers, on the stem of which were grouped together the seeds, in the form of a white, feathery coronal.

These loose, airy wool-flowers are very beautiful, and look like fine, snowy feathers or down. The children held them to their mouths and tried to blow away the whole coronal with one puff of the breath. They had been told by their grandmothers that whoever did so would be sure to have new clothes before the end of the year. The despised flower was by this raised to the position of a prophet, or foreteller of events.

"Do you see," said the sunbeam, "do you see the beauty of these flowers? Do you see their powers of giving pleasure?"

"Yes, to children," said the apple bough.

By and by an old woman came into the field and, with a blunt knife without a handle, began to dig round the roots of some of the dandelion plants and pull them up. With some she intended to make tea for herself, but the rest she was going to sell to the chemist and obtain money.

"But beauty is of higher value than all this," said the apple-tree branch; "only the chosen ones can be admitted into the realms of the beautiful. There is a difference between plants, just as there is a difference between men."

Then the sunbeam spoke of the boundless love of God as seen in creation and over all that lives, and of the equal distribution of His gifts, both in time and in eternity.

"That is your opinion," said the apple bough.

Then some people came into the room and among them the young countess—the lady who had placed the apple bough in the transparent vase, so pleasantly beneath the rays of sunlight. She carried in her hand something that seemed like a flower. The object was hidden by two or three great leaves which covered it like a shield so that no draft or gust of wind could injure it, and it was carried more carefully than the apple branch had ever been.

Very cautiously the large leaves were removed, and there appeared the feathery seed crown of the despised yellow dandelion. This was what the lady had so carefully plucked and carried home so safely covered, so that not one of the delicate feathery arrows of which its mistlike shape was so lightly formed should flutter away. She now drew it forth quite uninjured and wondered at its beautiful form, its airy lightness and singular construction so soon to be blown away by the wind.

"See," she exclaimed, "how wonderfully God has made this little flower. I will paint it in a picture with the apple branch. Every one admires the beauty of the apple bough, but this humble flower has been endowed by Heaven with another kind of loveliness, and although they differ in appearance both are children of the realms of beauty."

Then the sunbeam kissed both the lowly flower and the blooming apple branch, upon whose leaves appeared a rosy blush.

The Little Mermaid

Far out in the ocean, where the water is as blue as the prettiest cornflower and as clear as crystal, it is very, very deep; so deep, indeed, that no cable could sound it, and many church steeples, piled one upon another, would not reach from the ground beneath to the surface of the water above. There dwell the Sea King and his subjects.

We must not imagine that there is nothing at the bottom of the sea but bare yellow sand. No, indeed, for on this sand grow the strangest flowers and plants, the leaves and stems of which are so pliant that the slightest agitation of the water causes them to stir as if they had life. Fishes, both large and small, glide between the branches as birds fly among the trees here upon land.

In the deepest spot of all stands the castle of the Sea King. Its walls are built of coral, and the long Gothic windows are of the clearest amber. The roof is formed of shells that open and close as the water flows over them. Their appearance is very beautiful, for in each lies a glittering pearl which would be fit for the diadem of a queen.

The Sea King had been a widower for many years, and his aged mother kept house for him. She was a very sensible woman, but exceedingly proud of her high birth, and on that account wore twelve oysters on her tail, while others of high rank were only allowed to wear six.

She was, however, deserving of very great praise, especially for her care of the little sea princesses, her six granddaughters. They were beautiful children, but the youngest was the prettiest of them all. Her skin was as clear and delicate as a rose leaf, and her eyes as blue as the deepest sea; but, like all the others, she had no feet and her body ended in a fish's tail. All day long they played in the great halls of the castle or among the living flowers that grew out of the walls. The large amber windows were open, and the fish swam in, just as the swallows fly into our houses when we open the windows; only the fishes swam up to the princesses, ate out of their hands, and allowed themselves to be stroked.

Outside the castle there was a beautiful garden, in which grew bright-red and dark-blue flowers, and blossoms like flames of fire; the fruit glittered like gold, and the leaves and stems waved to and fro continually. The earth itself was the finest sand, but blue as the flame of burning sulphur. Over everything lay a peculiar blue radiance, as if the blue sky were everywhere, above and below, instead of the dark depths of the sea. In calm weather the sun could be seen, looking like a reddish-purple flower with light streaming from the calyx.

Each of the young princesses had a little plot of ground in the garden, where she might dig and plant as she pleased. One arranged her flower bed in the form of a whale; another preferred to make hers like the figure of a little mermaid; while the youngest child made hers round, like the sun, and in it grew flowers as red as his rays at sunset.

She was a strange child, quiet and thoughtful. While her sisters showed delight at the wonderful things which they obtained from the wrecks of vessels, she cared only for her pretty flowers, red like the sun, and a beautiful marble statue. It was the representation of a handsome boy, carved out of pure white stone, which had fallen to the bottom of the sea from a wreck.

She planted by the statue a rose-colored weeping willow. It grew rapidly and soon hung its fresh branches over the statue, almost down to the blue sands. The shadows had the color of violet and waved to and fro like the branches, so that it seemed as if the crown of the tree and the root were at play, trying to kiss each other.

Nothing gave her so much pleasure as to hear about the world above the sea. She made her old grandmother tell her all she knew of the ships and of the towns, the people and the animals.

To her it seemed most wonderful and beautiful to hear that the flowers of the land had fragrance, while those below the sea had none; that the trees of the forest were green; and that the fishes among the trees could sing so sweetly that it was a pleasure to listen to them. Her grandmother called the birds fishes, or the little mermaid would not have understood what was meant, for she had never seen birds.

"When you have reached your fifteenth year," said the grandmother, "you will have permission to rise up out of the sea and sit on the rocks in the moonlight, while the great ships go sailing by. Then you will see both forests and towns."

In the following year, one of the sisters would be fifteen, but as each was a year younger than the other, the youngest would have to wait five years before her turn came to rise up from the bottom of the ocean to see the earth as we do. However, each promised to tell the others what she saw on her first visit and what she thought was most beautiful. Their grandmother could not tell them enough—there were so many things about which they wanted to know.

None of them longed so much for her turn to come as the youngest—she who had the longest time to wait and who was so quiet and thoughtful. Many nights she stood by the open window, looking up through the dark blue water and watching the fish as they splashed about with their fins and tails. She could see the moon and stars shining faintly, but through the water they looked larger than they do to our eyes. When something like a black cloud passed between her and them, she knew that it was either a whale swimming over her head, or a ship full of human beings who never imagined that a pretty little mermaid was standing beneath them, holding out her white hands towards the keel of their ship.

At length the eldest was fifteen and was allowed to rise to the surface of the ocean.

When she returned she had hundreds of things to talk about.

But the finest thing, she said, was to lie on a sand bank in the quiet moonlit sea, near the shore, gazing at the lights of the near-by town, that twinkled like hundreds of stars, and listening to the sounds of music, the noise of carriages, the voices of human beings, and the merry pealing of the bells in the church steeples. Because she could not go near all these wonderful things, she longed for them all the more.

Oh, how eagerly did the youngest sister listen to all these descriptions! And afterwards, when she stood at the open window looking up through the dark-blue water, she thought of the great city, with all its bustle and noise, and even fancied she could hear the sound of the church bells down in the depths of the sea.

In another year the second sister received permission to rise to the surface of the water and to swim about where she pleased. She rose just as the sun was setting, and this, she said, was the most beautiful sight of all. The whole sky looked like gold, and violet and rose-colored clouds, which she could not describe, drifted across it. And more swiftly than the clouds, flew a large flock of wild swans toward the setting sun, like a long white veil across the sea. She also swam towards the sun, but it sank into the waves, and the rosy tints faded from the clouds and from the sea.

The third sister's turn followed, and she was the boldest of them all, for she swam up a broad river that emptied into the sea. On the banks she saw green hills covered with beautiful vines, and palaces and castles peeping out from amid the proud trees of the forest. She heard birds singing and felt the rays of the sun so strongly that she was obliged often to dive under the water to cool her burning face. In a narrow creek she found a large group of little human children, almost naked, sporting about in the water. She wanted to play with them, but they fled in a great fright; and then a little black animal—it was a dog, but she did not know it, for she had never seen one before—came to the water and barked at her so furiously that she became frightened and rushed back to the open sea. But she said she should never forget the beautiful forest, the green hills, and the pretty children who could swim in the water although they had no tails.

The fourth sister was more timid. She remained in the midst of the sea, but said it was quite as beautiful there as nearer the land. She could see many miles around her, and the sky above looked like a bell of glass. She had seen the ships, but at such a great distance that they looked like sea gulls. The dolphins sported in the waves, and the great whales spouted water from their nostrils till it seemed as if a hundred fountains were playing in every direction.

The fifth sister's birthday occurred in the winter, so when her turn came she saw what the others had not seen the first time they went up. The sea looked quite green, and large icebergs were floating about, each like a pearl, she said, but larger and loftier than the churches built by men. They were of the most singular shapes and glittered like diamonds. She had seated herself on one of the largest and let the wind play with her long hair. She noticed that all the ships sailed past very rapidly, steering as far away as they could, as if they were afraid of the iceberg. Towards evening, as the sun went down, dark clouds covered the sky, the thunder rolled, and the flashes of lightning glowed red on the icebergs as they were tossed about by the heaving sea. On all the ships the sails were reefed with fear and trembling, while she sat on the floating iceberg, calmly watching the lightning as it darted its forked flashes into the sea.

Each of the sisters, when first she had permission to rise to the surface, was delighted with the new and beautiful sights. Now that they were grown-up girls and could go when they pleased, they had become quite indifferent about it. They soon wished themselves back again, and after a month had passed they said it was much more beautiful down below and pleasanter to be at home.

Yet often, in the evening hours, the five sisters would twine their arms about each other and rise to the surface together. Their voices were more charming than that of any human being, and before the approach of a storm, when they feared that a ship might be lost, they swam before the vessel, singing enchanting songs of the delights to be found in the depths of the sea and begging the voyagers not to fear if they sank to the bottom. But the sailors could not understand the song and thought it was the sighing of the storm. These things were never beautiful to them, for if the ship sank, the men were drowned and their dead bodies alone reached the palace of the Sea King.

When the sisters rose, arm in arm, through the water, their youngest sister would stand quite alone, looking after them, ready to cry—only, since mermaids have no tears, she suffered more acutely.

"Oh, were I but fifteen years old!" said she. "I know that I shall love the world up there, and all the people who live in it."

At last she reached her fifteenth year.

"Well, now you are grown up," said the old dowager, her grandmother. "Come, and let me adorn you like your sisters." And she placed in her hair a wreath of white lilies, of which every flower leaf was half a pearl. Then the old lady ordered eight great oysters to attach themselves to the tail of the princess to show her high rank.

"But they hurt me so," said the little mermaid.

"Yes, I know; pride must suffer pain," replied the old lady.

Oh, how gladly she would have shaken off all this grandeur and laid aside the heavy wreath! The red flowers in her own garden would have suited her much better. But she could not change herself, so she said farewell and rose as lightly as a bubble to the surface of the water.

The sun had just set when she raised her head above the waves. The clouds were tinted with crimson and gold, and through the glimmering twilight beamed the evening star in all its beauty.

The sea was calm, and the air mild and fresh. A large ship with three masts lay becalmed on the water; only one sail was set, for not a breeze stirred, and the sailors sat idle on deck or amidst the rigging. There was music and song on board, and as darkness came on, a hundred colored lanterns were lighted, as if the flags of all nations waved in the air.

The little mermaid swam close to the cabin windows, and now and then, as the waves lifted her up, she could look in through glass window-panes and see a number of gayly dressed people.

Among them, and the most beautiful of all, was a young prince with large, black eyes. He was sixteen years of age, and his birthday was being celebrated with great display. The sailors were dancing on deck, and when the prince came out of the cabin, more than a hundred rockets rose in the air, making it as bright as day. The little mermaid was so startled that she dived under water, and when she again stretched out her head, it looked as if all the stars of heaven were falling around her.

She had never seen such fireworks before. Great suns spurted fire about, splendid fireflies flew into the blue air, and everything was reflected in the clear, calm sea beneath. The ship itself was so brightly illuminated that all the people, and even the smallest rope, could be distinctly seen. How handsome the young prince looked, as he pressed the hands of all his guests and smiled at them, while the music resounded through the clear night air!

It was very late, yet the little mermaid could not take her eyes from the ship or from the beautiful prince. The colored lanterns had been extinguished, no more rockets rose in the air, and the cannon had ceased firing; but the sea became restless, and a moaning, grumbling sound could be heard beneath the waves. Still the little mermaid remained by the cabin window, rocking up and down on the water, so that she could look within. After a while the sails were quickly set, and the ship went on her way. But soon the waves rose higher, heavy clouds darkened the sky, and lightning appeared in the distance. A dreadful storm was approaching. Once more the sails were furled, and the great ship pursued her flying course over the raging sea. The waves rose mountain high, as if they would overtop the mast, but the ship dived like a swan between them, then rose again on their lofty, foaming crests. To the little mermaid this was pleasant sport; but not so to the sailors. At length the ship groaned and creaked; the thick planks gave way under the lashing of the sea, as the waves broke over the deck; the mainmast snapped asunder like a reed, and as the ship lay over on her side, the water rushed in.

The little mermaid now perceived that the crew were in danger; even she was obliged to be careful, to avoid the beams and planks of the wreck which lay scattered on the water. At one moment it was pitch dark so that she could not see a single object, but when a flash of lightning came it revealed the whole scene; she could see every one who had been on board except the prince. When the ship parted, she had seen him sink into the deep waves, and she was glad, for she thought he would now be with her. Then she remembered that human beings could not live in the water, so that when he got down to her father's palace he would certainly be quite dead.

No, he must not die! So she swam about among the beams and planks which strewed the surface of the sea, forgetting that they could crush her to pieces. Diving deep under the dark waters, rising and falling with the waves, she at length managed to reach the young prince, who was fast losing the power to swim in that stormy sea. His limbs were failing him, his beautiful eyes were closed, and he would have died had not the little mermaid come to his assistance. She held his head above the water and let the waves carry them where they would.

In the morning the storm had ceased, but of the ship not a single fragment could be seen. The sun came up red and shining out of the water, and its beams brought back the hue of health to the prince's cheeks, but his eyes remained closed. The mermaid kissed his high, smooth forehead and stroked back his wet hair. He seemed to her like the marble statue in her little garden, so she kissed him again and wished that he might live.

Presently they came in sight of land, and she saw lofty blue mountains on which the white snow rested as if a flock of swans were lying upon them. Beautiful green forests were near the shore, and close by stood a large building, whether a church or a convent she could not tell. Orange and citron trees grew in the garden, and before the door stood lofty palms. The sea here formed a little bay, in which the water lay quiet and still, but very deep. She swam with the handsome prince to the beach, which was covered with fine white sand, and there she laid him in the warm sunshine, taking care to raise his head higher than his body. Then bells sounded in the large white building, and some young girls came into the garden. The little mermaid swam out farther from the shore and hid herself among some high rocks that rose out of the water. Covering her head and neck with the foam of the sea, she watched there to see what would become of the poor prince.

It was not long before she saw a young girl approach the spot where the prince lay. She seemed frightened at first, but only for a moment; then she brought a number of people, and the mermaid saw that the prince came to life again and smiled upon those who stood about him. But to her he sent no smile; he knew not that she had saved him. This made her very sorrowful, and when he was led away into the great building, she dived down into the water and returned to her father's castle.

She had always been silent and thoughtful, and now she was more so than ever. Her sisters asked her what she had seen during her first visit to the surface of the water, but she could tell them nothing. Many an evening and morning did she rise to the place where she had left the prince. She saw the fruits in the garden ripen and watched them gathered; she watched the snow on the mountain tops melt away; but never did she see the prince, and therefore she always returned home more sorrowful than before.

It was her only comfort to sit in her own little garden and fling her arm around the beautiful marble statue, which was like the prince. She gave up tending her flowers, and they grew in wild confusion over the paths, twining their long leaves and stems round the branches of the trees so that the whole place became dark and gloomy.

At length she could bear it no longer and told one of her sisters all about it. Then the others heard the secret, and very soon it became known to several mermaids, one of whom had an intimate friend who happened to know about the prince. She had also seen the festival on board ship, and she told them where the prince came from and where his palace stood.

"Come, little sister," said the other princesses. Then they entwined their arms and rose together to the surface of the water, near the spot where they knew the prince's palace stood. It was built of bright-yellow, shining stone and had long flights of marble steps, one of which reached quite down to the sea. Splendid gilded cupolas rose over the roof, and between the pillars that surrounded the whole building stood lifelike statues of marble. Through the clear crystal of the lofty windows could be seen noble rooms, with costly silk curtains and hangings of tapestry and walls covered with beautiful paintings. In the center of the largest salon a fountain threw its sparkling jets high up into the glass cupola of the ceiling, through which the sun shone in upon the water and upon the beautiful plants that grew in the basin of the fountain.

Now that the little mermaid knew where the prince lived, she spent many an evening and many a night on the water near the palace. She would swim much nearer the shore than any of the others had ventured, and once she went up the narrow channel under the marble balcony, which threw a broad shadow on the water. Here she sat and watched the young prince, who thought himself alone in the bright moonlight.

She often saw him evenings, sailing in a beautiful boat on which music sounded and flags waved. She peeped out from among the green rushes, and if the wind caught her long silvery-white veil, those who saw it believed it to be a swan, spreading out its wings.

Many a night, too, when the fishermen set their nets by the light of their torches, she heard them relate many good things about the young prince. And this made her glad that she had saved his life when he was tossed about half dead on the waves. She remembered how his head had rested on her bosom and how heartily she had kissed him, but he knew nothing of all this and could not even dream of her.

She grew more and more to like human beings and wished more and more to be able to wander about with those whose world seemed to be so much larger than her own. They could fly over the sea in ships and mount the high hills which were far above the clouds; and the lands they possessed, their woods and their fields, stretched far away beyond the reach of her sight. There was so much that she wished to know! but her sisters were unable to answer all her questions. She then went to her old grandmother, who knew all about the upper world, which she rightly called "the lands above the sea."

"If human beings are not drowned," asked the little mermaid, "can they live forever? Do they never die, as we do here in the sea?"

"Yes," replied the old lady, "they must also die, and their term of life is even shorter than ours. We sometimes live for three hundred years, but when we cease to exist here, we become only foam on the surface of the water and have not even a grave among those we love. We have not immortal souls, we shall never live again; like the green seaweed when once it has been cut off, we can never flourish more. Human beings, on the contrary, have souls which live forever, even after the body has been turned to dust. They rise up through the clear, pure air, beyond the glittering stars. As we rise out of the water and behold all the land of the earth, so do they rise to unknown and glorious regions which we shall never see."

"Why have not we immortal souls?" asked the little mermaid, mournfully. "I would gladly give all the hundreds of years that I have to live, to be a human being only for one day and to have the hope of knowing the happiness of that glorious world above the stars."

"You must not think that," said the old woman. "We believe that we are much happier and much better off than human beings."

"So I shall die," said the little mermaid, "and as the foam of the sea I shall be driven about, never again to hear the music of the waves or to see the pretty flowers or the red sun? Is there anything I can do to win an immortal soul?"

"No," said the old woman; "unless a man should love you so much that you were more to him than his father or his mother, and if all his thoughts and all his love were fixed upon you, and the priest placed his right hand in yours, and he promised to be true to you here and hereafter—then his soul would glide into your body, and you would obtain a share in the future happiness of mankind. He would give to you a soul and retain his own as well; but this can never happen. Your fish's tail, which among us is considered so beautiful, on earth is thought to be quite ugly. They do not know any better, and they think it necessary, in order to be handsome, to have two stout props, which they call legs."

Then the little mermaid sighed and looked sorrowfully at her fish's tail. "Let us be happy," said the old lady, "and dart and spring about during the three hundred years that we have to live, which is really quite long enough. After that we can rest ourselves all the better. This evening we are going to have a court ball."

It was one of those splendid sights which we can never see on earth. The walls and the ceiling of the large ballroom were of thick but transparent crystal. Many hundreds of colossal shells,—some of a deep red, others of a grass green,—with blue fire in them, stood in rows on each side. These lighted up the whole salon, and shone through the walls so that the sea was also illuminated. Innumerable fishes, great and small, swam past the crystal walls; on some of them the scales glowed with a purple brilliance, and on others shone like silver and gold. Through the halls flowed a broad stream, and in it danced the mermen and the mermaids to the music of their own sweet singing.

No one on earth has such lovely voices as they, but the little mermaid sang more sweetly than all. The whole court applauded her with hands and tails, and for a moment her heart felt quite gay, for she knew she had the sweetest voice either on earth or in the sea. But soon she thought again of the world above her; she could not forget the charming prince, nor her sorrow that she had not an immortal soul like his. She crept away silently out of her father's palace, and while everything within was gladness and song, she sat in her own little garden, sorrowful and alone. Then she heard the bugle sounding through the water and thought: "He is certainly sailing above, he in whom my wishes center and in whose hands I should like to place the happiness of my life. I will venture all for him and to win an immortal soul. While my sisters are dancing in my father's palace I will go to the sea witch, of whom I have always been so much afraid; she can give me counsel and help."

Then the little mermaid went out from her garden and took the road to the foaming whirlpools, behind which the sorceress lived. She had never been that way before. Neither flowers nor grass grew there; nothing but bare, gray, sandy ground stretched out to the whirlpool, where the water, like foaming mill wheels, seized everything that came within its reach and cast it into the fathomless deep. Through the midst of these crushing whirlpools the little mermaid was obliged to pass before she could reach the dominions of the sea witch. Then, for a long distance, the road lay across a stretch of warm, bubbling mire, called by the witch her turf moor.

Beyond this was the witch's house, which stood in the center of a strange forest, where all the trees and flowers were polypi, half animals and half plants. They looked like serpents with a hundred heads, growing out of the ground. The branches were long, slimy arms, with fingers like flexible worms, moving limb after limb from the root to the top. All that could be reached in the sea they seized upon and held fast, so that it never escaped from their clutches.

The little mermaid was so alarmed at what she saw that she stood still and her heart beat with fear. She came very near turning back, but she thought of the prince and of the human soul for which she longed, and her courage returned. She fastened her long, flowing hair round her head, so that the polypi should not lay hold of it. She crossed her hands on her bosom, and then darted forward as a fish shoots through the water, between the supple arms and fingers of the ugly polypi, which were stretched out on each side of her. She saw that they all held in their grasp something they had seized with their numerous little arms, which were as strong as iron bands. Tightly grasped in their clinging arms were white skeletons of human beings who had perished at sea and had sunk down into the deep waters; skeletons of land animals; and oars, rudders, and chests, of ships. There was even a little mermaid whom they had caught and strangled, and this seemed the most shocking of all to the little princess.

She now came to a space of marshy ground in the wood, where large, fat water snakes were rolling in the mire and showing their ugly, drab-colored bodies. In the midst of this spot stood a house, built of the bones of shipwrecked human beings. There sat the sea witch, allowing a toad to eat from her mouth just as people sometimes feed a canary with pieces of sugar. She called the ugly water snakes her little chickens and allowed them to crawl all over her bosom.

"I know what you want," said the sea witch. "It is very stupid of you, but you shall have your way, though it will bring you to sorrow, my pretty princess. You want to get rid of your fish's tail and to have two supports instead, like human beings on earth, so that the young prince may fall in love with you and so that you may have an immortal soul." And then the witch laughed so loud and so disgustingly that the toad and the snakes fell to the ground and lay there wriggling.

"You are but just in time," said the witch, "for after sunrise to-morrow I should not be able to help you till the end of another year. I will prepare a draft for you, with which you must swim to land to-morrow before sunrise; seat yourself there and drink it. Your tail will then disappear, and shrink up into what men call legs.

"You will feel great pain, as if a sword were passing through you. But all who see you will say that you are the prettiest little human being they ever saw. You will still have the same floating gracefulness of movement, and no dancer will ever tread so light-ly. Every step you take, however, will be as if you were treading upon sharp knives and as if the blood must flow. If you will bear all this, I will help you."

"Yes, I will," said the little princess in a trembling voice, as she thought of the prince and the immortal soul.

"But think again," said the witch, "for when once your shape has become like a human being, you can no more be a mermaid. You will never return through the water to your sisters or to your father's palace again. And if you do not win the love of the prince, so that he is willing to forget his father and mother for your sake and to love you with his whole soul and allow the priest to join your hands that you may be man and wife, then you will never have an immortal soul. The first morning after he marries another, your heart will break and you will become foam on the crest of the waves."

"I will do it," said the little mermaid, and she became pale as death.

"But I must be paid, also," said the witch, "and it is not a trifle that I ask. You have the sweetest voice of any who dwell here in the depths of the sea, and you believe that you will be able to charm the prince with it. But this voice you must give to me. The best thing you possess will I have as the price of my costly draft, which must be mixed with my own blood so that it may be as sharp as a two-edged sword."

"But if you take away my voice," said the little mermaid, "what is left for me?"

"Your beautiful form, your graceful walk, and your expressive eyes. Surely with these you can enchain a man's heart. Well, have you lost your courage? Put out your little tongue, that I may cut it off as my payment; then you shall have the powerful draft."

"It shall be," said the little mermaid.

Then the witch placed her caldron on the fire, to prepare the magic draft.

"Cleanliness is a good thing," said she, scouring the vessel with snakes which she had tied together in a large knot. Then she pricked herself in the breast and let the black blood drop into the caldron. The steam that rose twisted itself into such horrible shapes that no one could look at them without fear. Every moment the witch threw a new ingredient into the vessel, and when it began to boil, the sound was like the weeping of a crocodile. When at last the magic draft was ready, it looked like the clearest water.

"There it is for you," said the witch. Then she cut off the mermaid's tongue, so that she would never again speak or sing. "If the polypi should seize you as you return through the wood," said the witch, "throw over them a few drops of the potion, and their fingers will be torn into a thousand pieces." But the little mermaid had no occasion to do this, for the polypi sprang back in terror when they caught sight of the glittering draft, which shone in her hand like a twinkling star.

So she passed quickly through the wood and the marsh and between the rushing whirlpools. She saw that in her father's palace the torches in the ballroom were extinguished and that all within were asleep. But she did not venture to go in to them, for now that she was dumb and going to leave them forever she felt as if her heart would break. She stole into the garden, took a flower from the flower bed of each of her sisters, kissed her hand towards the palace a thousand times, and then rose up through the dark-blue waters.

The sun had not risen when she came in sight of the prince's palace and approached the beautiful marble steps, but the moon shone clear and bright. Then the little mermaid drank the magic draft, and it seemed as if a two-edged sword went through her delicate body. She fell into a swoon and lay like one dead. When the sun rose and shone over the sea, she recovered and felt a sharp pain, but before her stood the handsome young prince.

He fixed his coal-black eyes upon her so earnestly that she cast down her own and then became aware that her fish's tail was gone and that she had as pretty a pair of white legs and tiny feet as any little maiden could have. But she had no clothes, so she wrapped herself in her long, thick hair. The prince asked her who she was and whence she came. She looked at him mildly and sorrowfully with her deep blue eyes, but could not speak. He took her by the hand and led her to the palace.

Every step she took was as the witch had said it would be; she felt as if she were treading upon the points of needles or sharp knives. She bore it willingly, however, and moved at the prince's side as lightly as a bubble, so that he and all who saw her wondered at her graceful, swaying movements. She was very soon arrayed in costly robes of silk and muslin and was the most beautiful creature in the palace; but she was dumb and could neither speak nor sing.

Beautiful female slaves, dressed in silk and gold, stepped forward and sang before the prince and his royal parents. One sang better than all the others, and the prince clapped his hands and smiled at her. This was a great sorrow to the little mermaid, for she knew how much more sweetly she herself once could sing, and she thought, "Oh, if he could only know that I have given away my voice forever, to be with him!"

The slaves next performed some pretty fairy-like dances, to the sound of beautiful music. Then the little mermaid raised her lovely white arms, stood on the tips of her toes, glided over the floor, and danced as no one yet had been able to dance. At each moment her beauty was more revealed, and her expressive eyes appealed more directly to the heart than the songs of the slaves. Every one was enchanted, especially the prince, who called her his little foundling. She danced again quite readily, to please him, though each time her foot touched the floor it seemed as if she trod on sharp knives.

The prince said she should remain with him always, and she was given permission to sleep at his door, on a velvet cushion. He had a page's dress made for her, that she might accompany him on horseback. They rode together through the sweet-scented woods, where the green boughs touched their shoulders, and the little birds sang among the fresh leaves. She climbed with him to the tops of high mountains, and although her tender feet bled so that even her steps were marked, she only smiled, and followed him till they could see the clouds beneath them like a flock of birds flying to distant lands. While at the prince's palace, and when all the household were asleep, she would go and sit on the broad marble steps, for it eased her burning feet to bathe them in the cold sea water. It was then that she thought of all those below in the deep.

Once during the night her sisters came up arm in arm, singing sorrowfully as they floated on the water. She beckoned to them, and they recognized her and told her how she had grieved them; after that, they came to the same place every night. Once she saw in the distance her old grandmother, who had not been to the surface of the sea for many years, and the old Sea King, her father, with his crown on his head. They stretched out their hands towards her, but did not venture so near the land as her sisters had.

As the days passed she loved the prince more dearly, and he loved her as one would love a little child. The thought never came to him to make her his wife. Yet unless he married her, she could not receive an immortal soul, and on the morning after his marriage with another, she would dissolve into the foam of the sea.

"Do you not love me the best of them all?" the eyes of the little mermaid seemed to say when he took her in his arms and kissed her fair forehead.

"Yes, you are dear to me," said the prince, "for you have the best heart and you are the most devoted to me. You are like a young maiden whom I once saw, but whom I shall never meet again. I was in a ship that was wrecked, and the waves cast me ashore near a holy temple where several young maidens performed the service. The youngest of them found me on the shore and saved my life. I saw her but twice, and she is the only one in the world whom I could love. But you are like her, and you have almost driven her image from my mind. She belongs to the holy temple, and good fortune has sent you to me in her stead. We will never part.

"Ah, he knows not that it was I who saved his life," thought the little mermaid. "I carried him over the sea to the wood where the temple stands; I sat beneath the foam and watched till the human beings came to help him. I saw the pretty maiden that he loves better than he loves me." The mermaid sighed deeply, but she could not weep. "He says the maiden belongs to the holy temple, therefore she will never return to the world—they will meet no more. I am by his side and see him every day. I will take care of him, and love him, and give up my life for his sake."

Very soon it was said that the prince was to marry and that the beautiful daughter of a neighboring king would be his wife, for a fine ship was being fitted out. Although the prince gave out that he intended merely to pay a visit to the king, it was generally supposed that he went to court the princess. A great company were to go with him. The little mermaid smiled and shook her head. She knew the prince's thoughts better than any of the others.

"I must travel," he had said to her; "I must see this beautiful princess. My parents desire it, but they will not oblige me to bring her home as my bride. I cannot love her, because she is not like the beautiful maiden in the temple, whom you resemble. If I were forced to choose a bride, I would choose you, my dumb foundling, with those expressive eyes." Then he kissed her rosy mouth, played with her long, waving hair, and laid his head on her heart, while she dreamed of human happiness and an immortal soul.

"You are not afraid of the sea, my dumb child, are you?" he said, as they stood on the deck of the noble ship which was to carry them to the country of the neighboring king. Then he told her of storm and of calm, of strange fishes in the deep beneath them, and of what the divers had seen there. She smiled at his descriptions, for she knew better than any one what wonders were at the bottom of the sea.

In the moonlight night, when all on board were asleep except the man at the helm, she sat on deck, gazing down through the clear water. She thought she could distinguish her father's castle, and upon it her aged grandmother, with the silver crown on her head, looking through the rushing tide at the keel of the vessel. Then her sisters came up on the waves and gazed at her mournfully, wringing their white hands. She beckoned to them, and smiled, and wanted to tell them how happy and well off she was. But the cabin boy approached, and when her sisters dived down, he thought what he saw was only the foam of the sea.

The next morning the ship sailed into the harbor of a beautiful town belonging to the king whom the prince was going to visit. The church bells were ringing, and from the high towers sounded a flourish of trumpets. Soldiers, with flying colors and glittering bayonets, lined the roads through which they passed. Every day was a festival, balls and entertainments following one another. But the princess had not yet appeared. People said that she had been brought up and educated in a religious house, where she was learning every royal virtue.

At last she came. Then the little mermaid, who was anxious to see whether she was really beautiful, was obliged to admit that she had never seen a more perfect vision of beauty. Her skin was delicately fair, and beneath her long, dark eyelashes her laughing blue eyes shone with truth and purity.

"It was you," said the prince, "who saved my life when I lay as if dead on the beach," and he folded his blushing bride in his arms.

"Oh, I am too happy!" said he to the little mermaid; "my fondest hopes are now fulfilled. You will rejoice at my happiness, for your devotion to me is great and sincere."

The little mermaid kissed his hand and felt as if her heart were already broken. His wedding morning would bring death to her, and she would change into the foam of the sea.

All the church bells rang, and the heralds rode through the town proclaiming the betrothal. Perfumed oil was burned in costly silver lamps on every altar. The priests waved the censers, while the bride and the bridegroom joined their hands and received the blessing of the bishop. The little mermaid, dressed in silk and gold, held up the bride's train; but her ears heard nothing of the festive music, and her eyes saw not the holy ceremony. She thought of the night of death which was coming to her, and of all she had lost in the world.

On the same evening the bride and bridegroom went on board the ship. Cannons were roaring, flags waving, and in the center of the ship a costly tent of purple and gold had been erected. It contained elegant sleeping couches for the bridal pair during the night. The ship, under a favorable wind, with swelling sails, glided away smoothly and lightly over the calm sea.

When it grew dark, a number of colored lamps were lighted and the sailors danced merrily on the deck. The little mermaid could not help thinking of her first rising out of the sea, when she had seen similar joyful festivities, so she too joined in the dance, poised herself in the air as a swallow when he pursues his prey, and all present cheered her wonderingly. She had never danced so gracefully before. Her tender feet felt as if cut with sharp knives, but she cared not for the pain; a sharper pang had pierced her heart.

She knew this was the last evening she should ever see the prince for whom she had forsaken her kindred and her home. She had given up her beautiful voice and suffered unheard-of pain daily for him, while he knew nothing of it. This was the last evening that she should breathe the same air with him or gaze on the starry sky and the deep sea. An eternal night, without a thought or a dream, awaited her. She had no soul, and now could never win one.

All was joy and gaiety on the ship until long after midnight. She smiled and danced with the rest, while the thought of death was in her heart. The prince kissed his beautiful bride and she played with his raven hair till they went arm in arm to rest in the sumptuous tent. Then all became still on board the ship, and only the pilot, who stood at the helm, was awake. The little mermaid leaned her white arms on the edge of the vessel and looked towards the east for the first blush of morning—for that first ray of the dawn which was to be her death. She saw her sisters rising out of the flood. They were as pale as she, but their beautiful hair no longer waved in the wind; it had been cut off.

"We have given our hair to the witch," said they, "to obtain help for you, that you may not die to-night. She has given us a knife; see, it is very sharp. Before the sun rises you must plunge it into the heart of the prince. When the warm blood falls upon your feet they will grow together again into a fish's tail, and you will once more be a mermaid and can return to us to live out your three hundred years before you are changed into the salt sea foam. Haste, then; either he or you must die before sunrise. Our old grandmother mourns so for you that her white hair is falling, as ours fell under the witch's scissors. Kill the prince, and come back. Hasten! Do you not see the first red streaks in the sky? In a few minutes the sun will rise, and you must die."

Then they sighed deeply and mournfully, and sank beneath the waves.

The little mermaid drew back the crimson curtain of the tent and beheld the fair bride, whose head was resting on the prince's breast. She bent down and kissed his noble brow, then looked at the sky, on which the rosy dawn grew brighter and brighter. She glanced at the sharp knife and again fixed her eyes on the prince, who whispered the name of his bride in his dreams.

She was in his thoughts, and the knife trembled in the hand of the little mermaid—but she flung it far from her into the waves. The water turned red where it fell, and the drops that spurted up looked like blood. She cast one more lingering, half-fainting glance at the prince, then threw herself from the ship into the sea and felt her body dissolving into foam.

The sun rose above the waves, and his warm rays fell on the cold foam of the little mermaid, who did not feel as if she were dying. She saw the bright sun, and hundreds of transparent, beautiful creatures floating around her—she could see through them the white sails of the ships and the red clouds in the sky. Their speech was melodious, but could not be heard by mortal ears— just as their bodies could not be seen by mortal eyes. The little mermaid perceived that she had a body like theirs and that she continued to rise higher and higher out of the foam. "Where am I?" asked she, and her voice sounded ethereal, like the voices of those who were with her. No earthly music could imitate it.

"Among the daughters of the air," answered one of them. "A mermaid has not an immortal soul, nor can she obtain one unless she wins the love of a human being. On the will of another hangs her eternal destiny. But the daughters of the air, although they do not possess an immortal soul, can, by their good deeds, procure one for themselves. We fly to warm countries and cool the sultry air that destroys mankind with the pestilence. We carry the perfume of the flowers to spread health and restoration.

"After we have striven for three hundred years to do all the good in our power, we receive an immortal soul and take part in the happiness of mankind. You, poor little mermaid, have tried with your whole heart to do as we are doing. You have suffered and endured, and raised yourself to the spirit world by your good deeds, and now, by striving for three hundred years in the same way, you may obtain an immortal soul."

The little mermaid lifted her glorified eyes toward the sun and, for the first time, felt them filling with tears.

On the ship in which she had left the prince there were life and noise, and she saw him and his beautiful bride searching for her. Sorrowfully they gazed at the pearly foam, as if they knew she had thrown herself into the waves. Unseen she kissed the forehead of the bride and fanned the prince, and then mounted with the other children of the air to a rosy cloud that floated above.

"After three hundred years, thus shall we float into the kingdom of heaven," said she. "And we may even get there sooner," whispered one of her companions. "Unseen we can enter the houses of men where there are children, and for every day on which we find a good child that is the joy of his parents and deserves their love, our time of probation is shortened. The child does not know, when we fly through the room, that we smile with joy at his good conduct—for we can count one year less of our three hundred years. But when we see a naughty or a wicked child we shed tears of sorrow, and for every tear a day is added to our time of trial."

The Snowman

It is so delightfully cold that it makes my whole body crackle," said the Snow Man. "This is just the kind of wind to blow life into one. How that great red thing up there is staring at me!" He meant the sun, which was just setting. "It shall not make me wink. I shall manage to keep the pieces."

He had two triangular pieces of tile in his head instead of eyes, and his mouth, being made of an old broken rake, was therefore furnished with teeth. He had been brought into existence amid the joyous shouts of boys, the jingling of sleigh bells, and the slashing of whips.

The sun went down, and the full moon rose, large, round, and clear, shining in the deep blue.

"There it comes again, from the other side," said the Snow Man, who supposed the sun was showing itself once more. "Ah, I have cured it of staring. Now it may hang up there and shine, so that I may see myself. If I only knew how to manage to move away from this place—I should so like to move! If I could, I would slide along yonder on the ice, as I have seen the boys do; but I don't understand how. I don't even know how to run."

"Away, away!" barked the old yard dog. He was quite hoarse and could not pronounce "Bow-wow" properly. He had once been an indoor dog and lain by the fire, and he had been hoarse ever since. "The sun will make you run some day. I saw it, last winter, make your predecessor run, and his predecessor before him. Away, away! They all have to go."

"I don't understand you, comrade," said the Snow Man. "Is that thing up yonder to teach me to run? I saw it running itself, a little while ago, and now it has come creeping up from the other side."

"You know nothing at all," replied the yard dog. "But then, you've only lately been patched up. What you see yonder is the moon, and what you saw before was the sun. It will come again to-morrow and most likely teach you to run down into the ditch

291

by the well, for I think the weather is going to change. I can feel such pricks and stabs in my left leg that I am sure there is going to be a change."

"I don't understand him," said the Snow Man to himself, "but I have a feeling that he is talking of something very disagreeable. The thing that stared so hard just now, which he calls the sun, is not my friend; I can feel that too."

"Away, away!" barked the yard dog, and then he turned round three times and crept into his kennel to sleep.

There really was a change in the weather. Toward morning a thick fog covered the whole country and a keen wind arose, so that the cold seemed to freeze one's bones. But when the sun rose, a splendid sight was to be seen. Trees and bushes were covered with hoarfrost and looked like a forest of white coral, while on every twig glittered frozen dewdrops. The many delicate forms, concealed in summer by luxuriant foliage, were now clearly defined and looked like glittering lacework. A white radiance glistened from every twig. The birches, waving in the wind, looked as full of life as in summer and as wondrously beautiful. Where the sun shone, everything glittered and sparkled as if diamond dust had been strewn about; and the snowy carpet of the earth seemed covered with diamonds from which gleamed countless lights, whiter even than the snow itself.

"This is really beautiful," said a girl who had come into the garden with a young friend; and they both stood still near the Snow Man, contemplating the glittering scene. "Summer cannot show a more beautiful sight," she exclaimed, while her eyes sparkled.

"And we can't have such a fellow as this in the summer-time," replied the young man, pointing to the Snow Man. "He is capital."

The girl laughed and nodded at the Snow Man, then tripped away over the snow with her friend. The snow creaked and crackled beneath her feet, as if she had been treading on starch.

"Who are those two?" asked the Snow Man of the yard dog. "You have been here longer than I; do you know them?"

"Of course I know them," replied the yard dog; "the girl has stroked my back many times, and the young man has often given me a bone of meat. I never bite those two."

"But what are they?" asked the Snow Man.

"They are lovers," he replied. "They will go and live in the same kennel, by and by, and gnaw at the same bone. Away, away!"

"Are they the same kind of beings as you and I?" asked the Snow Man.

"Well, they belong to the master," retorted the yard dog. "Certainly people know very little who were only born yesterday. I can see that in you. I have age and experience. I know every one here in the house, and I know there was once a time when I did not lie out here in the cold, fastened to a chain. Away, away!"

"The cold is delightful," said the Snow Man. "But do tell me, tell me; only you must not clank your chain so, for it jars within me when you do that."

"Away, away!" barked the yard dog. "I'll tell you: they said I was a pretty little fellow, once; then I used to lie in a velvet-covered chair, up at the master's house, and sit in the mistress's lap; they used to kiss my nose, and wipe my paws with an embroidered handkerchief, and I was called 'Ami, dear Ami, sweet Ami.' But after a while I grew too big for them, and they sent me away to the housekeeper's room; so I came to live on the lower story. You can look into the room from where you stand, and see where I was once master—for I was, indeed, master to the housekeeper. It was a much smaller room than those upstairs, but I was more comfortable, for I was not continually being taken hold of and pulled about by the children, as I had been. I received quite as good food and even better. I had my own cushion, and there was a stove—it is the finest thing in the world at this season of the year. I used to go under the stove and lie down. Ah, I still dream of that stove. Away, away!"

"Does a stove look beautiful?" asked the Snow Man. "Is it at all like me?"

"It is just the opposite of you," said the dog. "It's as black as a crow and has a long neck and a brass knob; it eats firewood, and that makes fire spurt out of its mouth. One has to keep on one side or under it, to be comfortable. You can see it through the window from where you stand."

Then the Snow Man looked, and saw a bright polished thing with a brass knob, and fire gleaming from the lower part of it. The sight of this gave the Snow Man a strange sensation; it was very odd, he knew not what it meant, and he could not account for it. But there are people who are not men of snow who understand what the feeling is. "And why did you leave her?" asked the Snow Man, for it seemed to him that the stove must be of the female sex. "How could you give up such a comfortable place?"

"I was obliged to," replied the yard dog. "They turned me out of doors and chained me up here. I had bitten the youngest of my master's sons in the leg, because he kicked away the bone I was gnawing. 'Bone for bone,' I thought. But they were very angry, and since that time I have been fastened to a chain and have lost my voice. Don't you hear how hoarse I am? Away, away! I can't talk like other dogs any more. Away, away! That was the end of it all."

But the Snow Man was no longer listening. He was looking into the housekeeper's room on the lower story, where the stove, which was about the same size as the Snow Man himself, stood on its four iron legs. "What a strange crackling I feel within me," he said. "Shall I ever get in there? It is an innocent wish, and innocent wishes are sure to be fulfilled. I must go in there and lean against her, even if I have to break the window."

"You must never go in there," said the yard dog, "for if you approach the stove, you will melt away, away."

"I might as well go," said the Snow Man, "for I think I am breaking up as it is."

During the whole day the Snow Man stood looking in through

the window, and in the twilight hour the room became still more inviting, for from the stove came a gentle glow, not like the sun or the moon; it was only the kind of radiance that can come from a stove when it has been well fed. When the door of the stove was opened, the flames darted out of its mouth,—as is customary with all stoves,—and the light of the flames fell with a ruddy gleam directly on the face and breast of the Snow Man. "I can endure it no longer," said he. "How beautiful it looks when it stretches out its tongue!"

The night was long, but it did not appear so to the Snow Man, who stood there enjoying his own reflections and crackling with the cold. In the morning the window-panes of the housekeeper's room were covered with ice. They were the most beautiful ice flowers any Snow Man could desire, but they concealed the stove. These window-panes would not thaw, and he could see nothing of the stove, which he pictured to himself as if it had been a beautiful human being. The snow crackled and the wind whistled around him; it was just the kind of frosty weather a Snow Man ought to enjoy thoroughly. But he did not enjoy it. How, indeed, could he enjoy anything when he was so stove-sick?

"That is a terrible disease for a Snow Man to have," said the yard dog. "I have suffered from it myself, but I got over it. Away, away!" he barked, and then added, "The weather is going to change."

The weather did change. It began to thaw, and as the warmth increased, the Snow Man decreased. He said nothing and made no complaint, which is a sure sign.

One morning he broke and sank down altogether; and behold! where he had stood, something that looked like a broomstick remained sticking up in the ground. It was the pole round which the boys had built him.

"Ah, now I understand why he had such a great longing for the stove," said the yard dog. "Why, there's the shovel that is used for cleaning out the stove, fastened to the pole. The Snow Man had a stove scraper in his body; that was what moved him so. But it is all over now. Away, away!"

And soon the winter passed. "Away, away!" barked the hoarse yard dog, but the girls in the house sang:

"Come from your fragrant home, green thyme;
Stretch your soft branches, willow tree;
The months are bringing the sweet spring-time,
When the lark in the sky sings joyfully.
Come, gentle sun, while the cuckoo sings,
And I'll mock his note in my wanderings."

And nobody thought any more of the Snow Man.

The Wild Swans

Far away, in the land to which the swallows fly when it is winter, dwelt a king who had eleven sons, and one daughter, named Eliza.

The eleven brothers were princes, and each went to school with a star on his breast and a sword by his side. They wrote with diamond pencils on golden slates and learned their lessons so quickly and read so easily that every one knew they were princes. Their sister Eliza sat on a little stool of plate-glass and had a book full of pictures, which had cost as much as half a kingdom.

Happy, indeed, were these children; but they were not long to remain so, for their father, the king, married a queen who did not love the children, and who proved to be a wicked sorceress.

The queen began to show her unkindness the very first day. While the great festivities were taking place in the palace, the children played at receiving company; but the queen, instead of sending them the cakes and apples that were left from the feast, as was customary, gave them some sand in a teacup and told them to pretend it was something good. The next week she sent the little Eliza into the country to a peasant and his wife. Then she told the king so many untrue things about the young princes that he gave himself no more trouble about them.

"Go out into the world and look after yourselves," said the queen. "Fly like great birds without a voice." But she could not make it so bad for them as she would have liked, for they were turned into eleven beautiful wild swans.

With a strange cry, they flew through the windows of the palace, over the park, to the forest beyond. It was yet early morning when they passed the peasant's cottage where their sister lay asleep in her room. They hovered over the roof, twisting their long necks and flapping their wings, but no one heard them or saw them, so they at last flew away, high up in the clouds, and over the wide world they sped till they came to a thick, dark wood, which stretched far away to the seashore.

Poor little Eliza was alone in the peasant's room playing with a green leaf, for she had no other playthings. She pierced a hole in the leaf, and when she looked through it at the sun she seemed to see her brothers' clear eyes, and when the warm sun shone on her cheeks she thought of all the kisses they had given her.

One day passed just like another. Sometimes the winds rustled through the leaves of the rosebush and whispered to the roses, "Who can be more beautiful than you?" And the roses would shake their heads and say, "Eliza is." And when the old woman sat at the cottage door on Sunday and read her hymn book, the wind would flutter the leaves and say to the book, "Who can be more pious than you?" And then the hymn book would answer, "Eliza." And the roses and the hymn book told the truth.

When she was fifteen she returned home, but because she was so beautiful the witch-queen became full of spite and hatred toward her. Willingly would she have turned her into a swan like her brothers, but she did not dare to do so for fear of the king.

Early one morning the queen went into the bathroom; it was built of marble and had soft cushions trimmed with the most beautiful tapestry. She took three toads with her, and kissed them, saying to the first, "When Eliza comes to bathe seat yourself upon her head, that she may become as stupid as you are." To the second toad she said, "Place yourself on her forehead, that she may become as ugly as you are, and that her friends may not know her." "Rest on her heart," she whispered to the third; "then she will have evil inclinations and suffer because of them." So she put the toads into the clear water, which at once turned green. She next called Eliza and helped her undress and get into the bath.

As Eliza dipped her head under the water one of the toads sat on her hair, a second on her forehead, and a third on her breast. But she did not seem to notice them, and when she rose from the water there were three red poppies floating upon it. Had not the creatures been venomous or had they not been kissed by the witch, they would have become red roses. At all events they became flowers, because they had rested on Eliza's head and on her heart. She was too good and too innocent for sorcery to have any power over her.

When the wicked queen saw this, she rubbed Eliza's face with walnut juice, so that she was quite brown; then she tangled her beautiful hair and smeared it with disgusting ointment until it was quite impossible to recognize her.

The king was shocked, and declared she was not his daughter. No one but the watchdog and the swallows knew her, and they were only poor animals and could say nothing. Then poor Eliza wept and thought of her eleven brothers who were far away. Sorrowfully she stole from the palace and walked the whole day over fields and moors, till she came to the great forest. She knew not in what direction to go, but she was so unhappy and longed so for her brothers, who, like herself, had been driven out into the world, that she was determined to seek them.

She had been in the wood only a short time when night came on and she quite lost the path; so she laid herself down on the soft moss, offered up her evening prayer, and leaned her head against the stump of a tree. All nature was silent, and the soft, mild air fanned her forehead. The light of hundreds of glowworms shone amidst the grass and the moss like green fire, and if she touched a twig with her hand, ever so lightly, the brilliant insects fell down around her like shooting stars.

All night long she dreamed of her brothers. She thought they were all children again, playing together. She saw them writing with their diamond pencils on golden slates, while she looked at the beautiful picture book which had cost half a kingdom. They were not writing lines and letters, as they used to do, but descriptions of the noble deeds they had performed and of all that they had discovered and seen. In the picture book, too, everything was living. The birds sang, and the people came out of the book and spoke to Eliza and her brothers; but as the leaves were turned over they darted back again to their places, that all might be in order.

When she awoke, the sun was high in the heavens. She could not see it, for the lofty trees spread their branches thickly overhead, but its gleams here and there shone through the leaves like a gauzy golden mist. There was a sweet fragrance from the fresh verdure, and the birds came near and almost perched on her shoulders. She heard water rippling from a number of springs, all flowing into a lake with golden sands. Bushes grew thickly round the lake, and at one spot, where an opening had been made by a deer, Eliza went down to the water.

The lake was so clear that had not the wind rustled the branches of the trees and the bushes so that they moved, they would have seemed painted in the depths of the lake; for every leaf, whether in the shade or in the sunshine, was reflected in the water.

When Eliza saw her own face she was quite terrified at finding it so brown and ugly, but after she had wet her little hand and rubbed her eyes and forehead, the white skin gleamed forth once more; and when she had undressed and dipped herself in the fresh water, a more beautiful king's daughter could not have been found anywhere in the wide world.

As soon as she had dressed herself again and braided her long hair, she went to the bubbling spring and drank some water out of the hollow of her hand. Then she wandered far into the forest, not knowing whither she went. She thought of her brothers and of her father and mother and felt sure that God would not forsake her. It is God who makes the wild apples grow in the wood to satisfy the hungry, and He now showed her one of these trees, which was so loaded with fruit that the boughs bent beneath the weight. Here she ate her noonday meal, and then placing props under the boughs, she went into the gloomiest depths of the forest.

It was so still that she could hear the sound of her own footsteps, as well as the rustling of every withered leaf which she crushed under her feet. Not a bird was to be seen, not a sunbeam could penetrate the large, dark boughs of the trees. The lofty trunks stood so close together that when she looked before her it seemed as if she were enclosed within trelliswork. Here was such solitude as she had never known before!

The night was very dark. Not a glowworm was glittering in the moss. Sorrowfully Eliza laid herself down to sleep. After a while it seemed to her as if the branches of the trees parted over her head and the mild eyes of angels looked down upon her from heaven.

In the morning, when she awoke, she knew not whether this had really been so or whether she had dreamed it. She continued her wandering, but she had not gone far when she met an old woman who had berries in her basket and who gave her a few to eat. Eliza asked her if she had not seen eleven princes riding through the forest.

"No," replied the old woman, "but I saw yesterday eleven swans with gold crowns on their heads, swimming in the river close by." Then she led Eliza a little distance to a sloping bank, at the foot of which ran a little river. The trees on its banks stretched their long leafy branches across the water toward each other, and where they did not meet naturally the roots had torn themselves away from the ground, so that the branches might mingle their foliage as they hung over the water.

Eliza bade the old woman farewell and walked by the flowing river till she reached the shore of the open sea. And there, before her eyes, lay the glorious ocean, but not a sail appeared on its surface; not even a boat could be seen. How was she to go farther? She noticed how the countless pebbles on the shore had been smoothed and rounded by the action of the water. Glass, iron, stones, everything that lay there mingled together, had been shaped by the same power until they were as smooth as her own delicate hand.

"The water rolls on without weariness," she said, "till all that is hard becomes smooth; so will I be unwearied in my task. Thanks for your lesson, bright rolling waves; my heart tells me you will one day lead me to my dear brothers."

On the foam-covered seaweeds lay eleven white swan feathers, which she gathered and carried with her. Drops of water lay upon them; whether they were dewdrops or tears no one could say. It was lonely on the seashore, but she did not know it, for the ever-moving sea showed more changes in a few hours than the most varying lake could produce in a whole year. When a black, heavy cloud arose, it was as if the sea said, "I can look dark and angry too"; and then the wind blew, and the waves turned to white foam as they rolled. When the wind slept and the clouds glowed with the red sunset, the sea looked like a rose leaf. Sometimes it became green and sometimes white. But, however quietly it lay, the waves were always restless on the shore and rose and fell like the breast of a sleeping child.

When the sun was about to set, Eliza saw eleven white swans, with golden crowns on their heads, flying toward the land, one behind the other, like a long white ribbon. She went down the slope from the shore and hid herself behind the bushes. The swans alighted quite close to her, flapping their great white wings. As soon as the sun had disappeared under the water, the feathers of the swans fell off and eleven beautiful princes, Eliza's brothers, stood near her.

She uttered a loud cry, for, although they were very much changed, she knew them immediately. She sprang into their arms and called them each by name. Very happy the princes were to see their little sister again; they knew her, although she had grown so tall and beautiful. They laughed and wept and told each other how cruelly they had been treated by their stepmother.

"We brothers," said the eldest, "fly about as wild swans while the sun is in the sky, but as soon as it sinks behind the hills we recover our human shape. Therefore we must always be near a resting place before sunset; for if we were flying toward the clouds when we recovered our human form, we should sink deep into the sea.

"We do not dwell here, but in a land just as fair that lies far across the ocean; the way is long, and there is no island upon which we can pass the night—nothing but a little rock rising out of the sea, upon which, even crowded together, we can scarcely stand with safety. If the sea is rough, the foam dashes over us; yet we thank God for this rock. We have passed whole nights upon it, or we should never have reached our beloved fatherland, for our flight across the sea occupies two of the longest days in the year.

"We have permission to visit our home once every year and to remain eleven days. Then we fly across the forest to look once more at the palace where our father dwells and where we were born, and at the church beneath whose shade our mother lies buried. The very trees and bushes here seem related to us. The wild horses leap over the plains as we have seen them in our childhood. The charcoal burners sing the old songs to which we have danced as children. This is our fatherland, to which we are drawn by loving ties; and here we have found you, our dear little sister. Two days longer we can remain here, and then we must fly away to a beautiful land which is not our home. How can we take you with us? We have neither ship nor boat."

"How can I break this spell?" asked the sister. And they talked about it nearly the whole night, slumbering only a few hours.

Eliza was awakened by the rustling of the wings of swans soaring above her. Her brothers were again changed to swans. They flew in circles, wider and wider, till they were far away; but one of them, the youngest, remained behind and laid his head in his sister's lap, while she stroked his wings. They remained together the whole day.

Towards evening the rest came back, and as the sun went down they resumed their natural forms. "To-morrow," said one, "we shall fly away, not to return again till a whole year has passed. But we cannot leave you here. Have you courage to go with us? My arm is strong enough to carry you through the wood, and will not all our wings be strong enough to bear you over the sea?"

"Yes, take me with you," said Eliza. They spent the whole night in weaving a large, strong net of the pliant willow and rushes. On this Eliza laid herself down to sleep, and when the sun rose and her brothers again became wild swans, they took up the net with their beaks, and flew up to the clouds with their dear sister, who still slept. When the sunbeams fell on her face, one of the swans soared over her head so that his broad wings might shade her.

They were far from the land when Eliza awoke. She thought she must still be dreaming, it seemed so strange to feel herself being carried high in the air over the sea. By her side lay a branch full of beautiful ripe berries and a bundle of sweet-tasting roots; the youngest of her brothers had gathered them and placed them there. She smiled her thanks to him; she knew it was the same one that was hovering over her to shade her with his wings. They were now so high that a large ship beneath them looked like a white sea gull skimming the waves. A great cloud floating behind them appeared like a vast mountain, and upon it Eliza saw her own shadow and those of the eleven swans, like gigantic flying things. Altogether it formed a more beautiful picture than she had ever before seen; but as the sun rose higher and the clouds were left behind, the picture vanished.

Onward the whole day they flew through the air like winged arrows, yet more slowly than usual, for they had their sister to carry. The weather grew threatening, and Eliza watched the sinking sun with great anxiety, for the little rock in the ocean was not yet in sight. It seemed to her as if the swans were exerting themselves to the utmost. Alas! she was the cause of their not advancing more quickly. When the sun set they would change to men, fall into the sea, and be drowned.

Then she offered a prayer from her inmost heart, but still no rock appeared. Dark clouds came nearer, the gusts of wind told of the coming storm, while from a thick, heavy mass of clouds the lightning burst forth, flash after flash. The sun had reached the edge of the sea, when the swans darted down so swiftly that Eliza's heart trembled; she believed they were falling, but they again soared onward.

Presently, and by this time the sun was half hidden by the waves, she caught sight of the rock just below them. It did not look larger than a seal's head thrust out of the water. The sun sank so rapidly that at the moment their feet touched the rock it shone only like a star, and at last disappeared like the dying spark in a piece of burnt paper. Her brothers stood close around her with arms linked together, for there was not the smallest space to spare. The sea dashed against the rock and covered them with spray. The heavens were lighted up with continual flashes, and thunder rolled from the clouds. But the sister and brothers stood holding each other's hands, and singing hymns.

In the early dawn the air became calm and still, and at sunrise the swans flew away from the rock, bearing their sister with them. The sea was still rough, and from their great height the white foam on the dark-green waves looked like millions of swans swimming on the water. As the sun rose higher, Eliza saw before her, floating in the air, a range of mountains with shining masses of ice on their summits. In the center rose a castle that seemed a mile long, with rows of columns rising one above another, while around it palm trees waved and flowers as large as mill wheels bloomed. She asked if this was the land to which they were hastening. The swans shook their heads, for what she beheld were the beautiful, ever-changing cloud-palaces of the Fata Morgana, into which no mortal can enter.

Eliza was still gazing at the scene, when mountains, forests, and castles melted away, and twenty stately churches rose in their stead, with high towers and pointed Gothic windows. She even fancied she could hear the tones of the organ, but it was the music of the murmuring sea. As they drew nearer to the churches, these too were changed and became a fleet of ships, which seemed to be sailing beneath her; but when she looked again she saw only a sea mist gliding over the ocean.

One scene melted into another, until at last she saw the real land to which they were bound, with its blue mountains, its cedar forests, and its cities and palaces. Long before the sun went down she was sitting on a rock in front of a large cave, the floor of which was overgrown with delicate green creeping plants, like an embroidered carpet.

"Now we shall expect to hear what you dream of to-night," said the youngest brother, as he showed his sister her bedroom.

"Heaven grant that I may dream how to release you!" she replied. And this thought took such hold upon her mind that she prayed earnestly to God for help, and even in her sleep she continued to pray. Then it seemed to her that she was flying high in the air toward the cloudy palace of the Fata Morgana, and that a fairy came out to meet her, radiant and beautiful, yet much like the old woman who had given her berries in the wood, and who had told her of the swans with golden crowns on their heads.

"Your brothers can be released," said she, "if you only have courage and perseverance. Water is softer than your own delicate hands, and yet it polishes and shapes stones. But it feels no pain such as your fingers will feel; it has no soul and cannot suffer such agony and torment as you will have to endure. Do you see the stinging nettle which I hold in my hand? Quantities of the same sort grow round the cave in which you sleep, but only these, and those that grow on the graves of a churchyard, will be of any use to you. These you must gather, even while they burn blisters on your hands. Break them to pieces with your hands and feet, and they will become flax, from which you must spin and weave eleven coats with long sleeves; if these are then thrown over the eleven swans, the spell will be broken. But remember well, that from the moment you commence your task until it is finished, even though it occupy years of your life, you must not speak. The first word you utter will pierce the hearts of your brothers like a deadly dagger. Their lives hang upon your tongue. Remember all that I have told you."

And as she finished speaking, she touched Eliza's hand lightly with the nettle, and a pain as of burning fire awoke her.

It was broad daylight, and near her lay a nettle like the one she had seen in her dream. She fell on her knees and offered thanks to God. Then she went forth from the cave to begin work with her delicate hands. She groped in amongst the ugly nettles, which burned great blisters on her hands and arms, but she determined to bear the pain gladly if she could only release her dear brothers. So she bruised the nettles with her bare feet and spun the flax.

At sunset her brothers returned, and were much frightened when she did not speak. They believed her to be under the spell of some new sorcery, but when they saw her hands they understood what she was doing in their behalf. The youngest brother wept, and where his tears touched her the pain ceased and the burning blisters vanished. Eliza kept to her work all night, for she could not rest till she had released her brothers. During the whole of the following day, while her brothers were absent, she sat in solitude, but never before had the time flown so quickly.

One coat was already finished and she had begun the second, when she heard a huntsman's horn and was struck with fear. As the sound came nearer and nearer, she also heard dogs barking, and fled with terror into the cave. She hastily bound together the nettles she had gathered, and sat upon them. In a moment there came bounding toward her out of the ravine a great dog, and then another and another; they ran back and forth barking furiously, until in a few minutes all the huntsmen stood before the cave. The handsomest of them was the king of the country, who, when he saw the beautiful maiden, advanced toward her, saying, "How did you come here, my sweet child?"

Eliza shook her head. She dared not speak, for it would cost her brothers their deliverance and their lives. And she hid her hands under her apron, so that the king might not see how she was suffering.

"Come with me," he said; "here you cannot remain. If you are as good as you are beautiful, I will dress you in silk and velvet, I will place a golden crown on your head, and you shall rule and make your home in my richest castle." Then he lifted her onto his horse. She wept and wrung her hands, but the king said: "I wish only your happiness. A time will come when you will thank me for this."

He galloped away over the mountains, holding her before him on his horse, and the hunters followed behind them. As the sun went down they approached a fair, royal city, with churches and cupolas. On arriving at the castle, the king led her into marble halls, where large fountains played and where the walls and the ceilings were covered with rich paintings. But she had no eyes for all these glorious sights; she could only mourn and weep. Patiently she allowed the women to array her in royal robes, to weave pearls in her hair, and to draw soft gloves over her blistered fingers. As she stood arrayed in her rich dress, she looked so dazzlingly beautiful that the court bowed low in her presence.

Then the king declared his intention of making her his bride, but the archbishop shook his head and whispered that the fair young maiden was only a witch, who had blinded the king's eyes and ensnared his heart. The king would not listen to him, however, and ordered the music to sound, the daintiest dishes to be served, and the loveliest maidens to dance before them.

Afterwards he led her through fragrant gardens and lofty halls, but not a smile appeared on her lips or sparkled in her eyes. She looked the very picture of grief. Then the king opened the door of a little chamber in which she was to sleep. It was adorned with rich green tapestry and resembled the cave in which he had found her. On the floor lay the bundle of flax which she had spun from the nettles, and under the ceiling hung the coat she had made. These things had been brought away from the cave as curiosities, by one of the huntsmen.

"Here you can dream yourself back again in the old home in the cave," said the king; "here is the work with which you employed yourself. It will amuse you now, in the midst of all this splendor, to think of that time."

When Eliza saw all these things which lay so near her heart, a smile played around her mouth, and the crimson blood rushed to her cheeks. The thought of her brothers and their release made her so joyful that she kissed the king's hand. Then he pressed her to his heart.

Very soon the joyous church bells announced the marriage feast; the beautiful dumb girl of the woods was to be made queen of the country. A single word would cost her brothers their lives, but she loved the kind, handsome king, who did everything to make her happy, more and more each day; she loved him with her whole heart, and her eyes beamed with the love she dared not speak. Oh! if she could only confide in him and tell him of her grief. But dumb she must remain till her task was finished.

Therefore at night she crept away into her little chamber which had been decked out to look like the cave and quickly wove one coat after another. But when she began the seventh, she found she had no more flax. She knew that the nettles she wanted to use grew in the churchyard and that she must pluck them herself. How should she get out there? "Oh, what is the pain in my fingers to the torment which my heart endures?" thought she. "I must venture; I shall not be denied help from heaven."

Then with a trembling heart, as if she were about to perform a wicked deed, Eliza crept into the garden in the broad moonlight, and passed through the narrow walks and the deserted streets till she reached the churchyard. She prayed silently, gathered the burning nettles, and carried them home with her to the castle.

One person only had seen her, and that was the archbishop—he was awake while others slept. Now he felt sure that his suspicions were correct; all was not right with the queen; she was a witch and had bewitched the king and all the people. Secretly he told the king what he had seen and what he feared, and as the hard words came from his tongue, the carved images of the saints shook their heads as if they would say, "It is not so; Eliza is innocent."

But the archbishop interpreted it in another way; he believed that they witnessed against her and were shaking their heads at her wickedness. Two tears rolled down the king's cheeks. He went home with doubt in his heart, and at night pretended to sleep. But no real sleep came to his eyes, for every night he saw Eliza get up and disappear from her chamber. Day by day his brow became darker, and Eliza saw it, and although she did not understand the reason, it alarmed her and made her heart tremble for her brothers. Her hot tears glittered like pearls on the regal velvet and diamonds, while all who saw her were wishing they could be queen.

In the meantime she had almost finished her task; only one of her brothers' coats was wanting, but she had no flax left and not a single nettle. Once more only, and for the last time, must she venture to the churchyard and pluck a few handfuls. She went, and the king and the archbishop followed her. The king turned away his head and said, "The people must condemn her." Quickly she was condemned to suffer death by fire.

Away from the gorgeous regal halls she was led to a dark, dreary cell, where the wind whistled through the iron bars. Instead of the velvet and silk dresses, they gave her the ten coats which she had woven, to cover her, and the bundle of nettles for a pillow. But they could have given her nothing that would have pleased her more. She continued her task with joy and prayed for help, while the street boys sang jeering songs about her and not a soul comforted her with a kind word.

Toward evening she heard at the grating the flutter of a swan's wing; it was her youngest brother. He had found his sister, and she sobbed for joy, although she knew that probably this was the last night she had to live. Still, she had hope, for her task was almost finished and her brothers were come.

Then the archbishop arrived, to be with her during her last hours as he had promised the king. She shook her head and begged him, by looks and gestures, not to stay; for in this night she knew she must finish her task, otherwise all her pain and tears and sleepless nights would have been suffered in vain. The archbishop withdrew, uttering bitter words against her, but she knew that she was innocent and diligently continued her work.

Little mice ran about the floor, dragging the nettles to her feet, to help as much as they could; and a thrush, sitting outside the grating of the window, sang to her the whole night long as sweetly as possible, to keep up her spirits.

It was still twilight, and at least an hour before sunrise, when the eleven brothers stood at the castle gate and demanded to be brought before the king. They were told it could not be; it was yet night; the king slept and could not be disturbed. They threatened, they entreated, until the guard appeared, and even the king himself, inquiring what all the noise meant. At this moment the sun rose, and the eleven brothers were seen no more, but eleven wild swans flew away over the castle.

Now all the people came streaming forth from the gates of the city to see the witch burned. An old horse drew the cart on which she sat. They had dressed her in a garment of coarse sackcloth. Her lovely hair hung loose on her shoulders, her cheeks were deadly pale, her lips moved silently while her fingers still worked at the green flax. Even on the way to death she would not give up her task. The ten finished coats lay at her feet; she was working hard at the eleventh, while the mob jeered her and said: "See the witch; how she mutters! She has no hymn book in her hand; she sits there with her ugly sorcery. Let us tear it into a thousand pieces."

They pressed toward her, and doubtless would have destroyed the coats had not, at that moment, eleven wild swans flown over her and alighted on the cart. They flapped their large wings, and the crowd drew back in alarm.

"It is a sign from Heaven that she is innocent," whispered many of them; but they did not venture to say it aloud.

As the executioner seized her by the hand to lift her out of the cart, she hastily threw the eleven coats over the eleven swans, and they immediately became eleven handsome princes; but the youngest had a swan's wing instead of an arm, for she had not been able to finish the last sleeve of the coat.

"Now I may speak," she exclaimed. "I am innocent."

Then the people, who saw what had happened, bowed to her as before a saint; but she sank unconscious in her brothers' arms, overcome with suspense, anguish, and pain.

"Yes, she is innocent," said the eldest brother, and related all that had taken place. While he spoke, there rose in the air a fragrance as from millions of roses. Every piece of fagot in the pile made to burn her had taken root, and threw out branches until the whole appeared like a thick hedge, large and high, covered with roses; while above all bloomed a white, shining flower that glittered like a star. This flower the king plucked, and when he placed it in Eliza's bosom she awoke from her swoon with peace and happiness in her heart. Then all the church bells rang of themselves, and the birds came in great flocks. And a marriage procession, such as no king had ever before seen, returned to the castle.

The Pen and the Inkstand

In a poet's room, where his inkstand stood on the table, the remark was once made: "It is wonderful what can be brought out of an inkstand. What will come next? It is indeed wonderful."

"Yes, certainly," said the inkstand to the pen and to the other articles that stood on the table; "that's what I always say. It is wonderful and extraordinary what a number of things come out of me. It's quite incredible, and I really never know what is coming next when that man dips his pen into me. One drop out of me is enough for half a page of paper—and what cannot half a page contain?

"From me all the works of the poet are produced—all those imaginary characters whom people fancy they have known or met, and all the deep feeling, the humor, and the vivid pictures of nature. I myself don't understand how it is, for I am not acquainted with nature, but it is certainly in me. From me have gone forth to the world those wonderful descriptions of charming maidens, and of brave knights on prancing steeds; of the halt and the blind—and I know not what more, for I assure you I never think of these things."

"There you are right," said the pen, "for you don't think at all. If you did, you would see that you can only provide the means. You give the fluid, that I may place upon the paper what dwells in me and what I wish to bring to light. It is the pen that writes. No man doubts that; and indeed most people understand as much about poetry as an old inkstand."

"You have had very little experience," replied the inkstand. "You have hardly been in service a week and are already half worn out. Do you imagine you are a poet? You are only a servant, and before you came I had many like you, some of the goose family and others of English manufacture. I know a quill pen as well as I know a steel one. I have had both sorts in my service, and I

313

shall have many more as long as he comes—the man who performs the mechanical part—and writes down what he obtains from me. I should like to know what will be the next thing he gets out of me."

"Inkpot!" retorted the pen, contemptuously.

Late in the evening the poet returned home from a concert, where he had been quite enchanted by the admirable performance of a famous violin player.

The player had produced from his instrument a richness of tone that sometimes sounded like tinkling water drops or rolling pearls, sometimes like the birds twittering in chorus, and then again, rising and swelling like the wind through the fir trees. The poet felt as if his own heart were weeping, but in tones of melody, like the sound of a woman's voice. These sounds seemed to come not only from the strings but from every part of the instrument. It was a wonderful performance and a difficult piece, and yet the bow seemed to glide across the strings so easily that one would think any one could do it. The violin and the bow seemed independent of their master who guided them. It was as if soul and spirit had been breathed into the instrument. And the audience forgot the performer in the beautiful sounds he produced.

Not so the poet; he remembered him and wrote down his thoughts on the subject: "How foolish it would be for the violin and the bow to boast of their performance, and yet we men often commit that folly. The poet, the artist, the man of science in his laboratory, the general—we all do it, and yet we are only the instruments which the Almighty uses. To Him alone the honor is due. We have nothing in ourselves of which we should be proud." Yes, this is what the poet wrote. He wrote it in the form of a parable and called it "The Master and the Instruments."

"That is what you get, madam," said the pen to the inkstand when the two were alone again. "Did you hear him read aloud what I had written down?"

"Yes, what I gave you to write," retorted the inkstand. "That was a cut at you, because of your conceit. To think that you could not understand that you were being quizzed! I gave you a cut from within me. Surely I must know my own satire."

"Ink pitcher!" cried the pen.

"Writing stick!" retorted the inkstand. And each of them felt satisfied that he had given a good answer. It is pleasing to be convinced that you have settled a matter by your reply; it is something to make you sleep well. And they both slept well over it.

But the poet did not sleep. Thoughts rose within him, like the tones of the violin, falling like pearls or rushing like the strong wind through the forest. He understood his own heart in these thoughts; they were as a ray from the mind of the Great Master of all minds.

The Flying Trunk

There was once a merchant who was so rich that he could have paved a whole street with gold, and would even then have had enough left for a small alley. He did not do so; he knew the value of money better than to use it in this way. So clever was he that every shilling he put out brought him a crown, and so it continued as long as he lived.

His son inherited his wealth, and lived a merry life with it. He went to a masquerade every night, made kites out of five-pound notes, and threw pieces of gold into the sea instead of stones, making ducks and drakes of them.

In this manner he soon lost all his money. At last he had nothing left but a pair of slippers, an old dressing gown, and four shillings. And now all his companions deserted him. They would not walk with him in the streets, but one of them, who was very good-natured, sent him an old trunk with this message, "Pack up!"

"Yes," he said, "it is all very well to say 'pack up.'" But he had nothing left to pack, therefore he seated himself in the trunk.

It was a very wonderful trunk, for no sooner did any one press on the lock than the trunk could fly. He shut the lid and pressed the lock, when away flew the trunk up the chimney, with him in it, right up into the clouds. Whenever the bottom of the trunk cracked he was in a great fright, for if the trunk had fallen to pieces, he would have turned a tremendous somersault over the trees. However, he arrived safely in Turkey. He hid the trunk in a wood under some dry leaves and then went into the town. This he could do very well, for among the Turks people always go about in dressing gowns and slippers, just as he was.

He happened to meet a nurse with a little child. "I say, you Turkish nurse," cried he, "what castle is that near the town, with the windows placed so high?"

"The Sultan's daughter lives there," she replied. "It has been prophesied that she will be very unhappy about a lover, and therefore no one is allowed to visit her unless the king and queen are present."

"Thank you," said the merchant's son. So he went back to the wood, seated himself in his trunk, flew up to the roof of the castle, and crept through the window into the room where the princess lay asleep on the sofa. She awoke and was very much frightened, but he told her he was a Turkish angel who had come down through the air to see her. This pleased her very much. He sat down by her side and talked to her, telling her that her eyes were like beautiful dark lakes, in which the thoughts swam about like little mermaids; and that her forehead was a snowy mountain which contained splendid halls full of pictures. He related to her the story about the stork, who brings the beautiful children from the rivers. These stories delighted the princess, and when he asked her if she would marry him, she consented immediately.

"But you must come on Saturday," she said, "for then my parents will take tea with me. They will be very proud when they find that I am going to marry a Turkish angel. But you must think of some very pretty stories to tell them, for they like to hear stories better than anything. My mother prefers one that is deep and moral, but my father likes something funny, to make him laugh."

"Very well," he replied, "I shall bring you no other marriage portion than a story"; and so they parted. But the princess gave him a sword studded with gold coins, and these he could make useful.

He flew away to the town and bought a new dressing gown, and afterwards returned to the wood, where he composed a story so as to be ready by Saturday; and that was no easy matter. It was ready, however, when he went to see the princess on Saturday. The king and queen and the whole court were at tea with the princess, and he was received with great politeness.

"Will you tell us a story?" said the queen; "one that is instructive and full of learning."

"Yes, but with something in it to laugh at," said the king.

"Certainly," he replied, and commenced at once, asking them to listen attentively.

"There was once a bundle of matches that were exceedingly proud of their high descent. Their genealogical tree—that is, a great pine tree from which they had been cut—was at one time a large old tree in the wood. The matches now lay between a tinder box and an old iron saucepan and were talking about their youthful days. 'Ah! then we grew on the green boughs,' said they, 'and every morning and evening we were fed with diamond drops of dew. Whenever the sun shone we felt his warm rays, and the little birds would relate stories to us in their songs. We knew that we were rich, for the other trees only wore their green dresses in summer, while our family were able to array themselves in green, summer and winter. But the woodcutter came like a great disaster, and our family fell under the ax. The head of the house obtained a situation as mainmast in a very fine ship and can sail round the world whenever he will. Other branches of the family were taken to different places, and our own office now is to kindle a light for common people. This is how such highborn people as we came to be in a kitchen.'

"'Mine has been a very different fate,' said the iron pot, which stood by the matches. 'From my first entrance into the world I have been used to cooking and scouring. I am the first in this house when anything solid or useful is required. My only pleasure is to be made clean and shining after dinner and to sit in my place and have a little sensible conversation with my neighbors. All of us excepting the water bucket, which is sometimes taken into the courtyard, live here together within these four walls. We get our news from the market basket, but it sometimes tells us very unpleasant things about the people and the government. Yes, and one day an old pot was so alarmed that it fell down and was broken in pieces.'

"'You are talking too much,' said the tinder box; and the steel struck against the flint till some sparks flew out, crying, 'We want a merry evening, don't we?'

"'Yes, of course,' said the matches. 'Let us talk about those who are the highest born.'

"'No, I don't like to be always talking of what we are,' remarked the saucepan. 'Let us think of some other amusement; I will begin. We will tell something that has happened to ourselves; that will be very easy, and interesting as well. On the Baltic Sea, near the Danish shore—'

"'What a pretty commencement!' said the plates. 'We shall all like that story, I am sure.'

"'Yes. Well, in my youth I lived in a quiet family where the furniture was polished, the floors scoured, and clean curtains put up, every fortnight.'

"'What an interesting way you have of relating a story,' said the carpet broom. 'It is easy to perceive that you have been a great deal in society, something so pure runs through what you say.'

"'That is quite true,' said the water bucket; and it made a spring with joy and splashed some water on the floor.

"Then the saucepan went on with its story, and the end was as good as the beginning.

"The plates rattled with pleasure, and the carpet broom brought some green parsley out of the dust hole and crowned the saucepan. It knew this would vex the others, but it thought, 'If I crown him to-day, he will crown me to-morrow.'

"'Now let us have a dance,' said the fire tongs. Then how they danced and stuck one leg in the air! The chair cushion in the corner burst with laughter at the sight.

"'Shall I be crowned now?' asked the fire tongs. So the broom found another wreath for the tongs.

"'They are only common people after all,' thought the matches. The tea urn was now asked to sing, but she said she had a cold and could not sing unless she felt boiling heat within. They all thought this was affectation; they also considered it affectation that she did not wish to sing except in the parlor, when on the table with the grand people.

"In the window sat an old quill pen, with which the maid generally wrote. There was nothing remarkable about the pen, except that it had been dipped too deeply in the ink; but it was proud of that.

"'If the tea urn won't sing,' said the pen, 'she needn't. There's a nightingale in a cage outside, that can sing. She has not been taught much, certainly, but we need not say anything this evening about that.'

"'I think it highly improper,' said the teakettle, who was kitchen singer and half brother to the tea urn, 'that a rich foreign bird should be listened to here. Is it patriotic? Let the market basket decide what is right.'

"'I certainly am vexed,' said the basket, 'inwardly vexed, more than any one can imagine. Are we spending the evening properly? Would it not be more sensible to put the house in order? If each were in his own place, I would lead a game. This would be quite another thing.'

"'Let us act a play,' said they all. At the same moment the door opened and the maid came in. Then not one stirred; they remained quite still, although there was not a single pot among them that had not a high opinion of himself and of what he could do if he chose.

"'Yes, if we had chosen,' each of them thought, 'we might have spent a very pleasant evening.'

"The maid took the matches and lighted them, and dear me, how they spluttered and blazed up!

"'Now then,' they thought, 'every one will see that we are the first. How we shine! What a light we give!' But even while they spoke their lights went out."

"What a capital story!" said the queen. "I feel as if I were really in the kitchen and could see the matches. Yes, you shall marry our daughter."

"Certainly," said the king, "thou shalt have our daughter." The king said "thou" to him because he was going to be one of the family. The wedding day was fixed, and on the evening before, the whole city was illuminated. Cakes and sweetmeats were thrown among the people. The street boys stood on tiptoe and shouted "Hurrah," and whistled between their fingers. Altogether it was a very splendid affair.

"I will give them another treat," said the merchant's son. So he went and bought rockets and crackers and every kind of fireworks that could be thought of, packed them in his trunk, and flew up with it into the air. What a whizzing and popping they made as they went off! The Turks, when they saw the sight, jumped so high that their slippers flew about their ears. It was easy to believe after this that the princess was really going to marry a Turkish angel.

As soon as the merchant's son had come down to the wood after the fireworks, he thought, "I will go back into the town now and hear what they think of the entertainment." It was very natural that he should wish to know. And what strange things people did say, to be sure! Every one whom he questioned had a different tale to tell, though they all thought it very beautiful.

"I saw the Turkish angel myself," said one. "He had eyes like glittering stars and a head like foaming water."

"He flew in a mantle of fire," said another, "and lovely little cherubs peeped out from the folds."

He heard many more fine things about himself and that the next day he was to be married. After this he went back to the forest to rest himself in his trunk. It had disappeared! A spark from the fireworks which remained had set it on fire. It was burned to ashes. So the merchant's son could not fly any more, nor go to meet his bride. She stood all day on the roof, waiting for him, and most likely she is waiting there still, while he wanders through the world telling fairy tales—but none of them so amusing as the one he related about the matches.

What Happened to the Thistle

Around a lordly old mansion was a beautiful, well-kept garden, full of all kinds of rare trees and flowers. Guests always expressed their delight and admiration at the sight of its wonders. The people from far and near used to come on Sundays and holidays and ask permission to see it. Even whole schools made excursions for the sole purpose of seeing its beauties.

Near the fence that separated the garden from the meadow stood an immense thistle. It was an uncommonly large and fine thistle, with several branches spreading out just above the root, and altogether was so strong and full as to make it well worthy of the name "thistle bush."

No one ever noticed it, save the old donkey that pulled the milk cart for the dairymaids. He stood grazing in the meadow hard by and stretched his old neck to reach the thistle, saying: "You are beautiful! I should like to eat you!" But the tether was too short to allow him to reach the thistle, so he did not eat it.

There were guests at the Hall, fine, aristocratic relatives from town, and among them a young lady who had come from a long distance—all the way from Scotland. She was of old and noble family and rich in gold and lands—a bride well worth the winning, thought more than one young man to himself; yes, and their mothers thought so, too!

The young people amused themselves on the lawn, playing croquet and flitting about among the flowers, each young girl gathering a flower to put in the buttonhole of some one of the gentlemen.

The young Scotch lady looked about for a flower, but none of them seemed to please her, until, happening to glance over the fence, she espied the fine, large thistle bush, full of bluish-red, sturdy-looking flowers. She smiled as she saw it, and begged the son of the house to get one of them for her.

"That is Scotland's flower," she said; "it grows and blossoms in our coat of arms. Get that one yonder for me, please."

And he gathered the finest of the thistle flowers, though he pricked his fingers as much in doing so as if it had been growing on a wild rosebush.

She took the flower and put it in his buttonhole, which made him feel greatly honored. Each of the other young men would gladly have given up his graceful garden flower if he might have worn the one given by the delicate hands of the Scotch girl. As keenly as the son of the house felt the honor conferred upon him, the thistle felt even more highly honored. It seemed to feel dew and sunshine going through it.

"It seems I am of more consequence than I thought," it said to itself. "I ought by rights to stand inside and not outside the fence. One gets strangely placed in this world, but now I have at least one of my flowers over the fence—and not only there, but in a buttonhole!"

To each one of its buds as it opened, the thistle bush told this great event. And not many days had passed before it heard—not from the people who passed, nor yet from the twittering of little birds, but from the air, which gives out, far and wide, the sounds that it has treasured up from the shadiest walks of the beautiful garden and from the most secluded rooms at the Hall, where doors and windows are left open—that the young man who received the thistle flower from the hands of the Scottish maiden had received her heart and hand as well.

"That is my doing!" said the thistle, thinking of the flower she had given to the buttonhole. And every new flower that came was told of this wonderful event.

"Surely I shall now be taken and planted in the garden," thought the thistle. "Perhaps I shall be put into a flowerpot, for that is by far the most honorable position." It thought of this so long that it ended by saying to itself with the firm conviction of truth, "I shall be planted in a flowerpot!"

It promised every little bud that came that it also should be placed in a pot and perhaps have a place in a buttonhole—that being the highest position one could aspire to. But none of them got into a flowerpot, and still less into a gentleman's buttonhole.

They lived on light and air, and drank sunshine in the day and dew at night. They received visits from bee and hornet, who came to look for the honey in the flower, and who took the honey and left the flower.

"The good-for-nothing fellows," said the thistle bush. "I would pierce them if I could!"

The flowers drooped and faded, but new ones always came.

"You come as if you had been sent," said the thistle bush to them. "I am expecting every moment to be taken over the fence."

A couple of harmless daisies and a huge, thin plant of canary grass listened to this with the deepest respect, believing all they heard. The old donkey, that had to pull the milk cart, cast long-ing looks toward the blooming thistle and tried to reach it, but his tether was too short. And the thistle bush thought and thought, so much and so long, of the Scotch thistle—to whom it believed itself related—that at last it fancied it had come from Scotland and that its parents had grown into the Scottish arms.

It was a great thought, but a great thistle may well have great thoughts.

"Sometimes one is of noble race even if one does not know it," said the nettle growing close by—it had a kind of presentiment that it might be turned into muslin, if properly treated.

The summer passed, and the autumn passed; the leaves fell from the trees; the flowers came with stronger colors and less per-fume; the gardener's lad sang on the other side of the fence:

"Up the hill and down the hill,
That's the way of the world still."

The young pine trees in the wood began to feel a longing for Christmas, though Christmas was still a long way off.

"Here I am still," said the thistle. "It seems that I am quite for-gotten, and yet it was I who made the match. They were engaged, and now they are married—the wedding was a week ago. I do not make a single step forward, for I cannot."

Some weeks passed. The thistle had its last, solitary flower, which was large and full and growing down near the root. The wind blew coldly over it, the color faded, and all its glory disap-peared, leaving only the cup of the flower, now grown to be as large as the flower of an artichoke and glistening like a silvered sunflower.

The young couple, who were now man and wife, came along the garden path, and as they passed near the fence, the bride, glancing over it, said, "Why, there stands the large thistle! it has no flowers now."

"Yes, there is still the ghost of the last one," said her husband, pointing to the silvery remains of the last flower—a flower in itself.

"How beautiful it is!" she said. "We must have one carved in the frame of our picture."

And once more the young man had to get over the fence, to break off the silvery cup of the thistle flower. It pricked his fingers for his pains, because he had called it a ghost. And then it was brought into the garden, and to the Hall, and into the drawing room. There stood a large picture—the portraits of the two, and in the bridegroom's buttonhole was painted a thistle. They talked of it and of the flower cup they had brought in with them—the last silver-shimmering thistle flower, that was to be reproduced in the carving of the frame.

The air took all their words and scattered them about, far and wide.

"What strange things happen to one!" said the thistle bush. "My first-born went to live in a buttonhole, my last-born in a frame! I wonder what is to become of me."

The old donkey, standing by the roadside, cast loving glances at the thistle and said, "Come to me, my sweetheart, for I cannot go to you; my tether is too short!"

But the thistle bush made no answer. It grew more and more thoughtful, and it thought as far ahead as Christmas, till its budding thoughts opened into flower.

"When one's children are safely housed, a mother is quite content to stay beyond the fence."

"That is true," said the sunshine; "and you will be well placed, never fear."

"In a flowerpot or in a frame?" asked the thistle.

"In a story," answered the sunshine. And here is the story!

The Old Street Lamp

Did you ever hear the story of the old street lamp? It is not remarkably interesting, but for once you may as well listen to it.

It was a most respectable old lamp, which had seen many, many years of service and now was to retire with a pension. It was this very evening at its post for the last time, giving light to the street. Its feelings were something like those of an old dancer at the theater who is dancing for the last time and knows that on the morrow she will be in her garret, alone and forgotten.

The lamp had very great anxiety about the next day, for it knew that it had to appear for the first time at the town hall to be inspected by the mayor and the council, who were to decide whether it was fit for further service; whether it was good enough to be used to light the inhabitants of one of the suburbs, or in the country, at some factory. If the lamp could not be used for one of these purposes, it would be sent at once to an iron foundry to be melted down. In this latter case it might be turned into anything, and it wondered very much whether it would then be able to remember that it had once been a street lamp. This troubled it exceedingly.

Whatever might happen, it seemed certain that the lamp would be separated from the watchman and his wife, whose family it looked upon as its own. The lamp had first been hung up on the very evening that the watchman, then a robust young man, had entered upon the duties of his office. Ah, well! it was a very long time since one became a lamp and the other a watchman. His wife had some little pride in those days; she condescended to glance at the lamp only when she passed by in the evening—never in the daytime. But in later years, when all of them—the watchman, the wife, and the lamp—had grown old, she had attended to it, cleaning it and keeping it supplied with oil. The old people were thoroughly honest; they had never cheated the lamp of a single drop of the oil provided for it.

This was the lamp's last night in the street, and to-morrow it must go to the town hall—two very dark things to think of. No wonder it did not burn brightly. How many persons it had lighted on their way, and how much it had seen! As much, very likely, as the mayor and corporation themselves! None of these thoughts were uttered aloud, however, for the lamp was good and honorable and would not willingly do harm to any one, especially to those in authority. As one thing after another was recalled to its mind, the light would flash up with sudden brightness. At such moments the lamp had a conviction that it would be remembered.

"There was a handsome young man, once," thought the lamp; "it is certainly a long while ago, but I remember that he had a little note, written on pink paper with a gold edge. The writing was elegant, evidently a lady's. Twice he read it through, and kissed it, and then looked up at me with eyes that said quite plainly, 'I am the happiest of men!' Only he and I know what was written on this, his first letter from his lady-love. Ah, yes, and there was another pair of eyes that I remember; it is really wonderful how the thoughts jump from one thing to another! A funeral passed through the street. A young and beautiful woman lay on a bier decked with garlands of flowers, and attended by torches which quite overpowered my light. All along the street stood the people from the houses, in crowds, ready to join the procession. But when the torches had passed from before me and I could look around, I saw one person standing alone, leaning against my post and weeping. Never shall I forget the sorrowful eyes that looked up at me."

These and similar reflections occupied the old street lamp on this the last time that its light would shine. The sentry, when he is relieved from his post, knows, at least, who will be his successor, and may whisper a few words to him. But the lamp did not know its successor, or it might have given him a few hints respecting rain or mist and might have informed him how far the moon's rays would reach, and from which side the wind generally blew, and so on.

On the bridge over the canal stood three persons who wished to recommend themselves to the lamp, for they thought it could give the office to whomsoever it chose. The first was a herring's head, which could emit light in the darkness. He remarked that it would be a great saving of oil if they placed him on the lamp-post. Number two was a piece of rotten wood, which also shines in the dark. He considered himself descended from an old stem, once the pride of the forest. The third was a glowworm, and how he found his way there the lamp could not imagine; yet there he was, and could really give light as well as the others. But the rotten wood and the herring's head declared most solemnly, by all they held sacred, that the glowworm only gave light at certain times and must not be allowed to compete with them. The old lamp assured them that not one of them could give sufficient light to fill the position of a street lamp, but they would believe nothing that it said. When they discovered that it had not the power of naming its successor, they said they were very glad to hear it, for the lamp was too old and worn out to make a proper choice.

At this moment the wind came rushing round the corner of the street and through the air-holes of the old lamp. "What is this I hear?" it asked. "Are you going away to-morrow? Is this evening the last time we shall meet? Then I must present you with a farewell gift. I will blow into your brain, so that in future not only shall you be able to remember all that you have seen or heard in the past, but your light within shall be so bright that you will be able to understand all that is said or done in your presence."

"Oh, that is really a very, very great gift," said the old lamp. "I thank you most heartily. I only hope I shall not be melted down."

"That is not likely to happen yet," said the wind. "I will also blow a memory into you, so that, should you receive other similar presents, your old age will pass very pleasantly."

"That is, if I am not melted down," said the lamp. "But should I, in that case, still retain my memory?"

"Do be reasonable, old lamp," said the wind, puffing away.

At this moment the moon burst forth from the clouds. "What will you give the old lamp?" asked the wind.

"I can give nothing," she replied. "I am on the wane, and no lamps have ever given me light, while I have frequently shone upon them." With these words the moon hid herself again behind the clouds, that she might be saved from further importunities. Just then a drop fell upon the lamp from the roof of the house, but the drop explained that it was a gift from those gray clouds and perhaps the best of all gifts. "I shall penetrate you so thoroughly," it said, "that you will have the power of becoming rusty, and, if you wish it, can crumble into dust in one night."

But this seemed to the lamp a very shabby present, and the wind thought so, too. "Does no one give any more? Will no one give any more?" shouted the breath of the wind, as loud as it could. Then a bright, falling star came down, leaving a broad, luminous streak behind it.

"What was that?" cried the herring's head. "Did not a star fall? I really believe it went into the lamp. Certainly, when such high-born personages try for the office we may as well go home."

And so they did, all three, while the old lamp threw a wonder-fully strong light all around.

"This is a glorious gift," it said. "The bright stars have always been a joy to me and have always shone more brilliantly than I ever could shine, though I have tried with my whole might. Now they have noticed me, a poor old lamp, and have sent me a gift that will enable me to see clearly everything that I remember, as if it still stood before me, and to let it be seen by all those who love me. And herein lies the truest happiness, for pleasures which we cannot share with others are only half enjoyed."

"That sentiment does you honor," said the wind; "but for this purpose wax lights will be necessary. If these are not lighted in you, your peculiar faculties will not benefit others in the least. The stars have not thought of this. They suppose that you and every other light must be a wax taper. But I must go down now." So it laid itself to rest.

"Wax tapers, indeed!" said the lamp; "I have never yet had these, nor is it likely I ever shall. If I could only be sure of not being melted down!"

The next day—well, perhaps we had better pass over the next day. The evening had come, and the lamp was resting in a grandfather's chair; and guess where! Why, at the old watchman's house. He had begged as a favor that the mayor and corporation would allow him to keep the street lamp in consideration of his long and faithful service, as he had himself hung it up and lighted it on the day he first commenced his duties, four and twenty years ago. He looked upon it almost as his own child. He had no children, so the lamp was given to him.

There lay the lamp in the great armchair near the warm stove. It seemed almost to have grown larger, for it appeared quite to fill the chair. The old people sat at their supper, casting friendly glances at it, and would willingly have admitted it to a place at the table. It is quite true that they dwelt in a cellar two yards below ground, and had to cross a stone passage to get to their room. But within, it was warm and comfortable, and strips of list had been nailed round the door. The bed and the little window had curtains, and everything looked clean and neat. On the window seat stood two curious flowerpots, which a sailor named Christian had brought from the East or West Indies. They were of clay, and in the form of two elephants with open backs; they were filled with earth, and through the open space flowers bloomed. In one grew some very fine chives or leeks; this was the kitchen garden. The other, which contained a beautiful geranium, they called their flower garden. On the wall hung a large colored print, representing the Congress of Vienna and all the kings and emperors. A clock with heavy weights hung on the wall and went "tick, tick," steadily enough; yet it was always rather too fast, which, however, the old people said was better than being too slow. They were now eating their supper, while the old street lamp, as we have heard, lay in the grandfather's armchair near the stove.

It seemed to the lamp as if the whole world had turned round. But after a while the old watchman looked at the lamp and spoke of what they had both gone through together—in rain and in fog, during the short, bright nights of summer or in the long winter nights, through the drifting snowstorms when he longed to be at home in the cellar. Then the lamp felt that all was well again. It saw everything that had happened quite clearly, as if the events were passing before it. Surely the wind had given it an excellent gift!

The old people were very active and industrious; they were never idle for even a single hour. On Sunday afternoons they would bring out some books, generally a book of travels which they greatly liked. The old man would read aloud about Africa, with its great forests and the wild elephants, while his wife would listen attentively, stealing a glance now and then at the clay elephants which served as flowerpots. "I can almost imagine I am seeing it all," she said.

Ah! how the lamp wished for a wax taper to be lighted in it, for then the old woman would have seen the smallest detail as clearly as it did itself; the lofty trees, with their thickly entwined branches, the men on horseback, and whole herds of elephants treading down bamboo thickets with their broad, heavy feet.

"What is the use of all my capabilities," sighed the old lamp, "when I cannot obtain any wax lights? They have only oil and tallow here, and these will not do." One day a great heap of wax-candle ends found their way into the cellar. The larger pieces were burned, and the smaller ones the old woman kept for waxing her thread. So there were now candles enough, but it never occurred to any one to put a little piece in the lamp.

"Here I am now, with my rare powers," thought the lamp. "I

have faculties within me, but I cannot share them. They do not know that I could cover these white walls with beautiful tapestry, or change them into noble forests or, indeed, to anything else they might wish."

The lamp, however, was always kept clean and shining in a corner, where it attracted all eyes. Strangers looked upon it as lumber, but the old people did not care for that; they loved it. One day—it was the watchman's birthday—the old woman approached the lamp, smiling to herself, and said, "I will have an illumination to-day, in honor of my old man." The lamp rattled in its metal frame, for it thought, "Now at last I shall have a light within me." But, after all, no wax light was placed in the lamp—only oil, as usual.

The lamp burned through the whole evening and began to perceive too clearly that the gift of the stars would remain a hidden treasure all its life. Then it had a dream; for to one with its faculties, dreaming was not difficult. It dreamed that the old people were dead and that it had been taken to the iron foundry to be melted down. This caused the lamp quite as much anxiety as on the day when it had been called upon to appear before the mayor and the council at the town hall. But though it had been endowed with the power of falling into decay from rust when it pleased, it did not make use of this power. It was therefore put into the melting furnace and changed into as elegant an iron candlestick as you could wish to see—one intended to hold a wax taper. The candlestick was in the form of an angel holding a nosegay, in the center of which the wax taper was to be placed. It was to stand on a green writing table in a very pleasant room, where there were many books scattered about and splendid paintings on the walls.

The owner of the room was a poet and a man of intellect. Everything he thought or wrote was pictured around him. Nature showed herself to him sometimes in the dark forests, sometimes in cheerful meadows where the storks were strutting about, or on the deck of a ship sailing across the foaming sea, with the clear, blue sky above, or at night in the glittering stars.

"What powers I possess!" said the lamp, awaking from its dream. "I could almost wish to be melted down; but no, that must not be while the old people live. They love me for myself alone; they keep me bright and supply me with oil. I am as well off as the picture of the Congress, in which they take so much pleasure." And from that time it felt at rest in itself, and not more so than such an honorable old lamp really deserved to be.

Sunshine Stories

"I am going to tell a story," said the Wind.

"I beg your pardon," said the Rain, "but now it is my turn. Have you not been howling round the corner this long time, as hard as ever you could?"

"Is this the gratitude you owe me?" said the Wind; "I, who in honor of you turn inside out—yes, even break—all the umbrellas, when the people won't have anything to do with you."

"I will speak myself," said the Sunshine. "Silence!" and the Sunshine said it with such glory and majesty that the weary Wind fell prostrate, and the Rain, beating against him, shook him, as she said:

"We won't stand it! She is always breaking through—is Madame Sunshine. Let us not listen to her; what she has to say is not worth hearing." And still the Sunshine began to talk, and this is what she said:

"A beautiful swan flew over the rolling, tossing waves of the ocean. Every one of its feathers shone like gold; and one feather drifted down to the great merchant vessel that, with sails all set, was sailing away.

"The feather fell upon the light curly hair of a young man, whose business it was to care for the goods in the ship—the supercargo he was called. The feather of the bird of fortune touched his forehead, became a pen in his hand, and brought him such luck that he soon became a wealthy merchant, rich enough to have bought for himself spurs of gold—rich enough to change a golden plate into a nobleman's shield, on which," said the Sunshine, "I shone."

"The swan flew farther, away and away, over the sunny green meadow, where the little shepherd boy, only seven years old, had lain down in the shade of the old tree, the only one there was in sight.

"In its flight the swan kissed one of the leaves of the tree, and falling into the boy's hand, it was changed to three leaves—to ten—to a whole book; yes, and in the book he read about all the wonders of nature, about his native language, about faith and knowledge. At night he laid the book under his pillow, that he might not forget what he had been reading.

"The wonderful book led him also to the schoolroom, and thence everywhere, in search of knowledge. I have read his name among the names of learned men," said the Sunshine.

"The swan flew into the quiet, lonely forest, and rested awhile on the deep, dark lake where the lilies grow, where the wild apples are to be found on the shore, where the cuckoo and the wild pigeon have their homes.

"In the wood was a poor woman gathering firewood—branches and dry sticks that had fallen. She bore them on her back in a bundle, and in her arms she held her little child. She too saw the golden swan, the bird of fortune, as it rose from among the reeds on the shore. What was it that glittered so? A golden egg that was still quite warm. She laid it in her bosom, and the warmth remained. Surely there was life in the egg! She heard the gentle pecking inside the shell, but she thought it was her own heart that was beating.

"At home in her poor cottage she took out the egg. 'Tick! tick!' it said, as if it had been a gold watch, but it was not; it was an egg— a real, living egg.

"The egg cracked and opened, and a dear little baby swan, all feathered as with the purest gold, pushed out its tiny head. Around its neck were four rings, and as this woman had four boys—three at home, and this little one that was with her in the lonely wood— she understood at once that there was one for each boy. Just as she had taken them the little gold bird took flight.

"She kissed each ring, then made each of the children kiss one of the rings, laid it next the child's heart awhile, then put it on his finger. I saw it all," said the Sunshine, "and I saw what happened afterward.

"One of the boys, while playing by a ditch, took a lump of clay in his hand, then turned and twisted it till it took shape and was like Jason, who went in search of the Golden Fleece and found it.

"The second boy ran out upon the meadow, where stood the flowers—flowers of all imaginable colors. He gathered a handful and squeezed them so tightly that the juice flew into his eyes, and some of it wet the ring upon his hand. It cribbled and crawled in his brain and in his hands, and after many a day and many a year, people in the great city talked of the famous painter that he was.

"The third child held the ring in his teeth, and so tightly that it gave forth sound—the echo of a song in the depth of his heart. Then thoughts and feelings rose in beautiful sounds,—rose like singing swans,—plunged, too, like swans, into the deep, deep sea. He became a great musical composer, a master, of whom every country has the right to say, 'He was mine, for he was the world's.'

"And the fourth little one—yes, he was the 'ugly duck' of the family. They said he had the pip and must eat pepper and butter like a sick chicken, and that was what was given him; but of me he got a warm, sunny kiss," said the Sunshine. "He had ten kisses for one. He was a poet and was first kissed, then buffeted all his life through.

"But he held what no one could take from him—the ring of fortune from Dame Fortune's golden swan. His thoughts took wing and flew up and away like singing butterflies—emblems of an immortal life."

"That was a dreadfully long story," said the Wind.

"And so stupid and tiresome," said the Rain. "Blow upon me, please, that I may revive a little."

And while the Wind blew, the Sunshine said: "The swan of fortune flew over the lovely bay where the fishermen had set their nets. The very poorest one among them was wishing to marry—and marry he did.

"To him the swan brought a piece of amber. Amber draws things toward itself, and this piece drew hearts to the house where the fisherman lived with his bride. Amber is the most wonderful of incense, and there came a soft perfume, as from a holy place, a sweet breath from beautiful nature, that God has made. And the fisherman and his wife were happy and grateful in their peaceful home, content even in their poverty. And so their life became a real Sunshine Story."

"I think we had better stop now," said the Wind. "I am dreadfully bored. The Sunshine has talked long enough."

"I think so, too," said the Rain.

And what do we others who have heard the story say?

We say, "Now the story's done."

About Hans Christian Andersen

Hans Christian Andersen was born in Odense, Denmark, in 1805. His parents encouraged his imagination, and as an adult, Andersen remembered fondly that his father read him tales from *The Thousand and One Nights*, one of the few books the family owned, and managed to take him to the theatre although they had little money for luxuries.

When he was 14, Andersen left home for Copenhagen in hopes of becoming an actor. He was protected by Copenhagen's theatrical community and given cheap lodgings, and he managed to earn some money singing in the homes of the city's wealthy residents. Although he tried to make a career as a performer, he never met with much success, and he turned to writing instead, publishing his first story, "The Ghost at Palnatoke's Grave," when he was only 17 and his first book when he was 22.

Andersen published his first collection of nine fairy tales— including some of his most-loved fables, "The Princess and the Pea," "Thumbelina," and "The Emperor's New Clothes" —in 1835. For many years, his fairy tales were much less popular than his novels and poetry, but they began to achieve acclaim from the 1840s, especially once they were translated into other languages. He continued writing fairy tales throughout his career, penning more than 200 and publishing his last one in 1872, three years before his death in 1875. Today, his fairy tales are available in more than 125 languages, inspiring popular movies, books, and films, and statues commemorate Hans Christian Andersen—and his imagination—in cities around the world.